# Show, Tell, Build

# Show, Tell, Build

## Twenty Key Instructional Tools and Techniques for Educating English Learners

Joyce W. Nutta
Carine Strebel
Florin M. Mihai
Edwidge Crevecoeur Bryant
Kouider Mokhtari

HARVARD EDUCATION PRESS
Cambridge, Massachusetts

Second Printing, 2019

Copyright © 2018 by the President and Fellows of Harvard College

All rights reserved. No part of this publication may be reproduced or transmitted in any form or by any means, electronic or mechanical, including photocopy, recording, or any information storage and retrieval systems, without permission in writing from the publisher.

Paperback ISBN 978-1-68253-222-5
Library Edition ISBN 978-1-68253-223-2

*Library of Congress Cataloging-in-Publication Data*

Names: Nutta, Joyce W., author. | Strebel, Carine, author. | Mihai, Florin, author. | Crevecoeur-Bryant, Edwidge, author. | Mokhtari, Kouider, author.
Title: Show, tell, build : twenty key instructional tools and techniques for educating English learners / Joyce W. Nutta, Carine Strebel, Florin M. Mihai, Edwidge Crevecoeur Bryant, Kouider Mokhtari.
Description: Cambridge, Massachusetts : Harvard Education Press, 2018. | Includes bibliographical references and index.
Identifiers: LCCN 2018023296| ISBN 9781682532225 (pbk.) | ISBN 9781682532232 (library edition)
Subjects: LCSH: Linguistic minorities—Educatio—United States. | Second language acquisition. | Education, Bilingual—United States. | Limited English-proficient students—United States. | English language—Study and teaching—United States.
Classification: LCC LC3725 .N87 2018 | DDC 370.117—dc23 LC record available at https://lccn.loc.gov/2018023296

Published by Harvard Education Press,
an imprint of the Harvard Education Publishing Group

Harvard Education Press
8 Story Street
Cambridge, MA 02138

Cover Design: Ciano Design
Cover Photo: oscarhdez/iStock/Getty Images
The typefaces used in this book are Aldine 401 BT, Museo Slab, and Univers

To Betty and Gloria, my first teachers.

—Joyce

✦

To my parents, Sonja and Max Strebel,
for a lifetime of love; and to my husband, Ray Halpern,
for selflessly supporting everything I do.

—Carine

✦

For my wife, Cristina, with love.

—Florin

✦

I dedicate this book to my husband, Thomas Bryant III,
for his encouragement and support as I pursue
my educational endeavors. Thank you, dear!

—Edwidge

✦

For teachers of English learners everywhere.

—Kouider

# Contents

# Introduction

Principal Finney dropped a pile of folders on the conference table and made eye contact with each teacher who was present for the mandatory meeting. The media center was at capacity, with most teachers seated together by grade and a few others standing alone, out of Mr. Finney's line of vision.

"We have some new data to discuss today," he said as he put on his reading glasses and opened the first folder. "Our learning gains did not hit our target. We're not too far off overall, but one group of students is underperforming." Teachers at the third-grade table looked up nervously. "Our English learners made negligible gains, well below expectations." A few heads turned toward the English language development teachers.

"We've been depending on our ELD teachers to address all of our English learners' needs, but the time has come for *all of us* to take responsibility for these students' achievement. I want *every* teacher who has one or more English learners to document the ELD strategies that they are using." He opened another folder and motioned to two nearby teachers to hand out the stack of papers.

The teachers at the kindergarten table looked over the handout, a page filled from edge to edge with "ELD Strategies." Number 3—Allow more time, Number 57—Scaffold writing assignments, Number 80—Use visuals. They all looked very familiar.

"The district has compiled this numbered list of strategies to make it easy for you to document what you're doing for your English learners. In your planner, make sure to include the number of the strategy you use for each lesson. As we focus on increasing our English learners' gains, I ask you to do all you can to use more district-approved strategies, and to use them more often. We need to see improvement, and we need it now."

"I think we are using most of these strategies already," a seasoned teacher asserted. "There are only a couple that I don't recognize."

Mr. Finney replied, "Good, then just do more of what you've been doing and document it. And if there are any strategies that you don't know, I'm sure our ELD teachers will be glad to answer your questions."

Many teachers in the room felt burdened by the latest obligation added to the school day, but nearly everyone agreed they had to do more to help their English learners succeed. Mr. Finney knew that his teachers' plates were more than full, but he felt reassured that they were already using many of the strategies. This new plan would require extra planning and documentation, but it would lead to better outcomes for their English learners, he reasoned. What he didn't realize was how unlikely it was that this additional effort would make any difference at all.

Mr. Finney's approach is a common response to a nationwide concern—the achievement gap of English learners (ELs). When educators determine that English learners in their districts and schools are not meeting expectations, they typically view teachers as first responders. And often they surmise that requiring teachers to do more, or to do something different, will lead to the needed improvements. The trouble is that the required changes may not address what teachers need to know and do to support their English learners' success in school. We believe that using and documenting so-called ELD (or ESOL) strategies often misses the mark.

## WHAT'S WRONG WITH USING ELD (OR ESOL) STRATEGIES?

There is nothing inherently wrong with consulting a list of suggested strategies when planning lessons in an EL-integrated classroom. The problem is that choosing a strategy that might be familiar because of its applicability to all students won't necessarily provide the support that English learners at different levels of English proficiency need. In other words, using a blanket approach to "EL-friendly" instructional practices is a hit-or-miss proposition in the EL-integrated classroom. We can, and must, be more deliberate than that.

So, how do we address more precisely the specific needs and varied backgrounds of English learners, including:

- Current levels of English proficiency (both oral language and literacy skills)
- Current age/grade level (and age of first exposure to English)
- Literacy in the first language (Can their first language literacy support their learning in a second language?)
- First language and its features (e.g., Does it have cognates with English? Does it have a similar word order?)
- Previous education in or outside of the United States (Are there knowledge gaps?)
- Cultural and experiential background (Are the students and families familiar with US customs and cultures?)

If we are going to adhere to any list to meet EL students' needs, the above six characteristics about each English learner should be the one. And once we know our EL students, we can be deliberate in which instructional approaches and supports we use because we will know why they work for their specific needs.

## A DIFFERENT APPROACH

Now, you might have gathered that we don't use the "S" word (strategies), and that's because we believe the word is used so broadly that it has lost its meaning. Instead, we refer to effective instructional practices for English learners as tools (what teachers and students use) and techniques (what teachers and students do and say) that provide communication support for ELs through showing and telling and that develop their language proficiency through building their skills; hence the title *Show, Tell, Build*.

This book is built upon the theoretical and practical foundation laid out in our previous book, *Educating English Learners: What Every Classroom Teacher Needs to Know.*[1] In *Show, Tell, Build* we focus on the instructional tools and techniques that teachers can use to support ELs' learning and to target language development instruction to their needs. The power to reach ELs where they are is not in the tools and techniques per se, but in *how* they are used for different levels and purposes.

In *Educating English Learners*, we compiled the most essential information that teachers in EL-integrated classrooms need to know to be able to support English learners' achievement in academic subjects and English language development. Organized around four English learners at different English proficiency levels in kindergarten, fourth, seventh, and tenth grades, *Educating English Learners* put second language acquisition theory and second language instructional practices into a familiar context for classroom teachers and addressed English learner challenges and attributes in concrete, realistic ways. Part I of the book discussed the theory and practice behind our approach to teaching academic subjects to English learners, and Part II highlighted the same for teaching language arts. All of the theory and practice was presented through the lens of the four case study students and how their teachers addressed their needs in different subjects and language domains. After conducting book studies with teachers and administrators at many schools, our team heard their main request loudly and clearly— they love the four EL students and the practical guidance for meeting their needs, and they want more nuts-and-bolts directions focused on exactly *what* they should do for their own EL students and *how* they should do it in their EL-integrated classrooms. *Show, Tell, Build* is the answer to this request.

## THE ACADEMIC SUBJECTS AND LANGUAGE ARTS PROTOCOLS

To help classroom teachers juggle and balance the needs of native English speakers alongside those of English learners, we developed two decision maps to plan and implement differentiated instruction for English learners, the Academic Subjects Protocol (ASP) and the Language Arts Protocol (LAP). The ASP and LAP were developed for the classroom teacher and collaborators to provide *accessible, targeted* instruction for ELs *within the context* of the EL-integrated classroom.[2]

After working with teachers of English learners for over twenty-five years, we created the two protocols to help teachers address English learners' needs in classrooms that include a mix of non–English learners (sometimes referred to as native speakers and/or former English learners) and English learners. We refer to this type of class as the EL-integrated classroom, or what some call mainstream or general classrooms. There are many good books and resources that explain how to teach English learners, but most of them do not fully explain how this can be done in classrooms with a majority of non-ELs. This is a challenge for teachers. The two protocols we created serve as an *overlay* to planning grade-level instruction in academic subjects (e.g., science, social studies, mathematics, etc.) and language arts (e.g., listening, speaking, reading, writing, and language conventions) that brings the needs of English learners at different proficiency levels into sharp focus and leads teachers in providing appropriate support and targeted instruction given the resources they have in their classrooms and schools.

Categorizing the protocols into academic subjects and language arts instruction does not mean that we consider the two areas as independent and separate. Indeed, we assert that language learning is part of academic subject learning, and vice versa. However, in academic subject instruction, the main goal is to learn the topics, concepts, and skills of the subject area. Learning the language of the discipline is essential, but not the main focus. In fact, in many cases with English learners, the language used in teaching and learning about academic subjects (learning through language)[3] can be a barrier to understanding the new content, so the Academic Subjects Protocol helps lower the language barrier while also helping EL students to rise above it. Our aim for academic subject teachers is to foster classroom communication (communication *for*, *between*, and *of* English learners) that reaches English learners at different proficiency levels (in academic subject instruction we suggest differentiating communication support for three levels of English proficiency—beginning, intermediate, and advanced).

The situation is parallel for language arts, or English language development (ELD) instruction, where learning language and learning about language is the main focus or point of instruction, and academic subject information may be the type of language that is being used during instruction. The point of language arts instruction, however, is not to teach a new concept in the academic subject through language, but rather to develop ELs' skills in listening, speaking, reading, and writing. It is this distinction in focus that defines the Language Arts Protocol's use, as well as our view that academic subject teachers who do not typically have extensive preparation in teaching language arts (e.g., secondary mathematics teachers) can do a lot to move EL students past language barriers, but it takes teachers with strong preparation in teaching language and literacy to adapt language and literacy instruction to meet the English language development needs of ELs at different proficiency levels (what we call *targeted language instruction* for ELs).[4] Our aim for language and literacy teachers is to target listening, speaking, reading, and writing instruction to ELs at their specific level of proficiency in each domain, which occurs by adjusting language and instructional features (what we call the four Ps of targeted language instruction—pitch, pace, portion, and perspective[5]). Because language development is sequential and incremental, we also suggest differentiating language and literacy instruction for six levels of English proficiency—WIDA levels Entering, Emerging, Developing, Expanding, Bridging, and Reaching.[6] This is a more complex type of differentiation than is necessary, for example, to make physics instruction accessible to English learners.

The tools and techniques presented in *Show, Tell, Build* are the substance of the ASP and LAP—they make academic subject instruction accessible, and they target English language development to specific proficiency levels of English learners. The ASP and LAP help classroom teachers and their collaborators to know which tools and techniques their ELs need and to plan how, when, and with whom to implement them.

In this book, the ASP is described in the introduction to part I, The Academic Subjects Protocol, and the LAP is explained in the introduction to part II, The Language Arts Protocol.

English learners need support throughout instruction and assessment in academic subjects and/or language arts, and in our experience the twenty tools and techniques in this book are excellent ways to provide it. We have field tested these tools and techniques in elementary, middle, and high school classrooms; with classroom teachers and ELD specialists; and for English learners from all backgrounds and levels of English proficiency. Our goal was to choose tools and techniques that work well in the EL-integrated classroom and to clearly lay out the steps of using each one for a variety of student needs and subject-matter demands. Assuming that the reader has little or no formal preparation in teaching ELs in the integrated classroom, we guide classroom teachers to use tools and techniques that experienced ELD teachers use, but within the context of the integrated classroom, in a collaborative school environment.

## HOW TO USE THIS BOOK

*Show, Tell, Build* is divided into two major sections: part I, which includes ten *Show* and *Tell* tools and techniques, and part II, which includes ten *Build* tools and techniques. *Show* and *Tell* refer to the two types of communication support, nonverbal and verbal, that are key to the Academic Subjects Protocol. *Build* refers to English language development, targeted to English learners' oral proficiency and literacy levels, which is the basis of the Language Arts Protocol.

Part I begins with an overview of the Academic Subjects Protocol, concisely discussing the major factors involved in teaching academic subjects to English learners. Following this overview of the ASP are descriptions of and instructions for using the four *Show* and six *Tell* tools and techniques. As with part I, part II starts by laying out the elements of the Language Arts Protocol, highlighting key elements in teaching language arts and literacy to English learners. The descriptions and instructions for the ten *Build* tools and techniques are categorized by which of the four language domains—listening, speaking, reading, or writing—is the primary focus.

This grouping of tools and techniques recognizes that their purpose for use is critical. Graphic organizers, for example, are presented in three different chapters because they are used differently to make key points of academic subject lessons comprehensible to ELs, to help ELs understand the structure of various types of text, and to organize ELs' main points and details for different types of essay writing.

We address each tool or technique separately to present not only its general features but also how it is used with English learners. Even if experienced teachers think they know the tool or technique already, what is presented here *will look different* because of its purpose for use and the way it is implemented.

Although we isolate twenty tools and techniques, our intention is for them to be used together. This can be done through what we term layering or sequencing. *Layering* involves using more than one tool and technique at the same time, depending on the English learners' level of proficiency, such as when a teacher uses diagrams, hands-on materials, and physical movement concurrently to demonstrate a concept. *Sequencing* indicates moving from one tool and technique to another, and sometimes back and forth, in a dynamic series of interactions with students, such as when a teacher responds to student writing by using leveled questioning and sentence framing to elicit the correct grammatical form from the student. These instructional practices will be discussed in more detail in each section.

Each tool and technique chapter can be consulted on an as-needed basis, like an instruction manual. However, the best way to get the most from this book is to read the appropriate introductory sections (the ASP and LAP descriptions) before reading a specific tool or technique. These introductory sections set the context for using the tools and techniques, and that is what is most different about using them with English learners versus other students. There is no specific order to reading each tool and technique, and it isn't necessary to read all of them to be able to use any one of them.

In the "Conclusion: Tools and Techniques in Practice," we provide suggestions on how to get started using the tools and techniques, combining them as needed and working with others at your school or independently as circumstances dictate. There are two appendices with crucial information: appendix A describes academic language in instruction and assessment and its challenges for ELs, and appendix B explains English proficiency levels and formal and informal ways to assess them and set goals to increase them.

To provide regularly updated resources for each chapter, we maintain a website, englishlearnerachievement.com. Click on the *Show, Tell, Build* cover to access links for the Additional Information and Resources presented at the end of the chapters 1–20 as well as additional, newly available resources and information.

We believe this book will help classroom teachers expand their teaching toolbox and develop a bigger repertoire of instructional techniques for the benefit of their English learners. We also believe that other educators, such as ELD specialists, bilingual paraprofessionals, literacy coaches, and school leaders, will gain valuable knowledge and skills to support ELs' academic success. We hope that reading and following the instructions in *Show, Tell, Build* will be an enjoyable and successful experience for all.

# THE ACADEMIC SUBJECTS PROTOCOL
## *Show* and *Tell* Tools and Techniques

Effective teachers of English learners (ELs) make numerous instructional moves every day to ensure they reach these learners where they are in terms of their cultural, experiential, and linguistic background knowledge. They recognize that teaching ELs is different from teaching non-ELs, and they understand the challenges these second language learners face. Important points to remember when teaching English through academic content are:

- Social language is different from academic language.
- Academic language consists of three dimensions: organization and thinking skills, sentences and grammar, and vocabulary.
- Subject-area vocabulary is an important component of academic language.
- Language demands are affected by both discipline and grade level.
- Academic language becomes increasingly challenging as grade levels rise.

There is a distinct relationship between academic subject learning and English language development. When English learners participate in academic subject instruction that provides appropriate communication support, they are also developing English proficiency. As depicted in figure I.1, the English language development (ELD) that occurs as part of EL-appropriate academic subject instruction improves ELs' subsequent

FIGURE I.1
**Purpose of Teaching Academic Subjects to ELs**

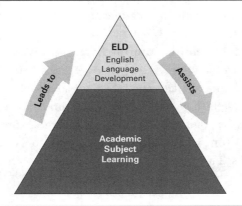

learning of academic subjects, and a cycle of learning both language and academic content continues.

In this section we present an overview of the Academic Subjects Protocol, a series of planning steps that help teachers in EL-integrated classrooms support communication for, between, and of English learners in academic subject instruction and that promote the continuous cycle of language development and academic achievement.

## THE ACADEMIC SUBJECTS PROTOCOL

The Academic Subjects Protocol (ASP) is one of the two protocols aimed at differentiating grade-level instruction for English learners that we presented in *Educating English Learners*.[1] It focuses on academic content areas other than language arts or literacy for the language needs of English learners. The ASP consists of a series of tasks and instructional decisions specific to English learners that teachers and curriculum experts make while designing challenging grade-level lessons. We break these decisions into two phases and a total of five steps that result in the delivery of the right types of support(s) that meet the needs of English learners in lessons originally designed for their non-EL peers.

Before we walk you through the Academic Subjects Protocol, however, we define some key terms that you will encounter both in the description of the ASP and later when we present the tools and techniques and their application with English learners.[2]

## KEY TERMS

✦ A communication **gap** is the divide between the language demands of a lesson and the language an English learner can process and produce at his or her current level of proficiency.

✦ **SLIDE** and **TREAD** are two mnemonic devices that help teachers locate areas in the lesson where the instruction is primarily given through either nonverbal or verbal means.

✦ Modifying instruction through different types of supports **narrows** this gap, although, by the nature of language proficiency, supports rarely close it altogether within a lesson.

✦ We use the terms **beginning**, **intermediate**, and **advanced** proficiency levels, which correspond to WIDA composite levels 1 and 2 for beginning, levels 3 and 4 for intermediate, and level 5 for advanced.

✦ **Use** refers to how the tools and techniques are implemented.

✦ **Time** relates to the point in the lesson the supports are provided.

✦ A **provider** is anyone who implements the chosen tool or technique with one or more ELs. The provider can be the classroom teacher, someone

✦ who collaborates with the classroom teacher, or even a technology-based resource. Collaborators may be ELD specialists, reading coaches, writing coaches, bilingual colleagues, bilingual aides, paraprofessionals, or classroom volunteers.[3]

✦ Depending on the size of the gap in the lesson for different proficiency levels, tools and techniques may need to be **layered**, meaning that several of them may be chosen concurrently for English learners at a lower proficiency level, while those at higher proficiency levels may require only one support or none.

✦ **Communication *for*** consists of the teacher explaining content or giving directions, or students receiving information through text or technology. In the field of second language acquisition, this is referred to as *input*.

✦ **Communication *between*** refers to interactions between the teacher and the EL students, the EL students and non-EL peers, or between ELs. This is referred to in second language acquisition theory as *interaction*.

✦ **Communication *of*** students is the way English learners show their understanding of the content through oral or written language. The term *output* is often used to describe this task.

With the above concepts in mind, we are now ready to describe the ASP, shown in figure I.2.[4]

## Phase I

Phase I of the ASP involves two steps. Step 1 consists of an analysis of the kinds and degrees of language demands of the lesson tasks. With this analysis in hand, the teacher moves on to step 2, which entails comparing the identified language demands with what English learners at the beginning, intermediate, and advanced levels can comprehend and produce. We have selected the WIDA Performance Definitions as the reference point for the language abilities of English learners at these three levels, which we have found to be a feasible number of levels that academic subject teachers can be expected to differentiate instruction for. Since the main purpose of academic subject instruction for ELs is to teach the academic subject, in terms of instructional differentiation we cluster the six WIDA levels as follows:

| | |
|---|---|
| Levels 1 & 2 | Beginning ELs |
| Levels 3 & 4 | Intermediate ELs |
| Level 5 | Advanced ELs |
| Level 6 | ELs exited from ELD services. We do not include this level in our discussion of the tools and techniques because their language abilities are close to those of grade-level non-ELs.[5] |

FIGURE I.2

**The Academic Subjects Protocol**

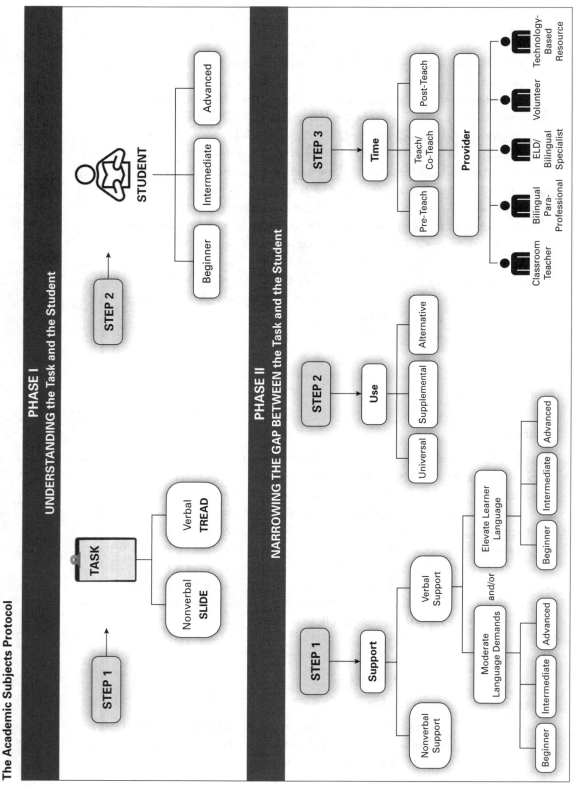

Together, steps 1 and 2 result in the determination of the gap between the language demands of a lesson and the ELs' language ability. It is important to note, as figure I.3 depicts, how the language demands increase along the preK–12 continuum. This means, for example, that an advanced-level English learner encounters a smaller gap in fourth grade than he would in tenth grade. How to determine the level of language demands is given in step 1 of phase I.

FIGURE I.3
**Classroom Communication Gap for ELs**

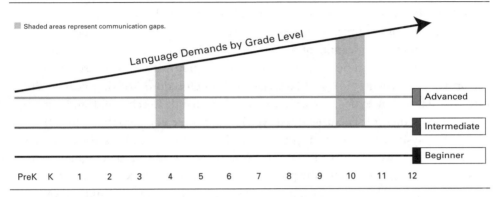

**STEP 1:** After designing a lesson or activity, the teacher reviews each instructional step and task, paying attention to the verbs that describe them. These verbs are then classified as either SLIDE or TREAD. SLIDE verbs point toward *less language-intensive* aspects of the lesson where the communication *between*, *for*, and *of* is not primarily conveyed through language. In other words, SLIDE verbs identify more nonverbal, and thus less language dependent, aspects already contained in the lesson plan. TREAD verbs, on the other hand, point to those areas where the information is provided primarily through language. We call these aspects *language intensive*. Table I.1 shows sample verbs that are included in the mnemonic devices SLIDE and TREAD.

TABLE I.1
**SLIDE and TREAD Verbs**

| **Less language-intensive** (not primarily language-conveyed) lesson aspects become visible by looking for the following verbs: | **More language-intensive** (primarily language-conveyed) lesson aspects tend to be described by verbs like: |
|---|---|
| • **S**how (also *watch, pantomime, model, display, project* [a picture/graphic])<br>• **L**ook (also *smell, taste, feel,* and other nonverbal senses)<br>• **I**nvestigate (also *measure, weigh, categorize, classify, connect*)<br>• **D**emonstrate (also *draw, design, act out*)<br>• **E**xperience (also *act, move, do, make, create*) | • **T**ell (also *present information, lecture, narrate, recount, go over, report out, share*)<br>• **R**ead (also *skim, scan, review*)<br>• **E**xplain (also *listen*)<br>• **A**sk/Answer (also *solicit, write, respond, predict*)<br>• **D**iscuss (also *describe, define, brainstorm*) |

In our practice, especially when working with preservice teachers, we have noticed that some verbs not listed in the mnemonic devices are ignored. This omission causes some of the instructional steps to remain unanalyzed, which may result in missing supports at pivotal events in the lesson or activity. Therefore, we remind educators to consider whether the information is conveyed predominantly through nonverbal, visual actions or largely through verbal ones, taking the spirit of the verbs and their synonyms into account.

Additionally, some verbs often used in lesson planning can fall under either SLIDE or TREAD. Examples are *find*, *locate*, *identify*, *provide*, and *give*. A student can be asked to find a partner to work with or to find evidence in the text that supports the author's claim, for example. In these—and really in all cases—we encourage you to consider the intended meaning of the verb used to describe a lesson step: Is information being conveyed through language or through action? Are students expected to perform a task through the use of language or through action? Looking at the main verbs in each sentence focuses teachers on exactly what the teacher and students are doing and whether it is language intensive. The first time you complete a SLIDE/TREAD analysis of a lesson plan, you will need to examine the plan sentence by sentence. Once you are comfortable with that process, you can scan each segment of the lesson (each task) and look for the predominant verbs in that task. After doing that a few times, you will be able to pick up any plan and skim it for verbal and nonverbal communication.

**STEP 2:**  In this step, the lesson designer compares the less language-intensive and the more language-intensive aspects to the language skill level(s) of the English learners in the class, in our case the WIDA Performance Definitions. When overlapped, the two show the size of the gap between what language skills are necessary to fully participate in the lesson and what English learners are capable of at the current time. For instance, a beginning-level EL would be able to *follow the sequence of events* of an earthquake if it is shown in a video, even though the explanation of the narrator would be considerably beyond that student's comprehension. On the other hand, a level 2 beginner, who can recognize general content words and expressions and cognates and recognize an idea with details in simple or compound sentence structures, would not be able to *comprehend the reasons why* the United States entered World War II presented in a video without support. The gap would obviously be smaller for an intermediate-level EL and even smaller for an advanced student than for the beginner. The determination of the gap size completes phase I of the ASP.

## Phase II

Phase II is where the instructional decisions take place. Here the teacher plans purposeful moves in the instructional cycle that afford English learners the chance to learn academic subject content and the necessary language to thrive.

**STEP 1:** The first step of phase II is to identify the type of support that is needed, keeping in mind that multiple layers of support may be necessary to fully assist the ELs in comprehending the content. The quickest decision is whether the addition of non-verbal support in the form of gestures, a picture, a graph, a movie, and so on would sufficiently mediate the gap.[6] We call the nonverbal supports presented in this book *Show* tools and techniques. If so, the teacher moves on to step 2. If, however, the addition of nonverbal support would be beneficial, but not adequate because the gap is too large, the decision is made as to what types of verbal supports should be chosen for the ELs to assure their active engagement in the lesson which, ultimately, will lead to learning. We call these verbal supports *Tell* tools and techniques.

When considering how to narrow the gap with verbal supports, it is important to understand that there are two directions in which *Tell* tools and techniques accomplish the task. Figure I.4 shows the constant increase of language demands from preK through grade 12 and highlights the directionality of the two types of supports.

The purpose of the first type of verbal support involves *moderating* (lowering or bringing down) the language demands. You can think of narrowing the gap as temporarily pulling down the language demands of a particular aspect of the lesson by reducing the linguistic complexity and/or the amount of language to slightly above the ELs' current proficiency level. Moderating the language demands may involve different types of supports for beginning, intermediate, and advanced English learners. Again, some supports may be layered to provide more support for beginners than for intermediate ELs who, in turn, require more support than the advanced ELs. In *Educating English Learners* we identified two support tools that narrow the gap by lowering the language demands: (1) leveled text (through simplification and elaboration described in chapter 8 in the *Tell* section) and (2) leveled questioning (described in chapter 6, also included in the *Tell* section).

FIGURE I.4
**Two Directions of Verbal Support**

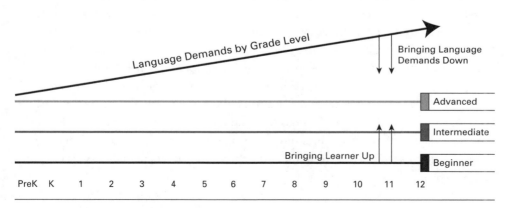

The opposite direction in which the gap can be narrowed is by temporarily *elevating* (bringing up) the ELs' ability to use language. Another way to think of this elevation is pushing students up from the language that can be comprehended and produced at their current level of proficiency. Note the use of the adverb *temporarily* in the first sentence of this paragraph. Although the tools and techniques to elevate learner language help ELs to better express their thinking and understanding of the content through language, the supports need to be provided *repeatedly and over a period of time* before the language features are fully absorbed and the ELs are able to use them independently. In *Educating English Learners* we identified two support tools that narrow the gap by elevating the student's language: (1) sentence frames and sentence starters and (2) word banks and glossaries. Both tools are also explained in chapter 10 in the *Tell* section.

Before moving to step 2 of the ASP, we would like to reiterate that multiple tools and techniques can be deployed in parallel, creating layered supports. These can be combined nonverbal and verbal supports or involve several nonverbal supports provided at the same time for ELs at particular proficiency levels. For instance, English learners, especially those at lower levels of proficiency, may need the addition of a word bank to sentence frames, with or without pictures to make the vocabulary easier to recognize. As students' listening, speaking, reading, and writing skills improve, sentence frames by themselves may provide enough support.

**STEP 2:** The second instructional decision to make consists of how the chosen support(s) should be used. We distinguish between three kinds of uses: (1) universal, (2) supplemental, and (3) alternative.

In universal use, support is added to the instruction for all students, not only English learners. The use of nonverbal support through gestures or pointing to a picture on the screen or smartboard are two examples of universal use. When the gap between the needs of advanced level ELs and those of their native English-speaking peers is small, sentence frames and sentence starters can be used universally for these two groups of students. More often, however, these tools should be differentiated to fit the proficiency of beginning and intermediate-level ELs.

Supplemental use implies that English learners are given a support that others—non-ELs or ELs at higher levels of proficiency—don't receive. Sentence frames or sentence starters, to show the different use of the tools just described, may be given to English learners, but not to non-ELs. Or a teacher may produce a word bank in conjunction with the universally applied sentence frames for an English learner. In these cases, the support is supplemental, or added to what other students in the class are given. Similarly, when teaching new vocabulary, the teacher may give a beginning-level EL a picture with the word and its definition, but decide that her peers at higher proficiency levels do not need this nonverbal support. In our experience, supplemental use of support is the most common of the three types and benefits all levels of English learners.

There are times when no amount of verbal or nonverbal support, not even multiple layers of it, results in narrowing the gap enough to teach the content. This is often the case with newcomers in higher grades where the language demands are too large to be bridged through supports. In these cases, the teacher needs different supports altogether, meaning that the newcomer watches a movie on the topic in the native language, or that a bilingual educator assumes responsibility for teaching the content. A second scenario that sometimes necessitates the use of alternative supports is when an EL student has a total lack of background knowledge or possesses very few or no literacy skills in either the native language or in English.[7] Again, this is most often the case when newcomers arrive in integrated classrooms during the middle or high school years.

**STEP 3:** Once the lesson designer has determined which support(s) mediate the gap enough for ELs to be active participants in the lesson and whether the support(s) can be incorporated universally, need to be given as a supplement, or require an alternative task, the final set of decisions can be made: (1) the best time(s) to provide the support and (2) who is the best person to provide it.

All general education teachers make decisions as to the most appropriate time to teach a concept on a daily basis and for all students. When working with English learners, deciding whether some components, such as vocabulary or building background knowledge, need to be pre-taught may be similar to determining which non-EL students require pulling aside to provide a head start to the lesson. This would be the case with struggling readers whose needs closely mirror those of ELs. Other times, the needs are so different that separate pre-teaching should be considered.

If the gap is not large and the chosen supports are likely adequate to narrow the gap, they can be used in a teaching/co-teaching setting. A third option is to teach/co-teach the lesson and follow up with post-teaching to assure that the content was understood to the level that permits moving forward the next day. The post-teaching session may reveal that some ELs are ready to go on, whereas others require reteaching to firm up the gained knowledge.

Depending on the type of program model, which could make other personnel such as ELD experts, paraprofessionals, bilingual aides, or volunteers available for collaboration with the classroom teacher, the teacher can decide which of these providers would be best suited to implement the supports and during what time (i.e., pre-teaching, teaching/co-teaching, or post-teaching). Teachers with limited access to qualified providers to collaborate with may need to make the hard choice as to whether pre-teaching or post-teaching is even possible.

## COLLABORATION AND ADVOCACY

In our recent experience working in schools, we became painfully aware how little interaction existed between the ELD specialists and general education teachers. If this is the case at your school, please seek the assistance of ELD experts, even if it is only to ask for a bilingual picture dictionary for a particular student. You may be surprised how quickly such requests can blossom into more frequent and deeper collaboration. Given the myriad administrative duties and service to the community that teachers perform in addition to their planning and teaching, finding time for coplanning on a regular basis is often difficult unless school leaders make the scheduling arrangements. However, with a little bit of effort, you and the ELD specialist or a bilingual teacher can find pockets of time when you can ask them for assistance interpreting standardized assessment scores, reviewing your leveled questions, or modifying a tricky text. As you build the relationship you may even find an opportunity to co-teach a lesson or ask them to conduct a focused observation when you try out a new tool or technique.

Although not providing ELs with important support(s) at specific times in the instructional cycle obviously doesn't give them full access to learning the content, we recognize that these are realities teachers encounter all too often. If this is your experience in your current assignment, we encourage you to advocate on behalf of the English learners—and yourself—and request additional support in the form of curricula, materials, or collaborators such as (bilingual) paraprofessionals or volunteers. Administrators in schools that have small EL populations often know little about the type of resources that would benefit their teachers who work with English learners. Your (repeated) request can change that! If your school does not have access to needed resources, find out who oversees programs and services for English learners at the district level and inquire about support for your school and classroom.

## MOVING FORWARD: *SHOW* AND *TELL* TOOLS AND TECHNIQUES

The next ten chapters will introduce you to tools and techniques rooted in second language acquisition research that you can add to your existing toolbox of supports (not ESOL strategies). A tool is something teachers and students use (e.g., a graphic organizer), and a technique is what they do (e.g., gesturing) that supports teaching and learning. The presentation of each tool or technique is organized by the considerations, phases, and steps of the Academic Subjects Protocol laid out in this part introduction (figure I.2). The tools and techniques are divided into several categories, depending on what type of nonverbal support they provide or which language skill is supported. These are the tools and techniques:

### *Show* Tools and Techniques

- *Images as support:* Graphic organizers for academic subjects
- *Images as support:* Infographics, diagrams, and animations
- *Objects as support:* Models, manipulatives, and realia
- *Actions as support:* Gestures, dramatization, and total physical response

### *Tell* Tools and Techniques

- *Support for listening:* Teacher talk
- *Support for listening:* Leveled questioning
- *Support for speaking*: Cooperative learning and academic discussions
- *Support for reading:* Leveled text

- *Support for reading:* Modified text
- *Support for writing:* Sentence starters, sentence frames, and word banks

As you review the tools and techniques and reflect on how they may fit into your current curriculum, instruction, and assessment, we invite you to occasionally return to this description of the ASP until you feel well versed in applying (some of) the tools and techniques to support your English learners at different levels of proficiency. Essential points you can easily keep in mind during your reading:

## ESSENTIAL POINTS

- Teaching English learners in an EL-integrated classroom is **different** from teaching non-ELs only.
- **Small gaps** may be bridged by the addition of universal support.
- **The larger the gap**, the **more substantive** the support(s) should be.
- Gaps can **vary** within activity or lesson phases. It all depends on the individual tasks.

## REFLECTION

At the beginning of each chapter, consider the following questions:

1. What do I know about this tool or technique?
2. How could this tool or technique help my ELs?

At the end of the chapter, consider the following questions:

1. Which of my ELs would benefit the most from this tool or technique?
2. If I had more time and resources to learn about and practice this tool or technique, whom would I ask for assistance (e.g., ELD specialist, more experienced peer)? For what purpose (e.g., planning, modeling, co-teaching)?

After you implement a tool or technique the first few times, reflect on the following questions:

1. What did I do today that helped my English learners comprehend and express comprehension of lesson content?
2. How successful was I in facilitating all ELs' comprehension and expression of comprehension of today's lesson? Were there any differences based on ELs' proficiency levels?

3. What could I have done better to help all ELs comprehend and express comprehension of lesson content? Do I need to consider adjusting support for ELs at specific proficiency levels?

4. How can I improve my application of this tool or technique moving forward? Are there any proficiency levels I should focus on more?

## Chapter 1

# Graphic Organizers for Academic Subjects

## DESCRIPTION

Graphic organizers show complex concepts and relationships pictorially, rather than describe them verbally. These tools include labels and brief descriptions, often with associated graphics, that show sequenced, organized, or connected elements of a topic or concept. The relationship of the elements is conveyed through their placement on the page or screen, proximity to one another, and the connectors drawn between them.

## PURPOSE

Graphic organizers can be used to present informational images to English learners or English learners can complete or create them to show what they know or learned. These tools can be used for many purposes, but this chapter focuses on their use in learning new content in academic subjects. For their use in developing literacy skills, please refer to the graphic organizers chapters 17 and 20 in the *Build* section of this book.

## CONTEXT FOR USE

Graphic organizers work very well to support comprehension of all academic subjects, but certain types are more appropriate for different disciplines. For example, a timeline format is used in teaching history, flowcharts in mathematics, cause-effect figures and charts and tables in science, and story maps in literature.

Many of the same types of graphic organizers are used at both elementary and secondary levels, but they vary in degree of complexity (and style flourishes) by grade. For example, a story map for primary grades might include the setting, the characters, and three sections describing the narrative arc—beginning, middle, and end. A secondary story map, however, might include rising action events, falling action events, conflict, and resolution.

Topics in science, social studies, literature, and other academic subjects can be previewed with concept maps, flowcharts, and other graphic organizers. This helps English learners whose oral proficiency is in the beginning stages of development get the big picture of the lesson topic. It also helps ELs whose oral proficiency is more advanced, but whose English literacy has not reached the same level, to anticipate key elements before reading a passage about the lesson topic.

Another way to apply these tools during instruction is to allow students to "check off" each segment of the graphic as it is taught, keeping on track ELs' global understanding of how the parts of the concept fit together. Providing empty templates of these tools for ELs to fill in, with either words or drawings, can be a less language-dependent means to assess attainment of the lesson objective. Alternatively, ELs can draw their own maps, charts, and organizers to show what they know about a topic, which teachers can use to access prior knowledge before a lesson or acquired knowledge after a lesson.

## MATERIALS AND PREPARATION

### Materials

Graphic organizers can be teacher- or ready-made. They can be given to students blank or completed, or students can create them from scratch. They are available as reproducible masters and as PDF files, and both you and/or the students can create them with computer programs such as Inspiration or Kidspiration. It's good to have plenty of blank pages and colorful markers to allow students to be creative with their maps, charts, and organizers.

### Preparation

When considering the lesson topic, review first the various types of graphic organizers available to see which ones fit the topic. For example, if the topic involves a process, a flowchart would be a good fit. If the topic includes a hierarchy of relationships, a concept map might be the best choice. If sorting is the goal, then a table would work well. Be sure to leave time to copy reproducible masters, download and print PDFs, or create Inspiration maps before your lesson. Once you've prepared them, you can reuse them when you teach the same topic again.

## HOW, WHEN, AND WITH WHOM TO USE

### Universal, Supplemental, and Alternative Uses

These tools are often used with non-ELs to highlight or summarize information. This is helpful to all ELs, but it may not be sufficient for ELs at lower levels of proficiency, who may also need first language support. For intermediate ELs, graphic organizers can supplement a presentation or a text. For ELs at beginning levels, these tools may be used in place of a text to limit the amount of language used to describe key points.

### Time and Provider (When and Who to Provide the Support)

The tools are equally applicable before, during, or after instruction. Before instruction graphic organizers can help ELs anticipate lesson main ideas, details, and their connection. They can also include native language labels for beginning ELs as appropriate. During instruction the classroom teacher or a collaborator can guide ELs in completing their own graphic organizers as key elements of the lesson are being explained, or a completed graphic organizer can be given as a supplement to a text that all students read. After instruction, the teacher or a collaborator can confirm comprehension by asking students to make their own graphic organizer.

## PRE-TEACHING PROCEDURES

Graphic organizers work well for pre-teaching and are great for giving an overview of the concept to be taught during the lesson. Through referring to completed maps, essential vocabulary, both discipline-specific and general, can be pre-taught so ELs are familiar with language that will be used in the lesson.

## TEACHING/CO-TEACHING PROCEDURES

### Communication *for* ELs

These tools provide a visual to refer to when presenting information to explain concepts. For example, as a history teacher plays a recording of a historic speech to his class, a collaborator can sit next to beginning ELs and point to an illustrated (or bilingual) map of the key points in the speech when the speaker makes them. If no additional provider is available, the teacher should routinely walk to the student's desk and indicate which part of the graphic organizer is being discussed at that moment. This not only gives a focus to listening to challenging rhetoric, but it also lowers the language load so that beginning ELs take away essential elements of the lesson and learn key words and phrases about them in English. If the main ideas map did not supplement the recorded speech, the amount of language that a beginning EL would need to sift through to understand the topic would be overwhelming.

### Communication *Between* Teacher and ELs, ELs and ELs, or ELs and Non-ELs

Continuing with the historic speech lesson, when the teacher pauses the recording to allow students to turn and talk about what they just heard, the teacher or additional provider can then ask the beginning and intermediate ELs leveled questions (see chapter 6) about the information on the graphic organizer to confirm comprehension. Having the key points and relationships laid out on the page succinctly, and in logical order, gives a concrete depiction and key language to refer to.

Another option at this point in the lesson is an activity where students complete a graphic organizer of their understanding of the topic so far, and the teacher or other provider asks beginning and intermediate ELs leveled questions about what they drew and wrote. If students complete the maps in pairs, communication between them is aided by referring to the drawings and words that they are able to produce, and it will be more successful for ELs than if they are told to discuss a question without any visual support.

## Communication *of* ELs

Filling out or drawing graphic organizers frees beginning-level ELs from having to rely solely on language to show their understanding of the topic. They can draw pictures and label them by copying words from the text or from a PowerPoint presentation. Intermediate ELs can represent their growing knowledge on the map, chart, or graphic, and then draft written descriptions, turning in both to the teacher. This can be done during the independent practice part of a lesson, after the lesson as a form of assessment, or as a follow-up assignment.

Graphic organizers are one of the main go-to tools teachers use to assess their ELs' comprehension of the lesson. Seeing a blank chart, map, or table is less daunting than an empty page or quiz questions for most students, but for ELs this is especially true. English learners, no matter what their level of proficiency, are capable of complex thought, but they may not be able to express those thoughts in English yet.

## POST-TEACHING/FOLLOW-UP PROCEDURES

Having students continue to add to a concept map that represents their developing understanding of a complex concept is a good follow-up for a lesson topic that is part of an ongoing instructional unit. For example, when learning about economic theories, ELs can start a concept map with main categories of theories, such as Keynesianism, Malthusianism, and so on during the lesson, and add details to their map during the follow-up session. Beginning ELs can include graphics and first language labels as well. Because their English language skills are in development, ELs sometimes latch on to new vocabulary details but lose focus of the big picture and the connections between them. Having a growing map to put everything together can help them comprehend global aspects they might otherwise miss.

## EXAMPLES

Example 1 is a completed concept map of a reading assignment. Students read an online account of the main eras and events of the women's suffrage movement in the United States, and the teacher provided the map, which had been created by students the semester before, to her beginning and intermediate English learners. The beginning ELs focused on the key events and reasons included in the graphic organizer, learning any new language listed within it (e.g., advocate for rights). Intermediate ELs used the graphic organizer as a checklist as they read the original online text detailing each part. Advanced ELs did not need the extra support to understand the original text, but they used Inspiration to create their own graphic organizer of the main points after reading the online content.

EXAMPLE 1

# Graphic Organizer of Women's Suffrage Movement in the United States (made with Inspiration)

**Women's Suffrage**
United States of America
1848–1920

Abolition of Slavery Movement → Seneca Falls Convention → Establishment of NWSA and AWSA → Founding of WCTU → NWSA & AWSA combine into NAWSA → Affiliation with Trade Union Movement → Establishment of National Women's Party → Women Win the Vote

**Sexism**
- Women were not considered persons.
- Men held the power inside & outside the home.

**Effects**
- Women had no rights.
- Women organized to advocate for their rights.

**People**
- Elizabeth Cady Stanton & Susan B. Anthony
- Sojourner Truth
- Alice Paul

Example 2 is a blank graphic organizer provided for all students to use while reading Susan B. Anthony's speech. Non-ELs read the original text, and advanced ELs were given a leveled text with elaboration of idioms in a glossary (see chapter 8). Both completed the organizer as they proceeded through the text. Instead of reading the entire text, intermediate ELs were given the following statements and were asked to write the sentences in their appropriate place:

All people formed the union.

Making men rulers over women is not a democracy.

Are women persons? If yes, they are citizens, and state laws cannot discriminate against them.

Susan B. Anthony, a woman, was arrested for voting.

Excluding half of the union from voting establishes a law that violates the Constitution.

She is giving a speech to defend herself.

She quotes the US Constitution: "We the people of the United States, in order to form a more perfect union . . ."

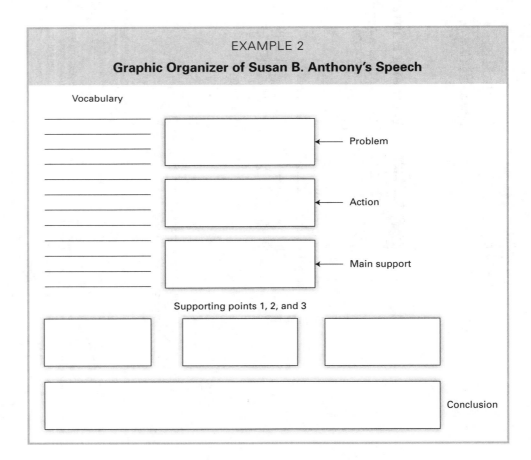

**EXAMPLE 2**

**Graphic Organizer of Susan B. Anthony's Speech**

Vocabulary

Problem

Action

Main support

Supporting points 1, 2, and 3

Conclusion

Beginning ELs are instructed to copy each sentence in the area indicated:

Problem: Susan B. Anthony, a woman, was arrested for voting.

Action: She is giving a speech to defend herself.

Main support: She quotes the US Constitution: "We the people of the United States, in order to form a more perfect union . . ."

Support point 1: All people formed the union.

Support point 2: Excluding half of the union from voting establishes a law that violates the Constitution.

Support point 3: Making men rulers over women is not a democracy.

Conclusion: Are women persons? If yes, they are citizens, and state laws cannot discriminate against them.

## ADDITIONAL INFORMATION AND RESOURCES

1. Houghton Mifflin Harcourt. "Graphic Organizers." www.eduplace.com/graphic organizer.

   This site offers thirty-nine reproducible graphic organizers in PDF format. Each file contains a brief instruction for the students. All graphic organizers are available in English and Spanish.

2. TeAchnology. "General Graphic Organizers Worksheets." www.teach-nology.com.

   This site offers reproducible graphic organizers in PDF format, with explanations of how to use each, as well as lesson plans that incorporate graphic organizers.

3. TeAchnology. "Graphic Organizer Maker." www.teach-nology.com.

   Customize common graphic organizers to fit your lesson and save them with a few simple steps.

4. Inspiration Software, Inc. "Visual Learning Overview." www.inspiration.com.

   This commercial software tool for visual learning allows teachers and students to build diagrams, visually brainstorm ideas, create outlines, and plan and deliver presentations. The website provides a brief description of each type of visual learning tool. A license is required.

5. The History Place. "Great Speeches Collection." www.history.com.

   This site contains texts of influential speeches, ranging from St. Francis of Assisi's 1220 "Sermon to the Birds" to Frederick Douglass's "The Hypocrisy of American Slavery" in 1852. Susan B. Anthony's 1873 speech "On Women's Right to Vote" was used as the basis for the graphic organizer in example 2 in this chapter.

6. Cox, Carol. "Using Graphic Organizers in Literature-Based Science Instruction." Reading Rockets. www.readingrockets.org.

   This article shows how graphic organizers can be used in different academic subjects and how they can be adapted for different grades. The author also includes links to a variety of resources.

7. Understood.org. "Graphic Organizers." www.understood.org.

   Through a partnership between fifteen nonprofit organizations and the National Center for Learning, this site provides resources to parents and teachers, such as reproducible organizers in PDF format to help kids with math or writing. Each file contains an example of how to use the organizer, followed by a blank copy for classroom use.

## Chapter 2

# Infographics, Diagrams, and Animations

## DESCRIPTION

Infographics, diagrams, and animations provide key information about topics, concepts, or processes in a concise, visual manner, helping to balance the language demands of a lesson by adding more nonverbal communication. They can be entirely nonverbal or may combine pictures of objects and their verbal descriptions.

## PURPOSE

Teachers use infographics, diagrams, and animations to present new information to English learners and to prompt students to discuss key points of the lesson topic with minimal information conveyed through language. Another purposeful application of these tools is to support ELs' interaction with peers to discuss, create, complete, or manipulate text and graphics to apply what has been introduced. For all students, infographics, diagrams, and animations can be good summaries to aid recall. Animated diagrams have the added benefit of movement.[1]

## CONTEXT FOR USE

Some lessons that are not specifically designed to address the needs of ELs at different English proficiency levels are by nature rich in images, and others may use no images whatsoever. Fortunately, any lesson can be designed or adapted to be more focused on ELs' success by incorporating *Show* support tools.

Infographics, diagrams, and animations are most commonly used for providing complex or key information in a concise visual format. The visual (nonverbal) element, including the sequence and placement of key components on the page or screen, carries a major part of the information. The verbal element, if any, provides essential details or explanation in the most straightforward, clear way possible. This means that complex processes that require complex language to describe and explain in text can be conveyed in less language-dependent ways. These visuals can be projected in a class PowerPoint presentation of the topic or concept of study, or if they will be referred to repeatedly in multiple lessons, infographics and diagrams can be put on chart paper or posters and displayed on the classroom wall.

In a social studies lesson about the history of Venice, for example, the general lesson plan included watching a fifteen-minute documentary in class, followed by a small-group discussion about its content and an individual writing assignment to summarize the main points. If the class includes ELs at beginning, intermediate, and advanced levels of English proficiency, adding the infographic in figure 2.1 and using it purposefully by English proficiency level and activity type to support ELs' comprehension and expression of the lesson content can make the difference between ELs' being engaged and meeting the lesson objective, or missing the point and tuning out.

The infographic examples in this chapter are from social studies, and history in particular, which is a subject that uses complex verb tenses that move from one point in the past to another and back to the present. This can be difficult for ELs to comprehend from language alone, so infographics and diagrams that include a visual depiction of time progression are especially helpful. Infographics, diagrams, and animations are widely available for scientific concepts as well. Regardless of the academic content area, these tools are especially useful for secondary students since their reading requirements are very demanding in academic subjects.

## MATERIALS AND PREPARATION

### Materials

Infographics, diagrams, and animations depicting the topic of instruction can be developed with software or on paper. Infographics and diagrams can be duplicated from books and printed or displayed from online resources. Apps such as Piktochart.com, Easel.ly, and Venngage.com offer free versions to make a variety of infographics, and apps such as Draw.io and software such as Inspiration.com are useful for creating diagrams. Canva.com is a helpful site to create different kinds of graphics. Sites like Dailyinfographic.com and Pinterest.com have banks of infographics explaining different topics. Google Images searches for specific topics, such as "history of Rome infographic" or "Roman history diagram," can lead to many resources. Students and teachers can create their own animations using Powtoon or Google's 3-D animation app Toontastic. Simple animations can be created with PowerPoint.

### Preparation

Handouts with infographics and diagrams can be prepared in advance for ELs (especially for beginning and intermediate ELs, who will need to look up terms and otherwise familiarize themselves with the content). Regardless of the specific tool, the creation of infographics, diagrams, and animations consists of three steps:

1. Before selecting the tool, review the lesson topic and objectives. Look at what students are expected to read (print or online), listen to (audio), and watch (video) for information about the topic, and identify the main concepts that they need to understand from these materials.

2. Make a list of simple sentences that depict the main concepts and highlight any keywords for focus.
3. Search infographics, diagrams, and animation banks for ready-made resources that illustrate the points. If none are available for the topic, use an app to make (or have English-proficient students make) one for the class. Incorporate the sentences and keywords from step 2.

Animations can be more time consuming to make, but luckily there are a number of free ready-made animations online, and apps such as Powtoon or Google's 3-D Toontastic do not require programming skills.

## HOW, WHEN, AND WITH WHOM TO USE

### Universal, Supplemental, and Alternative Uses

Because the use of infographics, diagrams, and animations does not detract from instruction for non-EL students and may help some non-EL students who benefit from images in addition to print, they are appropriate for whole-class instruction in classrooms that include one or more ELs. They also work well with groups or individuals to supplement activities or assignments that are text-dependent, providing key points in an abbreviated and image-supported format.

Infographics, diagrams, and animations benefit all ELs at all proficiency levels, but they are especially helpful for beginning ELs since they reduce the amount of language needed to comprehend or to show comprehension of key points, and they can be provided as a supplement or even an alternative to grade-level text. For intermediate ELs, they can serve as advance organizers before students read a text.

The amount and complexity of language included in these tools when used to supplement instruction or provide an alternative format can be adjusted by proficiency level. Student-completed infographics and diagrams enable English learners to show the depth of content comprehension by labeling or providing captions for an infographic or diagram instead of writing about the topic, as non-ELs may be asked to do.

### Time and Provider (When and Who to Provide the Support)

Support using infographics, diagrams, and animations can be provided before, during, or after the lesson by the teacher or by available providers, such as an English language development specialist or a bilingual paraprofessional.

## PRE-TEACHING PROCEDURES

Even though infographics, diagrams, and animations may reduce the language demands of introducing a new topic or concept, they may include terms or phrases that are unfamiliar to ELs. Before introducing the lesson topic, confirm comprehension of or familiarize the ELs (especially beginning and intermediate-level ELs) with key terms in the infographic, diagram, or animation and any prior knowledge necessary to learn the new content. For example, in an infographic available online by searching "Rome Ancient Supercity" (provided by History.com), for beginning ELs the word *stories* might be confused with the other meaning of the word (tales), or they might know the synonym for stories, *floors*, instead. Intermediate ELs might need clarification of the sentence "Engineers perfected a form of concrete, similar to today's cement, which they used to build . . ." by breaking it into its three parts and checking for comprehension with each: (1) *Engineers perfected a form of concrete*—explain or elicit by questioning the student that *perfected* is a verb that means "make perfect" and that here the word *form* means a "type"; (2) *similar to today's cement*—explain or elicit that concrete, a mixture of sand and paste that hardens, from ancient Rome was like the cement,[2] another word for concrete, that we use now; and (3) *which they used to build*—explain or elicit that *which* refers to cement and *they* refers to engineers. It is important to remember that even though the support tool may balance the lesson's language demands for English learners, some of the language used or the background knowledge assumed in the support tool may need explanation or unpacking for English learners, depending on the level of English proficiency and prior education.

## TEACHING/CO-TEACHING PROCEDURES

Continuing with the ancient Rome theme, a unit on the Roman Empire, a general lesson begins by the showing of a documentary about the engineering of Rome. After the video, groups of students refer to a section in their textbook that covers the same topic, which they had been assigned to read for homework, and they address its discussion questions. Then, individual students complete a written summary about the three most important engineering feats. To support English learners' comprehension and expression of the topic during this lesson, we can look at the lesson segments in terms of whether the communication is *for*, *between*, or *of* students and how the image tool, an infographic, can be added purposefully.

### Communication *for* ELs

When infographics, diagrams, and animations are provided for ELs, they can be used alongside or in place of reading passages (as a form of text modification) or spoken explanations (teacher or video presentations), which may use language that is too advanced for English learners. With beginning ELs, infographics, diagrams, and animations can be an alternative to the English text provided for non-ELs, limiting the amount of the new language that has to be deciphered. Coupling infographics, diagrams, or animations, which by their brevity may omit important information, with more detailed texts in beginning ELs' dominant language can provide opportunities for developing English proficiency as well as learning the key concepts of the academic subject of focus.

The Rome infographic can be a supplemental source of information to the reading that students were assigned, limiting the amount of text that ELs need to comprehend to learn the main facts of the lesson. For beginning English learners, the infographic may be assigned in lieu of the textbook reading, and a native language reading can be provided (from online materials) to more fully address details that are not represented in the infographic. Having the infographic during the documentary showing can help focus ELs on identifying key images and terms from the video while watching it.

## Communication *Between* Teacher and ELs, ELs and ELs, or ELs and Non-ELs

When ELs are paired or grouped with other students (ELs or non-ELs), they can struggle to talk about their task or contribute their insights in English. Asking them to speak extemporaneously without support, especially for beginning and intermediate ELs, can require more productive ability in English than they currently possess, so giving them an infographic, diagram, or animation with key terms and phrases can help provide the necessary language as well as graphics to refer to. Another way to use infographics for communication between students is to demonstrate a hands-on process, such as water erosion, and then have groups create an infographic showing and narrating the process (the beginning ELs can focus more on the illustrations).

For example, during the discussion phase of a lesson, English learners can be paired with ELs at different proficiency levels or with non-ELs and can answer level-appropriate questions (chapter 6) that the teacher prepared about the content of the infographic, having the visuals and reduced-language descriptions to refer to when answering. These two *Show* and *Tell* tools and techniques can be combined with sentence frames (chapter 10) to provide structure for lower-level ELs to use when answering.

## Communication *of* ELs

Developing or completing infographics, diagrams, or animations can be a less language-intensive task than writing one or more paragraphs. Students whose English proficiency is not advanced enough to write descriptive compositions can show understanding of the lesson topic through these tools. Beginning and intermediate ELs can be asked to label or write brief captions for infographics or diagrams in lieu of writing a description. Advanced English learners can use a ready-made infographic, diagram, or animation to organize their writing. Most students struggle with writing summaries of texts, not knowing how to select the key elements to include or how to phrase the summary without copying what was written in the text. Following an infographic, diagram, or animation can help the writer identify the most important information and organize it for writing the summary in his or her own words.

As an alternative to the writing assignment on the three most important engineering feats in Rome, beginning ELs could be given a variation of the infographic that includes images only (by masking the words) and be assigned to identify three of the images by writing simple captions for them. Intermediate ELs could complete the paragraph assignment through having the infographic to support their writing. Another alternative would be to have beginning or intermediate ELs create their own infographic that shows their three choices and illustrates and describes the reasons for selecting them.

## POST-TEACHING/FOLLOW-UP PROCEDURES

If the teacher or collaborator was not able to pre-teach the vocabulary or sufficiently check for comprehension through leveled questioning during class, this can be done with individuals after the lesson. In addition, a blank, simple infographic or diagram template can be printed for students to take home and complete with family members—for example, an infographic of historical events in their family's place of origin.

## EXAMPLES

The examples on the following pages are a teacher-made infographic about the history of Venice and a ready-made diagram of the water cycle from the United States Geological Survey.

## ADDITIONAL INFORMATION AND RESOURCES

1. Lankow, Jason, Josh Ritchie, and Ross Crooks. *Infographics: The Power of Visual Storytelling*. Hoboken, NJ: John Wiley & Sons, 2012.

   This book has easy-to-follow steps and tips and strategies to create compelling and shareable visual content. The strategies help students find stories in data and allow them to visually communicate information with others in a concise manner.

2. E-learning Infographics. "The Ultimate Math Cheat Sheet Infographic." 2014. elearninginfographics.com.

   This site includes various learning sheets that explain key math concepts in an easy manner.

3. Eaton, Thomas. *Infographic Guide to Life, the Universe and Everything*. London: Cassell, 2014.

   This book contains one hundred infographics that teach a variety of concepts in life and physical science.

EXAMPLE 1

**Teacher-Made Infographic**

# History of the Venetian Republic

### Founded AD 421

The first inhabitants of the lagoon communities were escaping the Lombards.

### Early Middle Ages

The Venetian Navy gained control over the Adriatic Sea.

### High Middle Ages

Venice became a wealthy republic that expanded beyond the Adriatic Sea to the Byzantine Empire.

### 15th Century

Doge Francesco Foscari led Venice to the height of its power.

### 17th Century

One third of the population died of the plague.

### Decline

In 1714 the Turks declared war on Venice. During the 1700s, the Venetian Navy was depleted.

### Fall of the Republic

Napolean's troops arrived at the lagoon, and Venice became part of Austria in 1797.

### Kingdom of Italy

In 1866, the Kingdom of Italy was created, and Venice became part of it.

### Italian Republic

In 1946, after World War II, the Italian Republic was formed. Since then, Venice has continued to be a major tourist destination.

**EXAMPLE 2**

**Diagram from the USGS**

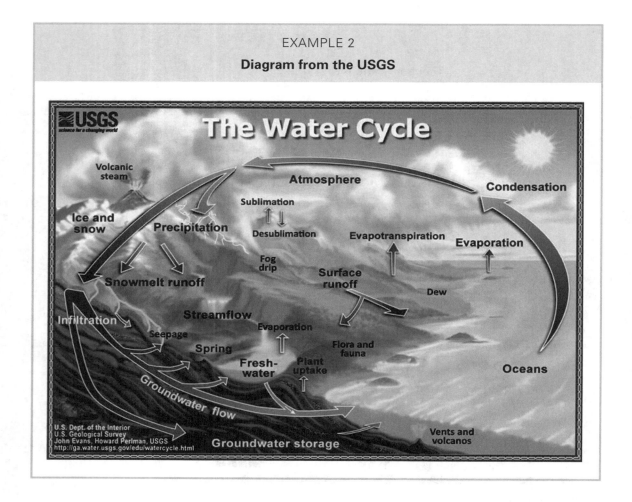

4. Higgins, Nadia. *The Solar System Through Infographics*. Minneapolis: Lerner Publications, 2018.

   This book helps students to understand the facts and key concepts of the solar system though charts, maps, and illustrations.

5. History Animated. historyanimated.com.

   This website contains animations of important wars the US fought, such as the American Civil War, World War II in the Pacific, World War II in Europe and Africa, and the Revolutionary War.

6. Free Math Animations. www.seemath.com.

   This website offers short number and algebra animations. The speed of the animation can be adjusted. Students click on the forward button when they have viewed and understood a screen.

7. Science Animations. science-animations.com.

   This website contains both math and physics games and simulations for teaching numbers, fractions, shapes, geometry, materials science, vibrations and waves, gravity, thermodynamics, and many more topics.

## Chapter 3

# Models, Manipulatives, and Realia

## DESCRIPTION

Models and manipulatives are physical objects that represent a system, concept, or thing and are natural elements when communicating new information during science, mathematics, history, and literature lessons. Computer-based versions of these tools include models, video clips, and 360-degree photographs or graphics. Realia are real objects used in teacher demonstrations or hands-on activities, such as different types of fruits, vegetables, and leaves.

## PURPOSE

Teachers use models, manipulatives, and realia to make learning experiences as concrete and realistic as possible.[1] These tools are especially helpful for ELs because they make content recognizable without language. For example, if a beginning EL is familiar with the solar system but doesn't know that term or the planet names in English, the student would be able to recognize that the lesson is about the solar system if a model of the solar system is shown in class.

Another purpose of these tools is for the teacher to refer to them or their elements during verbal explanations, which can connect new verbal expressions with model elements and processes. They can also be useful in providing ELs a concrete reference to point to when describing or explaining a process or concept, especially if they are not yet able to provide a complex verbal description or explanation.

The key for using these tools with ELs is not to assume that simply using objects will make instruction accessible. It will improve accessibility, but it won't guarantee comprehension. Pairing these objects with the language that describes them, and reinforcing that multiple times, will help comprehension of the topic and acquisition of the language.

## CONTEXT FOR USE

There is a plethora of objects for use in academic subject instruction. Science instruction includes many types of models, such as a solar system mechanical model (also called an *orrery*), a stream table for demonstrating the process of erosion, or an inclined plane and car to show principles of physics. Science also uses many types of realia in hands-on learning activities, such as leaves students gather from the ground and sort into bins labeled as deciduous or coniferous or bean plants students grow from seeds.

Manipulatives are very common in mathematics instruction. Pattern blocks, used to teach shapes and basics of geometry, as well as base ten blocks, used to teach place value, are materials found in most elementary classrooms. During mathematics instruction that uses manipulatives, you should indicate the functions or properties of the objects as you are talking about them. For example, if you hold up a square shape and say, "Squares have four equal sides," you should point to each side and indicate with your thumb and forefinger that each side is the same length. If you hold up only the square shape when describing the properties of a square, you risk excluding beginning ELs from understanding the concept and learning its language. Mathematics lessons also use realia—for example, asking students to identify and photograph objects in the classroom that are in the shape of a circle to apply new conceptual knowledge.

In subjects such as literature and social studies, teachers frequently use realia. Literature instruction might include dramatizing a scene from a play (see chapter 4), with the teacher or students wearing clothes of the era, acting in front of a backdrop depicting the setting. Social studies classes use realia such as currency from other countries and miniatures of historic buildings that classes have visited on field trips. Physical models such as dioramas are particularly well suited for social studies, showing, for example, how a battle advanced or how historic buildings were situated in relation to one another.

## MATERIALS AND PREPARATION

### Materials

Having the physical objects organized in bins or file folders makes them readily accessible. They can be organized by category if you plan to use them for more than one topic, by lesson if they are specific to only one lesson, or by EL proficiency level if they are needed only for ELs at a certain level. The time invested in setting up an organizational system will be more than regained in quick access when needed.

### Preparation

When planning a lesson, teachers of ELs can let their creativity flourish and incorporate as many touchable, movable objects as possible. Whenever you consider using a lesson plan, scan it to find opportunities to add models, manipulatives, and realia, and then gather them before teaching the lesson.

## HOW, WHEN, AND WITH WHOM TO USE

### Universal, Supplemental, and Alternative Uses

Models, manipulatives, and realia are primarily universal supports because they benefit non-ELs as well as ELs. English learners need even more such tools than other students because they reduce the language load of learning a new topic, and they help teach the language of the system, concept, or details.

## Time and Provider (When and Who to Provide the Support)

Because these tools are beneficial for all students, the classroom teacher is normally the main person who uses them with ELs. Although they have application for pre-teaching and post-teaching, they are easily incorporated into any lesson or activity and are commonly used with all students. Their use does not guarantee that ELs will acquire the associated language. The teacher or a collaborator can reinforce this by making explicit language and object connections before or after instruction.

## PRE-TEACHING PROCEDURES

It makes a big difference if the EL already knows the content of the lesson in his or her native language, so assessing prior knowledge using objects is highly beneficial. In this case, the cognitive demand can be dedicated to learning the language of the topic.[2] If the content is new to the EL, the student has to learn twice as much. To assess prior knowledge, use leveled questioning (chapter 6) about the objects, pointing to their components while referencing them. For beginning ELs especially, it's easier to talk about something in front of them.

## TEACHING/CO-TEACHING PROCEDURES

## Communication *for* ELs

When speaking about topics using objects, it's important to indicate the specific part or quality of the object as it's being referred to rather than just holding up the item. Doing so makes communication more precise, and it helps ELs learn the language associated with each object and what it represents.

An example is introducing the topic of erosion by using a stream table. After soil has been added to the table and has been elevated to create a slope, the teacher adds water to the upper end of the table; it then flows downward to the bottom and into a bucket, eroding the soil and demonstrating how a stream forms. Other materials can be added to the table, such as pebbles or pine needles, to see how they affect the water flow.

For beginning or intermediate ELs observing this process, it is clear that the lesson is about the formation of a stream even if they don't understand all the language used during the demonstration. Seeing this concrete process promotes ELs' comprehension of it.

During the demonstration, the teacher has a prime opportunity for teaching the language associated with the topic, but many teachers don't use this opportunity to its full advantage. Narrating each step and pointing to and holding up objects as they are named help not only ELs but all students to acquire academic language. We have seen teachers go through the process of setting the water in motion and watching it flow to the bottom, only to say, "Isn't that cool?!" or "Wow, look at that!" as it moved downward instead of stating what was happening or eliciting a description from the class. After the activity, the teacher asked the students to write what happened in their science journals and was surprised when her English learners wrote incomplete sentences without the proper terms. Instead, had the teacher narrated each step as it happened, pointing to each object and action as she described it, and written key words and phrases on a whiteboard as she stated them, the students would have had a great deal of language to draw from when writing their description of the process in their journals.

## Communication *Between* Teacher and ELs, ELs and ELs, or ELs and Non-ELs

When teachers work with ELs in small groups, they can use objects to facilitate discussion and language learning. For example, before a lesson about the three basic rock types—metamorphic, igneous, and sedimentary—the teacher can pre-teach the vocabulary with real rocks of each category, pointing out their features, followed by questioning the ELs about their differences. Having the rocks to refer to will help the ELs continue their descriptions even if they lack a word or the grammatical competency to phrase the description in English. If they don't know the word *layer* in English, for example, but they say "lines" while pointing to the layers in a sedimentary rock, the teacher can confirm their understanding of a feature of sedimentary rocks and also supply the proper word in English.

If ELs work with other students in hands-on activities such as sorting leaves into bins or measuring forces on an inclined plane, it's important to provide support for ELs to talk about the models. This can be done by providing supplementary word banks (such as *basic machine, force, angle, ramp*) and sentence frames (chapter 10) for the topic ("The object moves along the ramp with an incline of _____").[3]

## Communication *of* ELs

When ELs work independently, either as practice or for assessment, they can label and describe the parts of a model. If they are beginning ELs, they can create a model or can hold up or point to objects to answer identification questions or arrange parts of a model correctly.

Computer-based models are well suited to independent practice or assessment for ELs. For example, the app called the Elements provides a 360-degree perspective on gold and copper, including animations demonstrating what happens when they are exposed to heat or other factors that change their form. ELs can not only observe each element from all angles, but they can also access descriptions in English and multiple languages. PhET simulations are another excellent technology-based resource for ELs to study scientific and mathematical principles; these provide animations of processes such as graphing slope-intercepts and include descriptions in English and multiple languages. After reviewing these materials, the student can write descriptions in a journal and submit it to the teacher or another provider for review.

## POST-TEACHING/FOLLOW-UP PROCEDURES

Using models, manipulatives, and realia helps any provider, whether skilled in teaching English learners or not, because they have objects to refer to when talking with ELs, and they can also have ELs sort or arrange the objects if their English proficiency is at a beginning level. It is important to continue use of the objects during post-teaching, just as it is important during other phases of a lesson.

## ADDITIONAL INFORMATION AND RESOURCES

1. Gray, Theodore. The Elements. Touch Press Inc.

   This app has vivid images of the periodic table of the elements. It also includes written definitions and photos of related items. Available in the App Store (cost: $8.99). Knowledge of the elements can be tested with the free Elements Flashcard app.

2. Gray, Theodore. The Elements in Action. Touch Press Inc.

   This app describes each element's characteristics and shows a video of it in use. Available in the App Store (cost: $4.99).

3. Gray, Theodore. Molecules. Touch Press Inc.

   This app uses video and interactive images to show molecules in action. Available in the App Store (cost: $9.99).

4. PhET Interactive Simulations. "Interactive Simulations for Science and Math." University of Colorado Boulder. phet.colorado.edu.

   The animations on this site explain a variety of STEM concepts for all grade levels and are available in dozens of languages. Select the simulations and languages under Teacher Resources on the home page, where you can also learn how to best use the PhET simulations.

5. EAI Education. "Home." www.eaieducation.com.

   This publisher sells teaching supplies, classroom resources, manipulatives, and educational games for grades preK–12.

6. Lakeshore. "Blocks and Manipulatives." lakeshorelearning.com.

   In addition to hands-on objects, this publisher sells books, manipulatives, kits with rock samples, erosion tables, and other items used for instruction. Free reproducible teacher resources are also available.

7. Dredge, Stuart. "10 of the Best Virtual Reality Apps for your Smartphone." *The Guardian*, June 13, 2016. www.theguardian.com.

   This article lists ten apps that use virtual reality headsets or multiple projected environments, sometimes in combination with physical environments or props, to generate realistic images, sounds, and other sensations that simulate a user's physical presence in a virtual or imaginary environment.

8. Google Expeditions.

   This app includes a plethora of augmented reality scenes and models, including historic sites, human anatomy, and engineering processes. Available in the App Store (cost: free).

# Gestures, Dramatization, and Total Physical Response

## DESCRIPTION

The three techniques presented in this chapter are kinesthetic in nature. Gestures, dramatization, and Total Physical Response (TPR) enhance and complement spoken language by making a direct connection between speech and the topic through movement or action in real time. In TPR and dramatization, the main roles of learners are to be listeners and, at times, performers.

Gestures are movements of the hand, head, or posture that accompany speech to express an idea or emphasize parts of a statement. Dramatization takes gestures to the next level. In addition to body language through gestures, dramatization demonstrates action through larger body movement. Total Physical Response was originally a method developed for second language teaching, allowing students to learn new vocabulary or phrases without having to say them before they are ready to do so, but has found a steady following by teachers of all subjects and grade levels.[1]

## PURPOSE

Because of the connection between verbal instruction and physical movement, teachers use gestures, dramatization, and TPR to introduce new terms, teach new processes or routines, or to check for their ELs' comprehension when they have limited reading, writing, and especially speaking skills. By mimicking the teacher's body movements or acting upon the verbal command, English learners provide immediate feedback regarding their comprehension of the language used without being forced to verbalize in English right away.

## CONTEXT FOR USE

Most people naturally gesture to a certain extent in every verbal communication with others—even when the listener is not physically present, such as when speaking on the phone. When teaching English learners, gestures and dramatizations should be *more frequent and more pronounced*. Except for pointing to pictures or realia while speaking, this intensification may feel unnatural at first. Teachers often must remind themselves to act out the simple words or definitions of new vocabulary when they first start using gestures more deliberately. They might also have to overcome a bit of timidity about looking foolish. However, once teachers see the effect on English learners' comprehension, particularly those at beginning levels, they will quickly get into the habit of using gestures and dramatization whenever possible or warranted.

The TPR technique can be used by content-area teachers with ELs at all levels of proficiency. Initially, TPR was considered to be more suited for beginning ELs who needed to develop listening comprehension first.[2] Nevertheless, elements of TPR can be incorporated by teachers for ELs at intermediate and even advanced levels of proficiency to make content comprehensible and less abstract. A science teacher who has newcomer English learners can teach lab safety rules or steps of an experiment that includes "walk to the fume hood" through TPR. Not only are the English learners able to follow the directions, they will also recognize the sentences during subsequent lessons when the teacher directs them to the fume hood. See the "Communication *for*" section for a typical sequence of events in a TPR activity.

Dramatization and TPR are valuable techniques for introducing BICS (social) and CALP (academic) vocabulary (e.g., hypothesis, metamorphosis), as well as more abstract concepts (e.g., frustration, ecstasy) in all academic subject instruction by connecting them to physical movement.[3] One impactful use of dramatization would be to start a unit on the colonization of North America, the French Revolution of 1789, or an introduction to the periodic table dressed up as a Puritan, Louis XVI or Marie Antoinette, or Madame Curie, respectively. The characters, played either by the teacher only, or in concert with helpers, then present their accomplishments by enacting a pivotal event, exposing the students for the first time to technical terms, events, or other figures' names. Not only do the EL students get a first impression of the person or period, they become excited about the upcoming topic!

## MATERIALS AND PREPARATION

### Materials

Both dramatizations and TPR-based activities rely on a sensory-rich environment. For a TPR activity, the materials are illustrations or realia of the vocabulary that is to be introduced or reinforced during that lesson. For example, during the first lesson on angles in a math class, teachers could use images or drawings that depict the various angles, vocabulary, and degrees to introduce that vocabulary. Materials used for hands-on science or math manipulatives can also be utilized for TPR activities, and are typically already part of a teacher's collection of resources.

Elaborate reenactments like the ones described above entail securing of wigs, costumes, or period-appropriate trimmings. Dramatization to act out meanings of words typically does not require any props or realia at all, or only the kinds that would be readily available in the classroom or at home.

## Preparation

Acting out simple terms or short phrases such as *stand*, *touch*, *turn*, *stand in line*, even some sophisticated terms such as *exhausted* or *annoyed* do not involve rehearsal. After all, we perform them daily or at least see them in other people's body language somewhat regularly. As in all lessons, you first have to consider which words or phrases that non-ELs already know that should be explicitly taught, and which can be made comprehensible through gestures or dramatization.

When planning for TPR instruction, however, it is imperative that you have a well-structured lesson plan, since TPR-based activities tend to be fast paced. After deciding which terms will be the center of the TPR-based activity, follow these steps: (1) sequence the commands you will use to convey the vocabulary or phrases, (2) decide what gestures or larger body movements best express their meaning, and (3) write a script for each of the commands that are accompanied by your acting out. This detail of preparation allows you to concentrate on the moment and not have to come up with new command verbs or physical depictions during the actual activity.

Dramatizations that take the form of reenactments obviously take the most preparation. In addition to securing costumes and props, as already mentioned, a speech or introduction to the era or person must be written and memorized for the performance to meet the intended attention.

## HOW, WHEN, AND WITH WHOM TO USE

### Universal, Supplemental, and Alternative Uses

Many English learners rely on actively connecting visuals to everyday language. Such connections can easily be incorporated into lectures or explanations of concepts in real time through gestures and dramatization. Although these techniques are consciously implemented for ELs, we consider them universal uses because they can be seen by all students. When using and teaching academic language in whole-class instruction, applying gestures, dramatization, and TPR universally benefit both groups of students.

Explicit gestures and dramatizations often suffice to make content comprehensible to English learners in whole-class instructional settings. There are times, however, when English learners need to build prerequisite basic vocabulary or academic language that is already known to non-ELs. In these situations, a teacher may spend a few minutes with the ELs to go over the unfamiliar words and phrases, using gestures and dramatization to make that connection between language and the visible action. Similarly, a teacher may choose to devise a brief TPR activity just for English learners, to prepare them for the upcoming lesson.

### Time and Provider (When and Who to Provide the Support)

Because of their potential benefit for all students, activities that involve physical movement can be used in all academic content lessons by anybody who collaborates with the teacher. It is essential to remember that the new vocabulary should be reinforced until it is learned by ELs who may need more explicit language and object connections than their non-EL peers. Therefore, teachers should make time to introduce the vocabulary prior to the lesson or reinforce it afterward with the same technique that is used during the whole-group instruction.

## PRE-TEACHING PROCEDURES

Content-area teachers can assess prior knowledge using the visuals and realia to be utilized during the TPR activity. They can use leveled questioning (chapter 6) while pointing to them and give a command. Additionally, teachers should make sure that ELs are familiar with the command verbs to be used during the TPR activity so that language demands are reduced and ELs can focus on the new vocabulary.

## TEACHING/CO-TEACHING PROCEDURES

### Communication *for* ELs

Deliberate gestures and dramatization of actions while introducing new vocabulary and concepts enhance English learners' understanding of the new information because they make immediate connections between the academic language and the observed movements. In a TPR-based classroom activity, the teacher introduces new language and concepts in the form of commands or instructions while modeling appropriate actions. Then, all students are invited to respond to a command or instruction by mimicking the action, both in groups and individually. The instructor always makes sure that learners understand the commands before they are asked to respond to them. The students can also be invited to repeat the definition with the teacher, which obviously requires some spoken proficiency. The goal is to facilitate learning through watching others perform and then performing oneself without the pressure of producing language right away. For example, students can move shapes to make a structure by following commands such as (1) pick up the trapezoid, (2) put the trapezoid to the left of the square, (3) place the triangle on top of the trapezoid, and so on. Students can also act out events in a repetitive story that is read aloud, with pauses for student actions.

TPR can also be used for teaching more abstract vocabulary and concepts through the use of a strategy called TPR Storytelling (TPRS).[4] TPRS consists of three steps:

First, the teacher selects vocabulary and language structures and teaches them by establishing meaning, writing words and definitions on the board, and using gestures and nonverbal means, such as pictures or realia (see chapter 3). Next, the teacher tells a story that uses the vocabulary and language structure. This is done step by step, as if a comic strip were being shown one image at a time. It follows the same process as when teaching the vocabulary, only the teacher (1) says the sentence while performing the action, (2) says the sentence and performs it along with the students, (3) says the sentence and has the students perform it together, and (4) says the sentence and has individual students perform it one at a time. Finally, the teacher displays the text that contains the story with the story, leaving blanks for the vocabulary taught in the activity. The class first orally fills in the blanks together; then students write them in independently.

An example for using TPRS in science is stages of matter with the language function of cause and effect. While vocabulary such as *molecules* can be taught using pictures, demonstrating the different stages can be acted out through TPR, commanding the students to stand rigidly and close together, then stand at some distance, and so on. The storytelling part can then be utilized to teach how water changes from solid to liquid and to gas when the temperature changes.

TPR and TPRS present ongoing opportunities for assessing students' understanding. If you want to be sure that all students understand the commands without checking what their peers do first, tell the class to close their eyes; then give the commands. This allows you to see which students understand the vocabulary or phrases right away, and which ones need more modeling.

## Communication *Between* Teacher and ELs, ELs and ELs, or ELs and Non-ELs

Using gestures and dramatization is just as important in addressing ELs directly as it is during the input portions of the lesson. Communication *between* the teacher and the ELs even affords the opportunity to individualize the use of these two techniques based on the learners' oral proficiency levels. When checking understanding with lower-level ELs, a teacher may choose to act out everyday words that would not need to be emphasized with intermediate or advanced peers. For example, helping a beginning-level EL write brief sentences to accompany her drawing of Paul Revere's ride to Lexington could entail acting out the verbs *walk*, *run*, *skip*, and *ride* and gesturing adjectives like *slow* or *fast* to give the student word choices that best describe the image.

Teachers sometimes have to make a conscious effort to dramatize words or actions as they begin to use these techniques with English learners, and may also need to reassure students that acting out words they cannot yet independently produce is a valued means of communication. After all, when English learners understand the information or question coming from the teacher—with or without the addition of gestures or dramatization—but cannot get their point across to carry the conversation forward, the communication breaks down. Initially you may need to encourage and remind the ELs to use pointing or facial expressions while speaking. You may also want to tell them to act out actions alongside you as you introduce or reinforce new vocabulary. Once they develop the habit, they can apply the same technique during think-pair-share or small-group activities to facilitate their contribution to discussions.

## Communication *of* ELs

One of the best features of TPR and dramatization is that even ELs at the beginning levels can actively participate in class activities right away. The fact that, depending on their current oral language proficiency level, ELs may communicate through physical movement only or in combination with spoken language makes gestures, dramatization, and TPR effective techniques for assessing whether they understand what the teacher or their peers are communicating to them.

## POST-TEACHING/FOLLOW-UP PROCEDURES

One activity that incorporates physical movement a teacher can use to reinforce the new vocabulary is to write it on a small whiteboard and use it in a sentence (or associate it with a drawing for lower-level ELs). The students then act out the term, either by repeating the entire sentence or just by saying the word. To deepen ELs' understanding of new vocabulary introduced with explicit gestures or dramatization or through a TPR activity, students can also come up with their own gestures or body movements, sentences, or illustrations.

## ADDITIONAL INFORMATION AND RESOURCES

1. The Teacher Toolkit. "Total Physical Response (TPR)." www.theteachertoolkit.com.

   This toolkit describes the process of TPR and provides ideas for when to use it, as well as how to adapt it for students with varying needs.

2. ISL Collective. "158 Free ESL Kinethetics, TPR (Total Physical Response) Activities Worksheets." en.islcollective.com.

   This platform contains free-to-use worksheets developed by a community of language teachers from around the globe. Use the "Material Type" pull-down menu to access the TPR activities and worksheets. A free account is required for downloads.

3. Hamilton, Lindsay. "Total Physical Response Slope of a Line." TeacherTube, 2010. www.teachertube.com.

   This video shows a teacher demonstrating how to engage a group of students by using TPR for teaching math vocabulary.

4. Kranzush, Kate. "Math TPR." YouTube, 2015. www.youtube.com.

   Watch this video to find out how a teacher uses TPR to teach math concepts with a group of elementary students.

5. Madland, Jennifer. "Walker Middle School TPR Vocabulary." YouTube, 2012. www.youtube.com.

   Watch this video to see the branches of government taught through TPR.

## Chapter 5

# Teacher Talk

## DESCRIPTION

Through targeted talk, teachers model appropriate language in various contexts, adjusting it to their students' needs. This technique reinforces social and academic phrasing and enhances students' listening skills. There are three types of teacher talk[1]: (1) repeating; (2) rephrasing and paraphrasing; and (3) simpler, slower speech. Teacher talk moderates the language demands of a lesson but does not lower the cognitive expectations placed on the students; rather, it meets the students where they are in their oral language development.

## PURPOSE

The main purpose of repetition and rephrasing and paraphrasing is to expose students to vocabulary and situation-fitting phrasing multiple times and in multiple ways. Slower speech affords English learners the opportunity to catch up with what is said, while simpler speech renders the verbal communication more digestible because it adjusts the complexity of grammatical structures to the current level of proficiency.

Teacher talk gives teachers the flexibility to fine-tune this verbal support to the precise needs of individual English learners by combining different versions. For example, a teacher may adjust the rate of speech through pausing and, at the same time, utilize short, simple sentences when completing a comprehension check with an EL who just recently moved from beginning to intermediate proficiency level. For the student who has been at the intermediate level for some time already, breaking down the information from longer sentences into smaller chunks may suffice. The determining factor is the EL's current level of oral proficiency.

## CONTEXT FOR USE

Students are exposed to verbal language input throughout the school day. They hear and read new information and are asked to show their understanding in all types of classroom situations and all learning activities. Therefore, verbal language needs to be closely tied to proficiency levels in all content areas and at all grade levels.

Teachers often **repeat** themselves or recap using different phrasing to let students catch up to what was just said or asked. Teachers of English learners also use repetition to recycle student responses and to put emphasis on important vocabulary or phrasing, such as "Absolutely, atoms have *neutrons* and *electrons*. What else do you know about atoms?" In this instance, the teacher's feedback to the student's answer is not limited to an evaluative statement such as "correct," "good," "not quite," or "you're close" before moving on to the next question. Instead, the informal verbal assessment challenges the student to provide additional information, producing additional academic language, which is heard by all. Alternatively, repetition lets teachers expand on student responses. For example, a beginning English learner's answer, "molecule," can be turned into, "yes, two atoms *form a molecule* when they join together."

Like repetition, **rephrasing** takes place during the presentation of new material and when teachers react to student answers. Teachers restate their information, directions, or question using synonyms or different grammatical phrasing, yet keep the message similar. This technique especially benefits beginning and intermediate-level English learners because it gives a second chance to hear what was said. The alternative expressions achieved by paraphrasing have the biggest effect on advanced English learners, who are able to understand a variety of grammatical structures and who have a broader lexical base that includes technical and abstract content-area vocabulary. Not only do these students hear the explanation of a concept a second time, but they hear it in different wording and phrasing that uses a variety of complex grammatical structures.

**Simplifying and slowing down** speech are ways in which native speakers adjust their language when speaking with non-native speakers. In many ways, it is akin to parents or caregivers speaking with small children while they acquire their first language. Slowing down the speed of delivery creates digestible chunks of phrasing, which allows the ELs to catch up with what the teacher says or asks. It is accomplished by briefly pausing between phrases (e.g., "There are two [pause] different patterns [pause] in this drawing"). It takes no more than a conscious decision to insert short breaks within and between sentences to implement.

Teacher talk is a best practice for students in all grade levels and in all subjects. When used with English learners, either in one-on-one or small-group settings or in whole-class instruction, the technique must be carefully implemented if it is to reach the ELs at their proficiency levels. It is therefore important for teachers to familiarize themselves as much as possible with the amount and degree of difficulty of academic speech ELs at the beginning, intermediate, and advanced levels are able to comprehend.

By its very nature, teacher talk is in reaction to the needs ELs display during a lesson, and is thus a form of ongoing informal assessment. The teacher hears a student's response, reacts either by paraphrasing (may be corrective) or by repeating a question or rephrasing it in simpler, shorter terms when it is clear that the student did not understand the question. The teacher can keep notes on students' needs for repetition and rephrasing to track progress.

There are two ways to simplify speech for the learners' level of oral proficiency. The first way entails careful selection of vocabulary that is appropriate for the oral proficiency level of the ELs. For instance, intermediate-level English learners can process words and expressions with common collocations (words that go together such as *make a difference* or *take an exam*), but they are not yet able to recognize shades of meaning (e.g., *suspected* vs. *believed*). Simplified speech can also be produced by turning complex grammatical structures into shorter, simpler ones. Information is thus conveyed in grammatically comprehensible pieces, not only through vocabulary. This version is important for all levels of proficiency, but particularly so for beginning and intermediate English learners because they can process fewer types of sentence structures.

## MATERIALS AND PREPARATION

### Materials

No materials are needed to practice this set of techniques, since they are used orally, in reaction to one's own speech or to student questions and responses.

### Preparation

In the leveled questioning technique chapter (chapter 6), we recommend that you write down anticipated responses in addition to scripting the question when you start to use the technique. With these potential answers in mind, you can naturally augment the teacher-student exchange with repetition and rephrasing of questions and answers. While simplifying speech does not require scripting, we recommend that you consult with an ELD specialist a few times before implementing this technique to gain a more thorough understanding of the grammatical structures English learners can comprehend at beginning, intermediate, and advanced proficiency levels. Slowing down speech does not require any up-front preparation. However, you may want to remind yourself to monitor your rate and complexity of speech at the beginning of a lesson until you feel you are able to consistently implement this technique at the level of proficiency that benefits your ELs.

## HOW, WHEN, AND WITH WHOM TO USE

### Universal, Supplemental, and Alternative Uses

Teacher talk takes place throughout the lesson for ELs and non-ELs in whole-class or small-group instruction, or when checking on students working independently. Depending on the activity and the EL's proficiency level, teacher talk can be used universally or as a supplement or alternative to instruction for all in the EL-integrated classroom. When beginning and intermediate-level English learners are present, the teacher talk naturally becomes more pronounced and frequent because there is a larger gap between the regular rate of delivery and the amount and complexity of speech that the students can take in at once, but the rate and complexity difference is relatively small for ELs at the advanced level. In other words, as the English learner achieves higher proficiency levels, the need for substantial rewording in terms of language complexity decreases, and there is less need for repetition and slowing down the rate of speech. Using teacher talk that is appropriate for beginning ELs exclusively would not be appropriate in whole-class instruction because non-ELs and more proficient ELs need input that is appropriate for their listening comprehension skill levels.

## Time and Provider (When and Who to Provide the Support)

Teacher talk should be used throughout the day and by all instructional personnel. While general education teachers incorporate it into all their lessons, ELD specialists may use the technique as an exercise in reverse, asking students to rephrase two simpler sentences into a more complex one or by briefly teaching shades of meaning as they help students edit their academic papers.

## PRE-TEACHING PROCEDURES

Modifying verbal delivery through repeating, rephrasing, and moderating speech rate and grammatical complexity is an integral part of all instructional phases. Incorporating teacher talk into pre-teaching activities gives the English learner more support in getting prepared for the upcoming lesson than introducing vocabulary or a concept alone. Some teachers tend to slow down speech, repeat information, or select wording more carefully when they work with small groups of English learners, but then return to their regular speech pattern when the group joins the rest of the class. This practice limits the benefit of pre-teaching for beginning and intermediate-level English learners, so it is important to remember to carry the practice into the next phase of the instructional cycle.

## TEACHING/CO-TEACHING PROCEDURES

### Communication *for* ELs

When a teacher repeats or rephrases what she just explained or paraphrases the contribution of a peer at an appropriate rate and with phrasing targeted at specific oral proficiency levels, the content is communicated to the ELs in a comprehensible manner. Teacher talk thus enables ELs to add to their prior knowledge and more fully participate in the learning activity. For example, if a student told the class that matter is made up of atoms, the teacher could restate and paraphrase the phrasal verb *made up of*, which can be confusing for ELs because the whole term does not equal the sum of its words. After pausing, she could say, "Matter is made up of atoms. That means that atoms are the parts, or elements, of matter." When a teacher presents new information to ELs, teacher talk, which uses simple, clear, and slower-than-normal speech, can help beginning ELs comprehend the topic without being overwhelmed by the amount, complexity, or rate of normal speech. Adding images, objects, and movement to teacher talk makes it even more comprehensible to beginning ELs.

## Communication *Between* Teacher and ELs, ELs and ELs, or ELs and Non-ELs

In addition to repeating the information they share with the students, teachers should also repeat and rephrase questions or comments made by all students. This practice enables English learners to better understand their peers' contributions to the lesson. It also keeps them engaged while the teacher conducts comprehension checks because they have more time to think how they would respond if the teacher called on them. For example, when a student asks the teacher whether acids are bad for people, the teacher who responds with, "Hmm, let's see. What do you all think? [pauses to indicate that she is going to ask a question] Are acids bad [emphasizing *bad*] for people?" not only gives ELs a second chance at understanding the question, but invites them to form and share an opinion.

Adding gestures while repeating any student's answer—for example, "Yes, this is a square and this is a triangle" (pointing to or holding up each picture or objects when comparing them)—takes no time and further opens the beginning English learners' opportunity to grasp details of a concept. But the teacher can further enhance the input for ELs or reinforce a point by adding emphasis: "Absolutely. *This* angle [pointing to a drawn angle on the board or holding elbows together and spreading the arms apart] is only a *liiiittle* [holding up the hand with little space between thumb and index finger] bit *wider* than on this one [pointing to another angle triangle and holding elbows together and spreading the arms apart at a smaller angle]."

## Communication *of* ELs

A technique to support listening, teacher talk is not intended as a means to facilitate communication *of* English learners.

## POST-TEACHING/FOLLOW-UP PROCEDURES

Teacher talk is one of the go-to techniques, be it when building background knowledge, during instruction, or when firming up the understanding of the concepts taught after the lesson. As already stated, it not only gives the students an opportunity to hear the information a second time, but it also exposes them to the academic language that is associated with the content. To verify the depth of understanding an advanced-level EL gained from the lesson, you can ask the student to repeat or rephrase something you just stated, as this lets the student use the modeled academic vocabulary and phrasing immediately after it is given.

## ADDITIONAL INFORMATION AND RESOURCES

1. English Skills Learning Center. "ESL Teaching Strategies: 6 Tips for Using Repetition in the Classroom." Reading Horizons, 2012. www.readinghorizons.com.

   This blog explains when and how to use repetition to maximize English learners' exposure to and use of academic language.

2. Fisher, Douglas, Nancy Frey, and Carol Rothenberg. *Content-Area Conversations: How to Plan Discussion-Based Lessons for Diverse Language Learners.* Alexandria: ASCD, 2008.

   This publication is a practical, hands-on guide to creating and managing environments that spur sophisticated levels of student oral and written communication.

3. Mohr, Kathleen, and Eric Mohr. "Extending English-Language Learners' Classroom Interactions Using the Response Protocol." *Reading Teacher* 60, no. 5 (2007): 440–50. Reprinted on the Colorín Colorado website. www.colorincolorado.org.

   In this article the authors first describe the verbal interactions in a typical classroom, give question-answer-feedback examples for different situations, and then lay out a plan for increasing English learners' classroom talk through teacher modeling.

## Chapter 6

# Leveled Questioning

## DESCRIPTION

When teachers use leveled questioning with English learners, they pose questions phrased at their levels of oral proficiency, eliciting and expanding students' verbal and nonverbal responses in an ongoing exchange. Rather than focusing solely on matching questions to students' cognitive understanding of the topic, leveled questioning zeroes in on the linguistic complexity of questions so ELs can comprehend and respond to the question.

## PURPOSE

It is critical to address and engage English learners at all levels, not only to establish the students' sense of belonging and participation, but also to help them develop listening and speaking skills in English. Incorporating leveled questioning in any type of instruction, be it whole class, small group, or individual, moderates the language demands of the questions posed and enables English learners to show their understanding through verbal and nonverbal responses. The technique is an effective, dynamic, teacher-led means of assessing students' attainment of the lesson objective that helps the teacher explore whether the ELs' answers are limited due to limited understanding, or to limited language to express understanding. Leveled questioning helps teachers talk to English learners at different levels of proficiency and is a springboard to instructional conversations and academic discussions. In other words, leveled questioning is as much about helping ELs understand the language as the topic because if they don't understand the question, they can't give the right answer.

## CONTEXT FOR USE

Leveled questioning is one of the most applicable techniques as it is used for communicating about academic subjects, such as the phases of the water cycle, as well as everyday topics, such as whether a student rides the bus to, or is dropped off at, school. Teachers use questioning with all students throughout literally every type of instruction, so questions that are adapted to English proficiency levels enable ELs to participate when they might otherwise be passive observers of teacher-led questioning.

Because language and thought are closely intertwined, cognitive and linguistic complexity are mutually dependent. However, using leveled questioning does not limit beginning ELs to lower levels of cognitive complexity, because leveled questioning is one of many tools and techniques for engaging and checking comprehension of English learners.[1] Tools and techniques using images, objects, and actions to show complex concepts and relationships, such as concept maps and physical and computer-based models, can be combined with leveled questioning to enable ELs at all levels of English proficiency to participate fully in instruction. After posing a leveled question to beginning ELs, the teacher's response to students' answers moves to language-teaching mode, with clear verbal references to observable images, objects, and actions so the student becomes exposed to the language used to talk about them. Because beginning ELs are acquiring the building blocks to express their thoughts in English, using leveled questioning with them involves more teacher talk than student talk.

As ELs progress to intermediate and advanced levels of English proficiency, using leveled questioning means raising the level of linguistic complexity to the appropriate degree of challenge. Because the process of using leveled questioning is a series of meaningful exchanges between the teacher and student, if a question is not comprehensible, or if it does not prompt a response that uses the student's full command of the language and topic, the teacher engages the student by rephrasing and further elicitation. The ongoing conversation is the *-ing* in leveled questioning, meaning that it is a back-and-forth verbal co-construction of understanding new information rather than a question/answer/confirmation process, with the teacher guiding the EL to express his thoughts in English as fully and accurately as possible at the student's current level of English proficiency.

## MATERIALS AND PREPARATION

### Materials

There are no special materials necessary for leveled questioning, but images and objects to support questions and expansion of student responses are helpful.

### Preparation

Many teachers without background in English language development (ELD) are unsure how to communicate with English learners, especially those at beginning levels. Preparing and asking questions according to oral proficiency level helps teachers experience characteristics of the process of second language acquisition, and bring English proficiency descriptors and definitions to life.[2] For example, practicing leveled questioning can help teachers develop the ability to differentiate for different proficiency levels, which derives from experiencing, for example, how a question phrased improperly for the intended level leads to a lack of understanding on the part of the EL, and how rephrasing the question and supporting it with nonverbal tools leads to comprehension and response.

When first using leveled questioning, it is important to prepare questions for beginning, intermediate, and/or advanced English learners in the class in advance because it takes quite a bit of practice to be able to generate level-appropriate questions spontaneously. Once you have conversed at length with ELs at different levels, accumulating experience in understanding what ELs can comprehend and express at each level and how your questions and follow-up to those questions affect their performance, you will be able to come up with level-appropriate questions in the moment (although it's always good to plan some questions in advance for all students).

Steps in Preparing Leveled Questions

1. Find images and objects that depict the lesson topic. If images are not provided in the text, use Google Images or other resources.
2. Identify the places in your lesson where you would naturally stop to check for comprehension. Prepare three to five questions for each level of proficiency in your class, referencing the image elements for your beginning ELs.
3. Anticipate students' possible answers and your follow-ups. Consider leveled questioning a three-step cycle, with your question, the student's possible responses, and your follow-up to their response planned in advance. Once the cycle is complete, then you can move to your next questioning cycle.

## HOW, WHEN, AND WITH WHOM TO USE

### Universal, Supplemental, and Alternative Uses

This technique can be interwoven into any type of instruction or activity. Certain less linguistically complex questions would not be beneficial to non-ELs, so the technique can supplement grade-level instruction whether in whole-class instruction or with a small group of ELs while other students work in groups. Leveled questioning can also be an alternative to the instruction planned for the class for newcomers or students with interrupted schooling.

### Time and Provider (When and Who to Provide the Support)

Because leveled questioning can range from asking one question to sustaining a series of back-and-forth exchanges, it can be used at any time and by any provider who is skilled in using the technique. It is one of the main go-to techniques for EL-integrated classroom teachers, and they use it regularly with ELs during whole-class instruction and when working with ELs exclusively before or after the main lesson.

### PRE-TEACHING PROCEDURES

Leveled questioning can be used to ascertain ELs' prior knowledge before a lesson. By using this technique together with other appropriate tools and techniques to support ELs' communication during questioning (e.g., *Show* tools such as images, objects, and actions, first language support, etc.), teachers or other collaborators can get a sense of whether an English learner who moved from another school, district, or state has been exposed to the concepts that will be the focus of the lesson. In addition, there is the possibility that they have experienced interrupted schooling and its resulting knowledge gaps, so it is especially critical to determine if the ELs have familiarity with the topic so that native language support can be provided to help build the prior knowledge necessary to understand new content.

## TEACHING/CO-TEACHING PROCEDURES

### Communication *for* ELs

Leveled questioning is primarily interactive, with teachers' communication for ELs (asking level-appropriate questions) and with ELs (back-and-forth conversation, including language teaching or further elicitation and expansion) comprising the most frequent application of the technique. To illustrate the technique, we present examples of appropriate questions for different proficiency levels based on a lesson about the Statue of Liberty.

Using photos of the Statue of Liberty (a close-up photo facing the entire statue and a more long-range photo that includes Manhattan in the background), the teacher prepares questions for three levels of English proficiency.[3]

#### BEGINNING

For beginning ELs, write questions about what can be observed here and now in the classroom or in the images or objects of the lesson. Keep the phrasing simple and avoid extra words, including polite terms that lengthen sentences, such as "Could you please tell me what is in this picture?" For the beginner, the less polite, more direct approach—"What is this?"—while you point to the item is more comprehensible. Question types include simple yes/no (question E below), either/or (D), one-word response questions beginning with what, who, when, and where (i.e., wh- questions; A and C), and short common phrase response wh- questions (B). Students at this level can also respond by pointing to an item if they can't verbalize their answer in English. At this level, it's important to phrase questions and elicit answers using frequent, concrete vocabulary and common phrases.

    **A.** What is this (pointing to the statue)?
    **B.** Where is the statue?
    **C.** What is behind the statue (pointing to skyscrapers in Manhattan)? Rephrase as "What is this?" if not understood.
    **D.** Is the statue a woman or a man?
    **E.** Is this (pointing to the water) the Pacific Ocean?

#### INTERMEDIATE

Intermediate English learners can understand and answer questions whose language is more complex, using not only the present tense to describe what can be seen here and now, but also more complex verb tenses such as the present progressive (What is she holding?), the simple past (How was the statue built?), the past progressive (Was the statue decaying in 1970?), simple future (Will the statue be there in a hundred years?), and the present perfect (Have you visited the Statue of Liberty?). Intermediate ELs are able to explain and elaborate their answers to yes/no questions.

A.  What is she holding in her hand?

B.  What does the torch (light) symbolize (or mean)? What does the tablet (book) symbolize (or mean)?

C.  Why is the Statue of Liberty in New York?

D.  Tell me about the history of the Statue of Liberty. When was the Statue of Liberty built? Who built it? How was it built?

E.  What do you think the Statue of Liberty symbolizes (or means)? Does it symbolize the same thing to everyone? Explain your reasons.

### ADVANCED

In general, the advanced questions are identical to questions for non-English learners, but sometimes the phrasing or terminology might require paraphrasing (e.g., the term *second nature* might be misunderstood to mean unnatural if the EL hadn't learned that expression and reasoned that first nature would be natural and second nature would not) or cultural background information might need explaining (e.g., a sports analogy referring to baseball).

A.  If you could design a new Statue of Liberty, what would it be? Explain your reasons.

B.  In "The New Colossus," poet Emma Lazarus wrote that the Statue of Liberty cried with silent lips, "Give me your tired, your poor, your huddled masses yearning to breathe free." Who is the poem referring to and what does it mean?

C.  Has America lived up to the ideals represented by the Statue of Liberty? Explain your reasons.

D.  Imagine you were arriving a hundred years ago on a ship from across the ocean. How would you have felt when you first saw the statue in the distance? Why? Does it have the same effect today, when people arrive by airplane?

E.  Millions of dollars were raised to complete the statue from small donations given by children, the elderly, and the working poor. Would it have been better to give these donations directly to immigrants in need rather than to create the statue dedicated to welcoming them? Explain your reasons.

## Communication *Between* Teacher and ELs, ELs and ELs, or ELs and Non-ELs

The interactive part of leveled questioning is a skill that teachers develop and use regularly with English learners. The beginning, intermediate, and advanced paragraphs below describe the follow-up to the questions listed in the previous section, engaging and prompting responses of ELs by proficiency level.[4]

### BEGINNING

When beginning ELs are unable to understand the question or attempt to answer but lack the language necessary to respond, the teacher should move from questioning mode to basic language teaching mode. For example, if the student does not answer the question "Where is the statue?" after adequate wait time, the teacher can point to the statue and repeat the question more slowly, emphasizing the word *where* while raising her palms upward and making an inquisitive facial expression to show she is asking a question. If the student still does not respond or says, "Uh . . . " (ELs often use *uh* or *um* when they can't express their thoughts in English), the teacher can pose an either/or question, pointing to the photo and asking, "Is this San Francisco or New York?" After the student says "New York" (or if the student responds incorrectly with "San Francisco"), the teacher states the full correct sentence, "The Statue of Liberty is in New York," while pointing to the Manhattan skyline behind it. Then, while pointing to the water, she says, "This water is called New York Harbor. New York Harbor connects to (holding up her fists side-by-side and connecting them together) the Atlantic Ocean." If the student looks confused, the teacher can refer to a classroom map to show New York Harbor and the Atlantic Ocean.

### INTERMEDIATE

Students at the intermediate level are able to describe objects and explain reasoning in somewhat simple terms, often using developing, incorrect grammar. One hallmark of intermediate English learners' responses is a tendency to "trail off" when answering an open-ended question or one that requires explanation, beginning an answer with half a sentence and then saying "ummm" or "something like that" or becoming silent. It's important to try to determine whether the incomplete answer is due to (a) not understanding the question, (b) knowing the answer to the question but not how to say it in English, (c) or not knowing the answer in any language. This can be done through follow-up to the student's response. For (a), you can rephrase the question, using more frequent vocabulary and some description or examples. For (b), if the student responds to "Why is the Statue of Liberty in New York?" by stating, "big city," you can expand his answer, "You're right, New York is a big city. It's the biggest city in the United States, but there is another reason. The reason is part of the history of New York. When the Statue of Liberty was built, what was happening in New York?" If the student answers, "People come from other countries," you can tell that the student knows the answer but does not have the language to say that New York was the entry point for immigrants during the nineteenth century. Concluding that the student did not know the right answer because he first answered "big city" would be premature because those words might have been the only ones in English that he could articulate about New York without prompting and expansion.

ADVANCED

For advanced ELs, it is especially important to be sure that there was no confusion about the question. A simple confirmation can help determine if the language or cultural elements are unfamiliar. For example, asking, "Is the question, or any part of the question, stated in a way that is confusing?" followed by asking which part was confusing and paraphrasing it or explaining its meaning, can help determine whether the student doesn't understand the information or needs further language or cultural clarification to understand. Acknowledging that even advanced students can be tripped up by language and culture, and asking openly if either is impeding understanding, can help these students feel more supported.

## Communication *of* ELs

Although leveled questioning primarily supports communication *for* ELs and *between* the teacher and ELs, the comprehensibility of the question gives English learners the opportunity to respond—they may need help through elicitation and expansion of their utterances, or at lower levels they may need first language and *Show* tools and techniques to support their communication of prior and newly acquired knowledge.[5] Additionally, the phrasing of oral leveled questions can be posed to the English learners as writing prompts.

## POST-TEACHING/FOLLOW-UP PROCEDURES

Leveled questioning is great for post-teaching to check for comprehension. The teacher or a collaborator can work with groups of ELs or with individuals to determine if additional support is needed.

## EXAMPLES

Table 6.1, on the next page, provides brief descriptions of appropriate question phrasing, including verb tenses, question types, and examples for beginning, intermediate, and advanced proficiency levels.

## ADDITIONAL INFORMATION AND RESOURCES

1. Cotton, Kathleen. *Classroom Questioning. School Improvement Research Series.* Portland: Northwest Regional Educational Laboratory, 1988.

   This book provides practical guidance for teachers in how to ask questions that support student learning and engagement.

2. Hill, Jane D., and Kirsten B. Miller. *Classroom Instruction That Works with English Language Learners*, 2nd ed. Alexandria: ASCD, 2013.

   The authors offer evidence-based strategies for teaching English learners, including questioning techniques.

TABLE 6.1
**Leveled Questioning for Each Proficiency Level**

| Beginning Question Phrasing | |
|---|---|
| Short, simply phrased questions that use frequent vocabulary and verb tenses that focus on the here and now (simple present tense). | |
| **Question Type** | **Example** |
| Questions that elicit nonverbal responses | • Where is the equator? *Answer:* points to globe |
| Yes/no | • Is this a triangle? |
| Either/or | • Is this a triangle or a square? |
| Wh- questions that elicit one-word answers | • What is this? *Answer:* a triangle<br>• Who is this (point to drawing)? *Answer:* Galileo<br>• What is your name? *Answer:* student's name |
| Wh- questions that elicit two- or three-word phrase answers | • Where is the cup? *Answer:* on the table<br>• When is lunch? *Answer:* 11:30 or at 11:30 |
| **Frequently used, formulaic questions**<br>How much or How many | • How much does this cost?<br>• How many pencils are there? |
| **Intermediate Question Phrasing** | |
| Longer questions with more complex phrasing that use less frequent vocabulary and verb tenses that focus on the present, past, and future. | |
| **Question Type** | **Example** |
| Wh- questions that elicit description | • What does a metamorphic rock look like? |
| *How* and *why* questions that elicit explanation | • How is sedimentary rock formed?<br>• Why is erosion bad for the environment? |
| Questions using simple verb tenses:<br><br>    Present progressive<br>    Simple past<br>    Past progressive<br>    Simple future<br>    Present perfect | • What **is** the water **doing**?<br>• What **caused** the levees to break?<br>• What **was** the geologist **doing** when the rock cracked?<br>• How **will** she solve the problem?<br>• Why **has** pollution **increased** so much this century? |
| Negative questions | • When **isn't** water a liquid? |
| **Advanced Question Phrasing** | |
| Complexly phrased questions that use a wide range of vocabulary and verb tenses and that discuss sequences of events in the past or future, or are hypothetical/conditional. | |
| **Question Type** | **Example** |
| Hypothetical/conditional<br>past perfect | • What **would have happened** if the Allies had lost the Battle of Midway? |
| Future perfect | • **Will** scientists have completed exploration of Mars by the next century? Why or why not? |

3. Gast, Ged. "Effective Questioning and Classroom Talk." National Society for Education in Art and Design. www.nsead.org.

   This downloadable guide offers tips, tools, and resources for asking questions that increase student engagement in learning.

4. Fries-Gaither, Jessica. "Questioning Techniques: Research-Based Strategies for Teachers." Ohio State University. 2008. beyondpenguins.ehe.osu.edu.

   On the OSU site you will find links to articles, teacher blogs, and other resources to learn about questioning.

5. Finley, Todd. "Generating Effective Questions." Edutopia. 2017. www.edutopia .org/blog/new-classroom-questioning-techniques-todd-finley.

   This article presents four different approaches to writing questions.

## Chapter 7

# Cooperative Learning and Academic Discussions

## DESCRIPTION

Cooperative learning is an instructional strategy in which small groups of students interact or work together on a common task.[1] The task can be as simple as solving a multistep math problem together, or as complex as developing a design for a new vehicle or city.

Academic discussions are purposeful, sustained conversations about academic content that require students to work together to attain high levels of thinking and deep understanding about an academic topic.[2]

Both cooperative learning and academic discussions can take place in pairs or small groups of students. This chapter will focus on supporting English learners in these types of activities, either grouped by proficiency level or mixed with students at different proficiency levels or non-ELs.

## PURPOSE

Both cooperative learning and academic discussions are characterized by high student engagement and participation, as students talk and learn about relevant topics that allow for multiple and diverse perspectives. Academic discussions require cooperation, and cooperative learning requires discussion. Both of these techniques involve establishing procedures, then having students work in pairs or groups, following the procedures as the teacher monitors them.

Cooperative learning and academic discussions share several characteristics. First, they build on purposeful conversations focused on learning content. Second, they are based on grade-level texts and tasks that reflect academic standards. Third, students work together to co-construct knowledge and negotiate meaning with the purpose of understanding and applying academic knowledge. Finally, students use a variety of strategies that foster oral language development in academic contexts, such as asking for clarification, paraphrasing, and building on or disagreeing with a previous idea.

Classroom discussions, as well as cooperative learning, are conducted with the purpose of helping students (a) share their own thoughts, (b) deepen their reasoning, (c) engage with others' reasoning, (d) develop academic language and concepts, and (e) develop social and emotional learning competencies, including collaboration, risk taking, and social skills.[3]

## CONTEXT FOR USE

Pair and group work have the potential to provide great opportunities for ELs' oral academic language development. In pair/small-group activities, each student has more time to speak than in a whole-class discussion, and may feel less intimidated to talk with one peer or a small group of peers than to speak in front of the whole class.

To foster academic achievement through cooperative learning and academic discussions, it is necessary to provide additional supports for ELs when it comes to pair and group work. ELs may find group work challenging because there may be confusion about what their role is, and they may feel frustrated if they aren't able to express their thoughts and ideas fully because of their developing language proficiency.

## MATERIALS AND PREPARATION

### Materials

Academic area teachers will need to create handouts with task descriptions and discussion questions that will help guide the pair/group task and keep it focused as well as develop evaluation rubrics. Sentence starters, discussion templates, and differentiated sentence frames can help keep the discussion flowing.

### Preparation

To ensure the effectiveness and success of pair and group work in addressing academic standards for ELs, Zwiers and Crawford recommend four practices: "coming to the discussion prepared, using appropriate body language for discussions, participating by taking turns, and making connections to what others have said."[4]

Teachers can generate a rubric together with the class to determine how students will demonstrate these expectations, and group members can fill them out for themselves and other members. For example, coming to the discussion prepared might include reading and thinking about the materials in advance, bringing any confusion about the content to the teacher's attention before the discussion, planning major points to make, and so on.

Students can then model each behavior for the class, such as appropriate and inappropriate body language during discussions (for example, making eye contact).

## HOW, WHEN, AND WITH WHOM TO USE

### Universal, Supplemental, and Alternative Uses

Cooperative learning and academic discussion in pairs or groups help all students develop thinking skills and a deeper understanding of content from various perspectives. For ELs, these activities are essential for language and academic content development for a variety of reasons.[5] First, ELs need to be exposed to language in authentic and varied contexts. Teachers as well as students with higher English language proficiency serve as language models. Exposure to discipline-specific language is critical. Next, ELs need opportunities to produce language in contextualized and purposeful ways. They need practice combining form (e.g., grammar, vocabulary) and function (e.g., language used to clarify, explain, argue) to communicate and build ideas in academic areas. Finally, ELs benefit from repetition of ideas and vocabulary. Pair and group work allow for many opportunities to hear new concepts and content explained, analyzed, and interpreted repeatedly.

### Time and Provider (When and Who to Provide the Support)

Academic area teachers and collaborators provide support for ELs at the beginning of, during, and after pair/group work to ensure that the ELs understand their expected role in the task they are working on. This can be achieved by strategically assigning specific roles to ELs in pairs and groups and explaining in detail what those roles are. Additionally, teachers need to make sure ELs utilize and develop their language abilities by pre-teaching essential vocabulary, activating prior knowledge, and using graphic organizers with guiding questions.

## PRE-TEACHING PROCEDURES

Teachers can assess prior knowledge using illustrations and realia. If an EL already knows the content of the lesson in his or her native language, it will be easier to make the necessary connections between academic English vocabulary and the student's prior knowledge. If the content is new to the EL, the student has to learn not only the content but also the language associated with it. Leveled questioning (chapter 6) is useful in assessing prior knowledge.

## TEACHING/CO-TEACHING PROCEDURES

### Communication *for* ELs

One important element that makes pair/group work effective is setting up and giving directions that are comprehensible for ELs. It is important to provide simple, clear written directions that the teacher and/or student volunteers model for the entire class. Equally important is ensuring that ELs understand any discussion questions before they begin academic conversations. This can be done by conducting one-on-one comprehension checks with EL students prior to the group task, or by preparing translated versions in advance.

## Communication *Between* Teacher and ELs, ELs and ELs, or ELs and Non-ELs

For cooperative learning or academic discussion, teachers can establish base groups, usually with four students whose desks are placed together, which means that they will work as a team for an extended period. It's important to change the base groups at least once a term so students have the opportunity to work regularly with different people. If there are four desks, two students would be seated next to each other, and the other two would be seated in front, facing them. This allows for two main pairing options, shoulder partners (seated side-by-side) and face partners (seated across from each other).

Careful consideration of the English proficiency levels as well as the native languages of the base group members can make a big difference in whether a group functions successfully. The first consideration should be whether any of the group members are at beginning English proficiency levels. Students at that level need maximum support, through both *Show* tools and techniques such as infographics and graphic organizers and *Tell* Tools and Techniques such as sentence frames, modified texts, and leveled texts that address the same content as the grade-level materials that higher level ELs and non-ELs are using. Beginning English learners need this type of support for any part of a lesson, whether it is teacher presentation of new information, student interaction to apply or discuss the new information, or assessment to determine whether students met the lesson objective. The point here is that just putting EL students in pairs or groups is not a form of support in and of itself.

Pairs and small groups can build in a different type of support for English learners, however. By this we mean that how teachers prepare students to work together, and how they monitor and guide their interaction, will shape the way that other students help English learners, especially beginning ELs. If possible, the teacher can involve the whole class in an experience learning something new in an unknown language (ask for parent volunteers to help with this) and then discuss what it's like not knowing the language of instruction. It's important to stress that becoming bilingual is a goal everyone should have, and that being bilingual is an asset.

Additional preparation for pair and team work should be provided for each group with ELs at beginning to intermediate levels, explaining to ELs at higher proficiency levels and to non-ELs that their group works as a team, that there are students who are in the process of acquiring English, and that everyone has something to learn from each other. Native speakers and ELs who are more proficient can serve as language models for ELs at beginning to intermediate levels, and teachers can give everyone index cards with conversation support phrases such as, "Could you please repeat that?," "I'm not sure what you mean," and "Can you say that a different way?" so they can use these repair strategies when communication is stuck. They should also know to ask for the teacher's help when their attempts to fix breaks in communication are not succeeding.

Pairing ELs in small groups can result in a less intimidating experience as they can express their ideas to one person rather than to the entire group. Where possible, teachers can add a "share with a partner" step to a group share activity if a beginning EL is present. Once beginning to intermediate ELs are in their base groups, the teacher should consider pairing strategies within the group. Another student who is more proficient in English but has the willingness to help could be the shoulder partner of the EL in the group. If the EL's partner is conversant in the EL's home language, that will be a plus. Teachers should be careful to avoid assuming that pairing a beginning EL with another speaker of the same home language will address all the EL's learning needs. First, translating is difficult, and students may not know academic language in their home language. Second, translating is not teaching, so having a translator does not release the teacher from providing communication support. Third, it's not fair to the translator to be expected to be a language broker for every group activity.

Base group configurations that could be problematic include grouping ELs of the same proficiency level (e.g., all beginners) because they won't have the benefit of more proficient or native-English-speaking teammates to model the appropriate language. Another concern when grouping ELs who share the same first language is to be mindful of the other group members who may not speak that language. For example, we visited a classroom where two beginning ELs were in a group with a monolingual, native speaker of English and an advanced EL who spoke the beginning ELs' home language. When observing their interactions, we noticed that the three students who spoke the same home language worked together discussing their task in that language, and the native speaker of English worked alone.

In addition to base groups, temporary groups can be assembled for different tasks (see table 7.1). Homogeneous groups (i.e., ELs at the same proficiency level) can function well if the teacher uses this grouping to work closely with them on an issue that is especially affected by their level (writing individual reflections about a previous group discussion, for example). Other times the teacher may want to create temporary random groups for the whole class, so in those cases it could be helpful to pair a beginning EL with another student who the teacher knows would be a supportive partner, and then randomizing them as a pair when the groups are established. When heterogeneous groups are formed (with ELs and non-ELs), teachers can support the ELs by assigning specific roles for the task to each member, and giving the beginning EL a less language-intensive task, such as illustrating a brochure the group makes.

## KAGAN STRUCTURES FOR COOPERATIVE LEARNING

The Kagan Publishing and Professional Development organization offers a treasure trove of resources for cooperative learning. The following Kagan Structures are nonacademic and academic, respectively. Nonacademic activities, what Kagan refers to

TABLE 7.1

**Possible Cooperative Pairing and Grouping Strategies for ELs**

| Grouping Strategy | Group Type | Purpose | Additional Support |
|---|---|---|---|
| *Heterogeneous* Different level ELs and non-ELs | Base and random | Collaborate on an academic activity that is the same for ELs and non-ELs | Supplemental supports such as sentence frames and infographics, as well as pairing of beginning ELs with higher proficiency students in the group |
| *Homogeneous* ELs at the same level | As needed | Work on an alternative activity that meets the lesson's objectives but is not appropriate for non-ELs or ELs at other levels due to the size of the gap between the whole-class activity and the EL students' English proficiency | Teacher-guided group or technology-based activity |

as team-building structures, help build collaboration skills as well as social and emotional skills.

**Team-Building Structures:** Team-building activities are important to help group members relate to and communicate with each other. Including nonacademic team-building experiences throughout the year is important for helping English learners fit in with the groups they are part of. One team-building activity, Me and My Teammate, involves giving shoulder partners a paper with a Venn diagram. The teacher models the activity, using a document camera, with a volunteer so all students understand their task. In each pair, the more proficient student (the teacher has designated the more English-proficient partner as student 1 for each pair that includes a beginning to intermediate EL) begins by writing, in pencil, three facts about herself that she thinks are specific to her (e.g., birthday) in the left circle. Then she asks the beginning to intermediate EL student to share three facts about himself and to write them in the right circle. If the EL has difficulty writing, the other student can help. After they both have written in their circles, and if they determine that none of their individual facts apply to both, they try to find three facts that they have in common (e.g., they like soccer), and they write them in the intersection of the two circles. After they finish, they share with the other group members.

**Review Structures:** In a social studies class focused on the Lewis and Clark Expedition, students review the main points by using Team Mind Mapping. The teacher gives each team a large sheet of paper and a different color marker for each teammate. One teammate writes "Lewis and Clark Expedition" in the center of the page and draws a circle around it and four spokes pointing in different directions. Using Round Robin, the group members individually suggest a core concept (total of four) of the main topic that they will write in circles they draw at the end of the four main spokes of the bubble map. Individuals or pairs of students then add more lines and circles to their core concept, filling them with ideas and drawings. For example, if one core concept was for Lewis and Clark to gather information about the explored lands, bubbles could be filled with the words *plants*, *animals*, and *people* and could include drawings. After each individual added details and examples to the core concepts, the group members could use Round Robin to discuss their input with the group. With assistance from their teachers and peers, students support what they added by using evidence from the academic content they studied.

## Communication *of* ELs

When participating in pairs or group work, ELs must learn not only appropriate spoken and written language, but also the appropriate body language associated with academic-based discussions. Certain behaviors are expected, such as nodding yes to show attention when another is talking.[6] More specifically, ELs need to be introduced and practice the discourse behaviors or talk moves needed to participate in academic discussions. Kagan refers to these as "gambits" and offers a number of suggestions for creating index cards or "chips" that include phrases and sentences for asking for clarification, agreeing, disagreeing, asking for more details or evidence, and so on. Keeping a collection of these gambit cards at each group can facilitate greater expression.

In addition to general group and pair communication gambits, activity and discipline-specific sentence templates, starters, and frames (chapter 10) help elevate ELs' spoken language through these models and patterns that ELs can state and adapt until they can express that level of academic language unassisted. After ELs' repeated use of sentence templates, frames, and starters, the academic language phrasing of these *Tell* tools will become internalized and can eventually be expressed spontaneously, without support.

## POST-TEACHING/FOLLOW-UP PROCEDURES

It is especially important for teachers to follow up with their EL students after a cooperative learning or group discussion activity to check their comprehension of the lesson content and attainment of its objectives. Individual assessment of ELs at beginning through intermediate levels should be a follow-up step to make sure that none of the ELs were lost or disengaged during the group task due to English proficiency. Future grouping strategies and support can be adjusted accordingly if this occurred.

## ADDITIONAL INFORMATION AND RESOURCES

1. Clowes, Gavin. *"The Essential 5: A Starting Point for Kagan Cooperative Learning."* Kagan Online Magazine, Spring 2011. www.kaganonline.com

   In this article, learn about how to select the appropriate Kagan Structure aimed at promoting student engagement and learning for the purpose of your activity.

2. Jones, Lily. "Video Playlists: Engaging ELLs in Academic Conversations." Teaching Channel, 2014. www.teachingchannel.org.

   Find out what teachers are doing to engage EL students in academic conversations, using participation protocols to encourage students to talk more and learn from each other. View the video and read the blogs "Why Are Academic Discussions So Important for Our ELLs?" by Nicole Knight and "Key Strategies for Developing Oral Language" by Jeff Zwiers.

3. Kagan, Spencer, and Julie High. "Kagan Structures for English Language Learners," *ESL Magazine* (July/August 2002): 10–12.

   Read about five of Dr. Kagan's favorite structures with English learners and learn how they connect to best practices in second language acquisition.

4. Kamm, Carrie. "Building Common Core Skills: Beyond 'Turn and Talk.'" Teaching Channel, 2013. www.teachingchannel.org.

   In this blog, the author discusses strategies such as Turn and Talk or Think-Pair-Shares aimed at engaging students in complex conversations.

## Chapter 8

# Leveled Text

## DESCRIPTION

The technique of leveling text for English learners is closely related to oral leveled questioning (chapter 6). It entails making the core points of the passage assigned to non-ELs accessible to ELs at their current reading proficiency level in English because it adapts the vocabulary and grammatical complexity while maintaining cognitive demands. Therefore, it is considered a technique that moderates the language demands of the text.

## PURPOSE

As students transition from primary grades to upper elementary and on to secondary grades, they are expected to learn increasingly vast amounts of information through reading. English learners at all levels of proficiency, even advanced, often encounter difficulty in comprehending the central message because of linguistic complexity and length of text. Aligning the linguistic demands of a passage or book chapter with the reading skills needs of English learners at varying levels of English proficiency creates a space for them to interact with the content in a meaningful way and build academic language.

## CONTEXT FOR USE

Leveling text can be done in any grade level and in any subject area in addition to disseminating important everyday information, such as classroom rules or a request for volunteers to clean up the school garden. The technique can be utilized in whole-class, small-group, and individual instructional settings. Since the language demands increase along the K–12 continuum in both linguistic complexity and technical vocabulary, producing a leveled text for ELs in the secondary grades thus requires more substantive adjustments than it does in elementary school grades.

There are two categories of leveled text, although ELs up to intermediate proficiency may need a combination of both, with or without the addition of pictures or graphs, providing layered support.

**Text simplification** is a reduction in length and/or linguistic complexity of the passage. The simplified passage contains the same core information as the original text, but material that does not contribute to conveying the main content is removed. In addition to the elimination of extraneous wording, text simplification may also involve turning grammatically complex phrasing or dense text into simpler, shorter sentences.[1]

In **text elaboration**, the reader's attention is drawn to important vocabulary or phrasing that is familiar to non-ELs, but that would make comprehension difficult for English learners. Difficult terms are identified through a change in print (e.g., bold, italicized, underlined, highlighted), and a glossary is added in the margins next to where they occur or at the bottom of the text. The terms are then explained in English or the student's native language by providing a definition or an example, with the intention of providing necessary background information. This can also occur within the text as an appositive—for example, "The frog leaps, *or jumps*, in the grass."

The amount and type of necessary changes to the original text vary greatly and depend on several factors: (1) the length of the passage, (2) the vocabulary and phrasing used, (3) the grammatical complexity of the language used to present the information, and (4) the reading proficiency level of the students for whom the text is made accessible. They can range from inserting a few student-friendly definitions within the text or in a glossary to major rewriting of the passage. At the extreme end of the text-leveling continuum, a passage for beginning ELs might have nonessential information cut out, shortened and less complex sentences, as well as glossaries with translation in the native language. Pictures that clarify individual terms within the glossary or that depict the overall topic of the passage may also be added to provide the nonverbal support described in the *Show* section.

When students receive a simplified text, they typically also depend on a simplification in the wording of assessment questions to show the concepts they learned through the reading task. When this is done orally, teachers can apply the technique of leveled questioning, described in chapter 6. If the assessment is to be done through a written response, the writing prompt should be leveled to reflect the type of grammatical and phrasing complexity provided to the English learner during the reading portion of the lesson or unit.

## MATERIALS AND PREPARATION

### Materials

Leveling text does not require any particular materials or tools, other than images or a bilingual dictionary to create a glossary if the teacher is not fluent in the EL's native language. Commercially leveled texts can make text simplification and elaboration a little easier because some of the linguistic complexity has already been reduced and pertinent vocabulary has been identified. However, it is important to keep in mind that they typically are produced for struggling readers who are not ELs, and whose needs may differ considerably from those of English learners.

### Preparation

Logistically, leveling a text for ELs through glossing is easiest when a digital version is available, since it can be manipulated through word processing. We recommend that each paragraph be typed or pasted into the left cell of a two-column table and the glossary in the right column. This allows for horizontal alignment of the text with the glossed information. Shorter passages can be retyped in the table layout if no soft copy is available. If the text is lengthy, important vocabulary and phrasing can be highlighted on the printed version with the glossary written in the margins by hand or printed on an attached paper. Before starting to examine a text for parts that are difficult for English learners, we recommend that you consult with an ELD specialist or a bilingual educator because they are highly tuned to linguistic hurdles and can point out specific areas of concern. Similarly, until you have developed some practice in leveling text, you should ask these peers to examine whether your leveled text is sufficiently simplified or, on the other side, too much so for the intended proficiency level.[2] It is important to increase the linguistic complexity and length of leveled texts as each EL develops greater English proficiency.

Teachers with whom we have worked in the past feel more comfortable to start leveling text through elaboration than simplification because they have developed the habit of scanning a passage for vocabulary or phrasing that could trip up their non-EL students when they design the lesson or unit. Elaborating a text for ELs begins with the same examination, but it requires additional considerations. Which technical words that your non-ELs would understand might be unknown to your beginning and intermediate ELs? How about everyday words that a beginner would not yet have encountered? Are there any idioms (e.g., *the last straw*) or phrasal verbs (e.g., *put up with*)? Are the difficulties limited to some words or short phrases that don't need to be taught to the non-ELs in the class? In this case, adding a translation or a student-friendly definition in the margins may suffice, since new technical vocabulary and other difficult wording will likely be addressed with the whole class. If, however, the phrasing of the passage is dense and filled with grammatical features your intermediate or advanced ELs have not yet acquired, text simplification should be considered.[3] As stated above, complex text will require multiple types of simplifications and the addition of nonverbal support for newcomers and English learners at the beginning levels of proficiency.

## HOW, WHEN, AND WITH WHOM TO USE

### Universal, Supplemental, and Alternative Uses

A text that is slightly adjusted (i.e., a few student-friendly definitions inserted within the passage, a few glossed items included in the margins, or the shortening of a few sentences) is considered a supplemental support because the ELs are given information on top of that given to their non-EL peers. Even though the core message is the same, when the leveled text contains a substantial number of simplifications and elaborations to provide needed background information and make it linguistically accessible to English learners, its use is alternative.[4]

### Time and Provider (When and Who to Provide the Support)

Once a text has been simplified or elaborated to correspond to the proficiency level of an English learner, it can be implemented by any collaborator and at any time.

## PRE-TEACHING PROCEDURES

The process of leveling text, as stated above, begins with the analysis of novel or difficult vocabulary and dense, complex sentences that contain multiple clauses. With this information in mind, teachers or other providers can prepare the English learner for subsequent successful reading by pre-teaching the terms or grammatical features, either with or without the leveled text present.

## TEACHING/CO-TEACHING PROCEDURES

### Communication *for* ELs

Leveled text is primarily a means to provide comprehensible input to English learners at their current level of reading proficiency. Imagine a high school history unit on World War II during which the students analyze a series of primary sources. One of the documents the students examine is a speech Senator James Byrnes made on January 17, 1941. Here is the original text:

> There is nothing altruistic about the determination of the United States to aid those nations now defending themselves against the forces of aggression. We are moved by reasons more impelling. We know that our own Democracy is menaced by the forces that now seek to destroy those Democracies across the Atlantic. One conquest only whets the dictators' desire for more power. If Great Britain falls, the United States will stand practically alone on the brink of the precipice.[5]

Following is an example of a text that was leveled through both simplification and elaboration and would be appropriate for an intermediate-level student. It contains shorter, simpler sentence structures that are appropriate for this proficiency level (although the teacher may need to unpack the relative clause "nations that other powers"). Some of the considerations that led to the new wording were: (1) Would the message of the text be altered if terms and sentences such as *determination of, forces of aggression*, or *moved by reasons more impelling* were removed or reworded? (2) What grammatical structures are well above an intermediate EL's current competency? (3) What is unnecessary wording that would draw the students' attention away from the critical parts?

| | |
|---|---|
| The United States wants to **aid democratic** nations that other **powers** are attacking. We want to help these nations because it is good for our country. It is good because the other powers across the Atlantic Ocean (in Europe) **threaten** the American Democracy. If Great Britain loses the war, it will be a dangerous time for the United States. | **aid:** to help<br><br>**democratic:** countries that have a democracy<br><br>**powers:** other countries or governments<br><br>**threaten:** are dangerous to |

The leveled text still contains some challenging phrasing and vocabulary that students at the intermediate level of English proficiency should be exposed to. The brief explanations in the glossary help them grasp the meaning through words that they already know. The phrase *across the Atlantic* could have been eliminated altogether and replaced by *powers in Europe*. However, the addition of *Ocean* fills in the missing word that is evident to non-ELs, while exposing the student to the phrase *across [a location]*. The elaboration in parenthesis further drives home the point that a vast body of water separates the United States and Europe. If, however, the text were augmented with a map that points out the location of the United States, the Atlantic Ocean, and Europe, the original wording *across the Atlantic* would be appropriate.

No amount of leveling, even with visual support, could create a comprehensible version of this text for beginning ELs. First of all, how would you display the concept of democracy and powers or forces? Furthermore, if we were to turn the meaning of the first sentence into the type of simple sentences a beginner could process, we would end up with, for example, "The United States helps countries. Countries attack other countries." These sentences omit mention of democracy, which is necessary to understand later that the United States' democracy is in danger. Instead of leveled text, these students need an alternative form of the text altogether, a technique that is presented in chapter 9, as well as native language support.

For ELs at the advanced level of proficiency, the text would not need a lot of leveling, since non-ELs would have similar problems understanding the cumbersome phrasing and vocabulary such as "We are moved by reasons more impelling" or "on the brink of the precipice." With explicit unpacking of the text provided for all students, advanced-level ELs would be able to understand most of the original text with glossing of some words like *forces* or *menaced*.

## Communication *Between* Teacher and ELs, ELs and ELs, or ELs and Non-ELs

Reading text in the classroom does not occur in a vacuum. Whether a text is introduced in a whole-class setting or assigned to be read individually or in pairs or small groups, discussion takes place at several points in the lesson or unit. The leveled text allows English learners to ask questions about things they do not understand and participate in exchanges that deepen their understanding of the topic. Keep in mind, however, that some portions of the original text may have been left out because they did not contribute much, if anything, to the central message. When this is the case, your questions not only need to be linguistically formulated so that the EL can understand and respond to them, but they should include only information covered through the leveled text. This is especially important when pairing ELs with non-ELs or possibly also ELs of different proficiency levels who read substantially different texts; otherwise some students may be unable to fully contribute to the group discussion.

### Communication *of* ELs

Although leveled texts are created by the teacher, their usage is not limited to the communication *for* and communication *between* components of our ASP protocol. When students are instructed to write a summary of the main points of the text after thorough deconstruction and discussion, allow the beginning and intermediate-level ELs to consult the leveled text rather than requiring them to write what they remember. The support of the text enables them to use more accurate vocabulary and produce more linguistically complex responses.

## POST-TEACHING/FOLLOW-UP PROCEDURES

If time permits or if another provider is available, the same leveled text that was utilized during guided reading or independent practice can be picked up for post-teaching to firm up understanding of the overall text or to focus on specific vocabulary or phrasing. This second exposure to the leveled text provides the English learner with additional time to digest the information and to build important academic language skills. If it is evident that the student has gained a good understanding of the topic and is able to recognize or even use new vocabulary, small details that may have been eliminated when the text was created for this particular proficiency level can be added.

## ADDITIONAL INFORMATION AND RESOURCES

1. Ferlazzo, Larry. "The Best Places to Get the 'Same' Text Written for Different 'Levels'" (blog), 2014. larryferlazzo.edublogs.org.

   This blog contains sources where teachers can find texts. Most of them are not specifically leveled for English learners. We therefore recommend that you use them as a starting point from which to apply leveling for ELs at lower reading proficiency levels.

2. Houghton Mifflin Harcourt. "Leveled Readers and Bookrooms." www.hmhco.com.

   This publisher's catalog has a rich selection of engaging book titles that appeal to many students and includes options for both on-level and intervention instruction to help you meet rigorous standards.

3. Martini-Peterson, Gail. "How 2 Lower the Reading Level." WOW! Women on Writing. wow-womenonwriting.com.

   Read this article to learn how to determine the readability statistics of a text through Word, what these statistics mean, and how to adjust your text level at the word and sentence level.

4. Oxford University Press. "Graded Readers." www.elt.oup.com.

   The "English Language Teaching" part of this publisher's catalog includes graded readers intended for English learners. These include books at six different levels of English proficiency on a variety of academic subjects as well as literature classics such as *Moby Dick*. Some readers are available in packs that include an audiobook.

5. Reading A-Z. "ELL Edition." www.readinga-z.com.

   This publisher sells leveled texts specifically for English learners that are typically used for differentiated instruction. A subscription is needed to download the texts.

## Chapter 9

# Modified Text

## DESCRIPTION

Modified text conveys the material presented in longer passages or entire book chapters in an alternative format. Different from leveled text (see chapter 8), which retains much of the original text's layout, modified text presents the information in an *entirely different fashion*. The amount a student must read to obtain the information through a modified text is considerably reduced by the omission of nonessential details, but the crucial content to be learned remains the same. Modified texts range from mostly images (for beginning-level ELs) to a mix of images and text to mostly verbal, especially in the case of literary works where emotions or larger themes are not well conveyed through images.[1]

## PURPOSE

Teachers produce modified text to render assigned grade-level readings accessible to English learners who have not yet attained sufficient English proficiency and reading skills to understand the main message (and potentially associated details) in the text. Modified texts are most beneficial for ELs at the beginning and intermediate proficiency levels because of the gap that exists between their vocabulary knowledge, ability to comprehend complex grammatical structures and lengthy sentences, and grade-level text expectations. This is especially true from fourth grade on when the turn from learning to read to reading to learn takes place. The gap between a grade-level text passage and the reading ability of advanced-level English learners often is small enough that a leveled text is a better choice than a modified one.

When teachers moderate the language demands of the original through modifying text, ELs can focus on comprehending the pertinent material without being distracted by unnecessary details that contribute little to the understanding of the topic. Another reason for modifying a text is to prevent the English learners from becoming frustrated when the text uses more complex language than they can currently process or is considerably longer than they can realistically read in the time allocated for non-ELs. When ELs are provided the chance to concentrate on the central message, the modified version fulfills the same purpose for assigning the original text: learning of academic subject information and acquiring of associated academic language.

## CONTEXT FOR USE

As students advance through the grade levels, less content is provided by means of hands-on activities and explorations. Instead, students are tasked with acquiring knowledge through presentations, lectures, and expository text passages that gradually become longer and also contain increasingly complex grammatical and text organization structures.

To make text accessible to English learners at varying levels of English proficiency, we recommend the following formats of modified texts:

- **Outlines** can take two formats:
  - The first consists of summarizing each paragraph in two or three sentences.
  - The second kind of outline organizes the information by wh- question words.

  Although outlines work well for various content areas, the second one is most suitable for social studies and literature instruction.

- **Bulleted lists** shorten the amount of text more than outlines because the information does not have to be conveyed in full sentences. Subheadings from the text can be chosen as the main points, and details or supporting evidence are provided through indented bullets. This simple visual display of the relationship between a term or concept and the associated facts helps English learners organize their thoughts and make connections to larger topics. Depending on the English proficiency level of the reader, the teacher can include more or fewer details and decide whether some complex sentence structures can be kept. In this regard, bulleted lists provide greater flexibility to fine-tune the text for very specific needs of English learners.

We prefer PowerPoint slides over Word documents when modifying text through bulleted lists because the Notes feature allows the teacher to differentiate instruction for ELs who are almost, but not quite, ready to work with leveled text (see chapter 8). English learners who read more fluently than others at a similar proficiency level, can be assigned the slides and the Notes, whereas the less fluent readers would be given the slides, only. Another helpful tool in PowerPoint is the ability to record voice, giving the English learner the added benefit of hearing the text read fluently while reading along.

Pictures, drawings, illustrations, charts, and tables add nonverbal elements where the modified text does not provide sufficient detail or clarity. Teachers may choose to provide the same wording for an English learner nearing the intermediate proficiency level as for a beginner, but augment the text for the lower proficiency level with clip art or other graphic depictions, providing layered support where needed.

When modifying text for ELs with very low reading proficiency, teachers may find that reducing the passage to a bulleted list is still too challenging or results in so much loss of information that little understanding can be gained. In such cases *contextualized modified text*, which presents the bulk of the information in visual ways, would be a better option. In contextualized modified text the content is conveyed through various forms of graphics, such as photographs, drawings and illustrations, images, time lines, or flowcharts. Essential vocabulary is connected through labels, and links between events or sequences are indicated by arrows. Because of the concentration of visual representation, the use of language is limited, often consisting of little more than content-specific vocabulary or short phrases, which allows beginning English learners to gain meaning from the text.

## MATERIALS AND PREPARATION

### Materials

The most important equipment for text modification includes a word processer; presentation software; access to the internet for pictures, images, and so on; plus, if available, a scanner to include graphics from textbooks or magazines. You can also be creative by taking photographs (e.g., different types of clouds, birds, or equipment and materials used in the science lab, such as test tubes and beakers) with your phone and organizing them in electronic folders by subjects and topics so you can add them to any form of modified text you craft.

### Preparation

Access to an electronic copy of the selected grade-level text does not greatly reduce the amount of work to modify it, since the core message is conveyed in a different format. Prior to deciding which form of modification is more appropriate, it helps to read the passage three times.

1. In the first round, familiarize yourself with the text as a whole, its organization, its text features, and the author's point of view.
2. During the second reading, underline the critical information that must be included.
3. In the final pass, focus on crucial vocabulary or phrasing, underlining those pieces in a different color than in step 2.

Now that you have identified the potentially challenging portions for your English learners, the next step is to look over the WIDA Performance Definitions (www.WIDA .us/standards/eld.aspx). Consider the type of vocabulary and phrasing your English learners know, the variety of grammatical sentence constructions, and the amount and density of written text they can already process through reading. Now you can decide which type of modified text best meets the linguistic needs of your ELs, while presenting the information with sufficient breadth and depth. Are full sentences with grammatical variations alongside pictures appropriate, or would it be best to convey the information through images with labels or bullets, alone?

Most teachers are adept at selecting the main points of a topic and producing PowerPoint presentations to introduce or review content, so it makes sense to try text modifications in the form of bulleted lists first. When doing so, you should keep in mind, especially for ELs at the beginning level, that academic vocabulary presents substantial comprehension challenges, even if the information is conveyed through short sentences or sentence fragments. Therefore, where content-specific or technical terms are not essential for learning the concept, replace them with everyday words, such as knife instead of cleaver, so that the students' focus can be on the crucial information.

## HOW, WHEN, AND WITH WHOM TO USE

### Universal, Supplemental, and Alternative Uses

The best use of modified text is in settings where the teacher or other provider can help deconstruct the written information or make explicit links to images by talking through them. Even though outlines, bulleted lists, and contextualized modified texts contain the same basic information as the original passages or book, they are specific to serving English learners and are provided in lieu of the text given to non-ELs. Therefore, modified texts belong to the alternative support category.

A text that is modified for advanced ELs as an alternative may also be appropriate for non-ELs who are struggling readers who may miss too many details, or who wouldn't get through the entire grade-level text in the time allocated to the independent reading. One way to use these tools as a supplement, instead of an alternative, to grade-level texts, however, is when ELs are not yet able to sift through all the original material but would benefit from being challenged by having access to it in conjunction with a modified version. This is most likely the case with an intermediate English learner in the second or third grade or with an EL at the higher end of advanced proficiency where the gap between grade level and the modified text is small.

### Time and Provider (When and Who to Provide the Support)

Producing modified text is a complex task for generalist teachers who have limited experience working with English learners at varying levels of proficiency. Therefore, before you start to modify text alone, speak with your school's or district's ELD specialist, who can give you advice as to the amount and complexity of written language your ELs can process based on the ELD standards. You may even collaborate to create a few modified texts of upcoming lessons prior to going solo. Once the texts are modified, any provider can implement them at the appropriate time in the instructional cycle.

## PRE-TEACHING PROCEDURES

English learners benefit a great deal from time spent building background knowledge on the topics of upcoming lessons, introducing vocabulary, or making connections to previously covered materials. At times this can be done within the modified text itself, while other times it may be more appropriate to introduce vocabulary or concepts through different means in anticipation of the alternative format chosen for the passage. Whichever option fits the lesson objective and activities for the entire class, once the students have seen the text, it is easier to acquire the information at a deeper level and participate in discussions.

## TEACHING/CO-TEACHING PROCEDURES

### Communication *for* ELs

The purpose of a modified text is to provide written information to English learners by altering the format, the linguistic complexity, and the length of passages at their current reading proficiency level. Without access to an appropriately modified version of the text assigned to non-ELs, English learners are unable to gain sufficient understanding of the content.

The difficulty in comprehending science expository text, for instance, stems from text density, sentences with multiple subordinate clauses, and the frequency of verb and adjective nominalization (turning them into nouns/noun phrases).[2] Modified text can alleviate many of these challenges for ELs at all levels because these elements are mostly eliminated through the reduction of wording.

### Communication *Between* Teacher and ELs, ELs and ELs, or ELs and Non-ELs

Although modified texts have been shown to be effective for English learners, not all alternative formats lend themselves to collaboration between ELs and non-ELs. A text that includes very few details or supporting evidence and that is written in incomplete or short, simple sentences to meet the needs of a beginning-level EL may render collaboration with peers who can comprehend the original passage unproductive. Two ELs whose alternative formats contain the same or similar level of detail, however, would be able to further their understanding through text-based academic discussions, a technique discussed in chapter 7. It is important to note that when working in collaborative group settings, non-EL students should be directed to read their own (original) text, rather than pulling the pertinent information from the text modified for the EL group member.

The teacher or other providers can assist English learners in engaging with the text in various settings, regardless of the alternative form in which the information has been presented. Leveled questioning (see chapter 6) offers insights into the ELs' meaning-making process when they read the outlines, bulleted lists, or contextualized texts. Given this flexibility, we submit that modified texts can also be used for modified guided reading instruction where the teacher and ELs can discuss the information in greater detail than would be possible in whole-class instruction.

### Communication *of* ELs

Although we describe modified text as a *Tell* tool for reading comprehension, teachers can ask students to respond to writing prompts using a format similar to the one in which the concept was presented. For example, a beginning-level EL may be asked to produce a time line, mark main events with a label, and draw a picture (or search for an image online) to show their understanding of a historical event or period. An intermediate-level EL can be directed to write about the main events using bullets or complete the appropriate who, what, when, where, why, and how prompts. Sentence frames or sentence starters (see chapter 10) can greatly enhance the student's output.

English learners who recently arrived from another country often enroll in school with little or no official information about their prior schooling. While the teachers await standardized assessment data, they can use various formats of a text to gauge the EL's literacy skills in English by giving them comprehension questions leveled to their proficiency (see chapter 6). The results of such informal assessments then inform the type of modified text that is most appropriate for upcoming reading assignments.

## POST-TEACHING/FOLLOW-UP PROCEDURES

There is no difference between the ways that modified text and the original passage are used for post-teaching. The post-teaching typically includes the same version that was used during the instruction to explain vocabulary or deepen the understanding by providing additional examples. It is not the type of text but the questioning techniques that enable the learner to gain and show understanding of the material.

If the teacher or other providers notice during post-teaching that the EL has a fairly good grasp of the information included in the modified text, small details can be added in the same format by talking about them. If it becomes evident during the lesson that the modified text used was too low for the English learner, a different format of the same text that is longer and contains some complex sentence structures may be provided for follow-up.

## EXAMPLES

The modified text examples consist of five paragraphs in a series of authentic texts on hydropower.[3] In this environmental science unit on global warming, the students researched how countries around the globe use different types of renewable energy in collaborative groups and prepared a presentation of their findings. In this first text, the students were directed to collect information about the time frame(s) of development of this renewable energy, the amount of energy production, and how the energy is produced. From there, different groups were instructed to find out how energy is produced in the different types of power plants and present their findings to the class.[4]

---

### EXAMPLE 1

### Introduction to Hydropower in Switzerland—
### Beginning English Learner Modified Text

*A simple list with font formatting to emphasize most pertinent information*

Country: **Switzerland** (Europe)

<u>Why</u> hydropower in Switzerland?

- Much **rain** in Switzerland
- Many **rivers**
- Many **lakes in the mountains**

<u>Development</u> of hydropower plants:[5]

- **Started** in **1900**
- **Many** hydropower plants built **1945–1970**

<u>Number</u> of hydropower plants in Switzerland in 2017: **643**[6]

Average <u>energy production</u> for each hydropower station: **36,264** gigawatt hours per year (GWh/year)

<u>Types</u> of hydropower plants and production percentage: **run-of-river** = 48.2%, **storage** power plant = 47.5%, **pumped storage** = 4.3%

<u>Future</u> of hydropower plants in Switzerland: Use more power from hydropower plants. The government plans **new** hydropower plants.

---

### EXAMPLE 2

### Introduction to Hydropower in Switzerland—
### Intermediate English Learner Modified Text

*A summary of the content, organized by paragraph with bold font to draw attention to important information*

Paragraph 1: Switzerland uses **hydropower** because it **rains a lot** and there are many **rivers, lakes,** and **mountains**. Hydropower became **popular** around 1900, and many **small and big power plants were built** between 1945 and 1970.

Paragraph 2: At the beginning of the 1970s, 90% of electricity in Switzerland came from hydropower. After the first **nuclear power plants** were built, the production **fell to** 60%. Today, 56% of energy comes from hydropower. It is still the **most important source of renewable energy**.

Paragraph 3: In January 2017, there were **643 hydropower plants** that produced a minimum of 300 kilowatts power. The average hydropower plant

produced about 36,264 gigawatt hours each year (GWh/y). 48.2% was produced by **run-of-river power plants**, 47.5% was produced by **storage power
plants**, and 4.3% was produced with **pumped storage power plants**. Most
hydroelectricity (63%) is produced in 6 mountain cantons (= counties), but two
cities also produce a lot of power.

Paragraph 4: Hydropower is an important part of the **energy industry** in
Switzerland.

Paragraph 5: The government of Switzerland wants to use more hydropower
in the future. It looks at many different ways. It wants to **renovate old** hydropower plants and **build new** plants. The government's **goal** is to produce
2,000 **more** gigawatt hours (GWh) **than in 2000**.

## ADDITIONAL INFORMATION AND RESOURCES

1. Rewordify.com. "Understand What You Read." rewordify.com.

   This free online software simplifies text and calculates an estimated average
   difficulty score of both the original and the simplified text. Type a text into
   the box and see it analyzed and transformed.

2. The Florida Center for Instructional Technology. fcit.usf.edu.

   This website offers royalty-free illustrations, stock photographs, historic
   maps, and images for use in presentations.

3. Creative Commons. creativecommons.org.

   Members of this site share creative works. The search function provides
   the opportunity to narrow the search to specific entities such as Flickr CC,
   Open Clip Art Library, and Google Images for royalty-free images.

## Chapter 10

# Sentence Starters, Sentence Frames, and Word Banks

## DESCRIPTION

Sentence starters, sentence frames, and word banks supply academic language that ELs are able to recognize and apply but are not yet able to produce by themselves. Sentence starters give the beginning of an open-ended sentence, whereas sentence frames provide sentence templates that leave out content information, which learners complete. Word banks provide the vocabulary English learners need to complete a given task. These tools, because they furnish parts of the vocabulary or phrasing non-ELs are expected to use unassisted, temporarily elevate the EL students' language beyond their current proficiency level.

## PURPOSE

An increasing number of teachers display sentence starters and sentence frames of common academic language functions (e.g., ordering or sequencing, classifying, persuading) throughout the classroom to refer to when the writing prompt calls for them. Students can use sentence frames both to start their writing and to check the appropriate wording before they turn in their work. Although the goal is the attainment of the proper academic wording by all students, the purpose of using sentence starters and frames with English learners is different. When they are provided the language they would not be able to produce on their own, ELs can practice and show understanding of the concept and academic vocabulary while avoiding the struggle to write a coherent, grammatically correct response in a language they are still learning.

The purpose of word banks, which can also include phrases, is to supply the vocabulary being studied, permitting ELs to show their understanding of it by using it appropriately without having to worry about spelling or remembering the specific term. Combining word banks and sentence starters or frames provides full verbal support to students at the beginning and intermediate levels of English proficiency so they can focus on the message they are trying to convey.

The three tools are expressly created for a specific writing task, such as completing a worksheet or recapping a lesson. Vocabulary and phrases that occur and are supplied frequently eventually become so familiar to the learner that they are used automatically. When teachers notice their English learners applying the academic vocabulary and phrasing of focus on their own during spoken interactions, they can increase the number or length of blanks in sentence frames, move to sentence starters, and/or reduce the number of word bank items in subsequent writing activities.

## CONTEXT FOR USE

Sentence frames, sentence starters, and word banks are go-to tools teachers can implement in every content area and in every grade. They also lend themselves to zooming in on the exact needs of individual ELs because they are so adaptable. An example from a science lesson illustrates variations of sentence frames a teacher might prepare for beginning-level English learners: "_____, _____, and _____ belong to the Mammalia" and "The groups of Carnivora, _____, and _____ are in the class of Mammalia." The two sentences are not only grammatically simple, but call for the term of each group, only. The second sentence is slightly more complex and longer, and it includes the terms *group* and *class*, which English learners need to understand and distinguish. If the vocabulary to be filled in is provided in a word bank, both sentences would be attainable for beginning ELs. Without the word bank, lower-level ELs may or may not be able to complete the first, shorter sentence. The second sentence, however, would be too difficult for their current writing ability. Intermediate-level ELs would be able to produce the Latin terms of the groups on their own, but the following sentence frame would be more appropriate because it requires understanding of the terminology of hierarchy of animal classification *in addition to* the Latin terms of the group members: "The _____ Mammalia splits into different _____, which include _____, _____, and _____."

When deciding what words to include in a word bank, teachers should keep in mind that beginning and intermediate English learners struggle not only with specific and technical vocabulary, but also with everyday vocabulary.[1] Therefore, words that native English-speaking students would already know may also need to be placed on the word bank produced for ELs. In an exploration of the development of agriculture in early civilizations, for example, beginning-level English learners would likely be unfamiliar with the words *sheep* and *goats*, whereas non-ELs would only have to learn the term *herding animals*.

## MATERIALS AND PREPARATION

### Materials

There are several ways in which teachers can provide sentence starters and sentence frames to their English learners. While proficiency-level-appropriate versions of commonly used language functions, like the example provided at the end of this chapter, can be displayed on charts throughout the room, it is helpful to provide each EL with their own copy. We recommend laminating word banks or sentence starters and sentence frames that are to be used repeatedly for ELs to refer to when needed during partner work or during small-group instruction with the teacher or other providers.. When providing sentence frames, sentence starters, or word banks that are specific to an assignment, different versions of the worksheet or writing prompt are necessary.

Some teachers we have worked with look at the grade-level lists of terms and phrases in the Tennessee Vocabulary Project resource and consult previous grades to jumpstart the word banks for ELs at the beginning level.

## Preparation

Depending on the academic language of the content, teachers may adapt ready-made sentence starters or frames targeted to the topic and the needs of their ELs. They can also make them in a few easy steps. Either way, the process is the same. The first step is to identify the expressions they expect native English-speaking students to produce, followed by a simplification of sentence structure, if necessary, and the replacement of terms or phrases with blanks. It is this second step that is most sensitive to ELs' writing skills. Are they able to focus on completing the blanks because the sentence structure is appropriate for their proficiency level? Do the blanks pose sufficient, but not too much, challenge for English learners to show their understanding? These questions lead to the decision of whether to include a word bank, which would be the last step.

We recommend that teachers who produce sentence frames for ELs for the first time begin at the higher proficiency levels, since these students' academic language ability approaches that of their English-speaking peers. In many cases adapting sentence starters and sentence frames for advanced-level English learners requires only minor simplification of phrasing to reduce the complexity and density. When moving to the intermediate and then to the beginning level of proficiency, the sentences become increasingly shorter and grammatically less complex.

## HOW, WHEN, AND WITH WHOM TO USE

### Universal, Supplemental, and Alternative Uses

Anchor charts with sentence starters and sentence frames provide universal support for all learners. However, especially for beginning and intermediate-level English learners, these supports are typically insufficient. To make the charts more EL-friendly, you can add drawings or graphic organizers next to the phrases or provide simplified versions of the same chart. While beginning and intermediate ELs would not be able to independently add a lot of information, their attention is drawn to the charts each time the teacher uses nonverbal gestures by pointing to and then modeling the use of the sentence frames during instruction.

It is the use of sentence frames and starters as a supplemental support that serves English learners' development of academic language the most. We suggest that you tape them to the ELs' desks for the duration of the unit or co-create an interactive notebook or a vocabulary book with your English learners. This gives the students quick and easy access whenever they are tasked with producing the sentences or using the vocabulary, and you can remind the ELs to use them as you circle around the room checking on their writing progress.

Word banks fall under the category of supplemental support. They are provided for specific tasks, such as completing a worksheet or showing comprehension during assessment. As with sentence frames and sentence starters, the amount of information the students have to produce on their own increases as they progress toward proficiency, which, in turn, decreases the number of words that need to be provided.

## Time and Provider (When and Who to Provide the Support)

Sentence starters, sentence frames, and word banks can be selected or prepared by anyone who is familiar with the academic language of the lesson or unit and English language development standards. Bilingual teachers or volunteers can translate some of the vocabulary provided in the word bank to further support the beginning English learner.

## PRE-TEACHING PROCEDURES

Whenever possible, sentence starters and frames as well as word banks should be introduced and practiced prior to the beginning of a unit or lesson because they model the language that will be used in the immediate future. English learners can then participate more actively because they already recognize the phrases and words within the context of the lesson.

## TEACHING/CO-TEACHING PROCEDURES

Students acquire new terms and phrases in all phases of learning a concept. Once the vocabulary and academic phrasing related to the content has been practiced a few times, native English-speaking students depend on the universally used anchor charts with decreasing frequency. English learners, however depend on the accessibility and repeated encouragement to use sentence starters and frames along with word banks throughout the unit and, in some cases, even beyond.

## Communication *for* ELs

Sentence starters, sentence frames, and word banks enable ELs to express their understanding of a lesson's content and are thus not used as an input tool to provide new content.

## Communication *Between* Teacher and ELs, ELs and ELs, or ELs and Non-ELs

The purpose of sentence frames and starters and word banks for ELs is to provide a model of the type of language used in the academic subject. Although we describe their use as a support for writing, these tools can also be provided to facilitate discussions between the ELs and their peers, or between the ELs and the instructional leader as they practice the new material, which may culminate in a writing activity. For example, when students calculate the perimeter of various manipulatives, the teacher can prompt the intermediate-level EL to state how that is done by saying, "The _____ (gesturing perimeter) of this _____ (pointing to an object) is calculated by _____." If the student hesitates, the teacher can supply the vocabulary and have the student try again while the teacher repeats the sentence frame. For the same pair activity, intermediate-level English learners would benefit from a word bank that contains the vocabulary for the different shapes, and beginning-level ELs should get the word bank with images of the shapes.

## Communication *of* ELs

The power of sentence starters, sentence frames, and word banks becomes most evident when implemented for writing tasks. Not only can English learners demonstrate their knowledge within accurately formed sentences, but word banks also improve spelling accuracy when copied from the correct model. Another benefit of these three tools is that English learners can complete the assignment in the same time frames as their English-speaking peers, which gives them a sense of accomplishment.

## POST-TEACHING/FOLLOW-UP PROCEDURES

Whether the teacher or a collaborator can pre-teach the academic language or not, follow-up after a lesson to reinforce understanding and usage of the sentence starters and frames for the next lesson is time well spent. Contrary to lesson-specific vocabulary, which is learned relatively quickly, academic language at the phrase and sentence level requires repeated exposure over a period before the English learner is able to produce grammatically correct extended language independently. When ELs are able to complete the assignment within the time allocated in the lesson with the support of sentence frames, sentence starters, and word banks, the teacher or other providers can reinforce the language templates during post-teaching.

## EXAMPLES

The examples on the following pages show how word banks can provide an additional layer of support to sentence starters and sentence frames. In table 10.1, we provide a side-by-side comparison of the difference in sentence frames and word bank use for beginning, intermediate, and advanced-level English learners.

The three examples are variations of the same earth science writing task, adapted for beginning, intermediate, and advanced English learners.

TABLE 10.1

**Use of a Word Bank for a Geometry Problem**

| Beginning | Intermediate | Advanced |
|---|---|---|
| *Word bank: perimeter, string, pan, cut, measured, put* | *Word bank: perimeter, around, measured* | *No word bank* |
| • We think that the pan is _____ *[give a number]* centimeters around.<br><br>• First we _____ the _____ around the _____.<br><br>• Then we _____ the string.<br><br>• Then we _____ the string.<br><br>• The _____ of the pan is _____ *[give your number]* centimeters around. | • We _____ that the _____ is _____ *[give a number]* centimeters around.<br><br>• First we _____ around the _____.<br><br>• Then we _____ the string and _____ it.<br><br>• The _____ of the pan is _____ *[write your finding]* centimeters _____. | • We think that _____ *[write your estimate]* centimeters.<br><br>• After _____ the string, we _____ it.<br><br>• We discovered that the _____ is _____ *[write your finding]* _____. |

---

EXAMPLE 1

## Weather: Beginning English Learner Sentence Frame Handout

A very simplified reading passage with chunking, a sentence frame with one-word responses, and a word bank with limited choices

Will thinks rain falls from        melted clouds.

Marcus thinks rain falls from       heavy water drops in clouds.

Lorna thinks rain falls from        evaporated water in clouds.

Which friend do you agree with?
Explain your thinking:

    I agree with _____

    because _____ falls

    when the _____ droplets in the _____

    get too _____ to stay in the air.

**WORD BANK**

Lorna, Will, Marcus

snow, rain, ice, water

air, ground

heavy, light

Rewrite the entire sentence:

_____

_____

## EXAMPLE 2

**Weather: Intermediate English Learner Sentence Frame Handout**

A simplified reading passage with underlining, a sentence frame with open-ended responses, and word bank choices that exceed the number of blanks

Will thinks rain falls <u>when clouds melt</u>.

Marcus thinks rain falls <u>when water drops in the clouds get too heavy</u>.

Lorna thinks rain falls <u>when the evaporated water in clouds condenses</u>.

Which friend do you most agree with?
Explain your thinking:

I agree with _____ because _____

when _____

get too _____ to _____.

**WORD BANK**

Lorna, Will, Marcus, snow, rain, falls, stops, ice, water, air, ground, heavy, light, in the air, crystals, droplets, stay, leave, wind, air

Rewrite the entire sentence:

_____

_____.

## EXAMPLE 3

**Weather: Advanced English Learner Sentence Starter Handout**

The original reading passage and writing task for all students with an added sentence starter

Rain is caused by melting clouds, according to Will.

Marcus believes that rain falls when water drops in the clouds get too heavy.

Condensation of evaporated water in clouds is Lorna's explanation for rainfall.

Which friend do you most agree with? Explain your thinking:

I agree with _____ because _____

_____

_____.

## ADDITIONAL INFORMATION AND RESOURCES

1. Brewer, Stacy. "Using Sentence Frames to Jumpstart Writing." Teaching Channel. www.teachingchannel.org.

   Watch this teacher use sentence frames with her students to move them from talking about a topic to writing responses.

2. Sweetwater Union High School District. *Academic Language Functions Toolkit*. 2010. orh.sweetwaterschools.org.

   In this resource based on Kate Kinsella's work, find out how to teach English from the perspective of twelve language functions (e.g., sequencing, summarizing, and informing). Language frames and appropriate graphic organizers to use, an observation feedback tool for each function, and a guide to teach academic language round out the toolkit.

3. Hayward Unified School District. "Academic Response Frames and Writing Templates." www.husd.k12.ca.us.

   In this section of the district's website, you can read up on common language functions, learn about response frames for academic language learning, and download sentence frames and signal words for five commonly used language functions.

4. Idaho State Department of Education. "Sentence Frame Reference Sheet for Integrating ELD in Content Areas." sde.idaho.gov.

   In this three-page resource, you will find sentence frames and signal words for scientific language functions ranging from describing to identifying relationships.

5. Marzano and Associates. *The Tennessee Academic Vocabulary Project*. 2006. State of Tennessee Department of Education.

   This list of content-specific vocabulary assembled by grade level can help you determine how to differentiate a word bank for English learners at different proficiency levels. If the grade-level word is too advanced for an EL, look for a related term one or two grade levels lower to build the bridge.

6. Marzano Research. "Vocabulary for the New Science Standards Reproducibles." www.marzanoresearch.com.

   This resource includes a variety of science-oriented worksheets that help to guide student learning, regardless of grade level, in such topics as human body parts, the solar system, forms of matter, and even plant life cycles. A free account is required to access the worksheets.

# THE LANGUAGE ARTS PROTOCOL
## *Build* Tools and Techniques

Although all students grow in wording sophistication and gain reading comprehension skills in language arts/literacy classes between kindergarten and twelfth grade, native English speakers arrive in school with a burgeoning vocabulary and an already developed knowledge of grammatical features, which they started to acquire in early childhood. They understand and can produce a variety of grammatically complex sentences and learn to perfect their use of language through language arts/literacy instruction. English learners, on the other hand, have to first acquire those skills. Teaching language and literacy to English learners provides the benefits of instructed second language acquisition, enabling the selection of grammatical structures that the English learner is ready to acquire, as well as a focus on the form of those words and sentences (i.e., grammatical structures) during activities that develop ELs' listening, speaking, reading, and writing skills.

Instructional differentiation for English learners in language and literacy lessons, which focus on grammatical structures that ELs at specific English proficiency levels are ready to acquire, is different from instructional differentiation for ELs in academic subjects (the Academic Subjects Protocol), where successful communication *for*, *between*, and *of* English learners in academic subjects is promoted through modifying verbal (language) and nonverbal (everything but language) communication. The point of academic subject instruction is to *learn the subject through language* (and nonverbal means), whereas the point of language and literacy instruction is to *learn the language* and *learn about the language*.

We address teaching language arts (or English language development, also referred to as ELD) to English learners from the perspective of this main goal—to develop knowledge about and skills in using the English language. For English learners, ELD instruction supports second language acquisition in listening, speaking, reading, and writing, which in turn improves ELs' learning of academic subjects. As they gain knowledge and skills in academic subjects and language relevant to those subjects, their English language proficiency increases. In other words, English language arts instruction that is appropriate for ELs' English proficiency levels leads to gains in English proficiency that improve academic subject learning, and academic subject learning that provides support for English learners leads to development of English language proficiency, which is depicted in figure II.1.[1]

FIGURE II.1
**English Language Development**

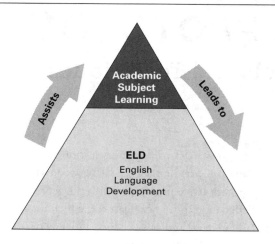

## THE LANGUAGE ARTS PROTOCOL

Like the Academic Subjects Protocol (ASP), the Language Arts Protocol (LAP) involves a series of planning decisions that generalist teachers follow to meet their English learners' needs. Also like the ASP, the underlying premise of the Language Arts Protocol is that lesson adjustments are made based on a gap—a gap between the language demands of grade-level instruction and English learners' current level of proficiency. The difference between the ASP and the LAP, then, is that the adjustments in language arts or literacy instruction require closer attention to language, calling for targeted instruction in all four language skills (i.e., listening, speaking, reading, and writing).

For those readers who start with the *Build* tool and techniques section, we provide an overview of key terms below. Readers who began with the *Show* and *Tell* tools and techniques section already know them, but we want to draw attention to several terms connected to the ASP that are not part of the LAP.

## KEY TERMS

❖ A natural **gap** exists between the language demands of a lesson and the language an English learner can process and produce at his or her current level of proficiency.

❖ Modifying instruction through different types of supports **narrows** this gap, although, given the nature of language proficiency, the supports rarely close it altogether within a lesson.

✦ **Use** refers to how the tools and techniques are implemented.

✦ **Time** relates to the point in the lesson when the supports are provided.

✦ A **provider** is anyone who implements the chosen tool or technique with one or more ELs. The provider can be the classroom teacher, someone who collaborates with the classroom teacher, or even a technology-based resource. Collaborators may be ELD specialists, reading coaches, writing coaches, bilingual colleagues, bilingual aides, paraprofessionals, or classroom volunteers.[2]

✦ Depending on the size of the gap in the lesson for different proficiency levels, tools and techniques may need to be **layered**, meaning that several of them may be chosen concurrently for English learners at a lower proficiency level, while those at higher proficiency levels may require only one support or none.

At this point it may be helpful to explore why it is necessary to have a protocol to teach language arts to English learners rather than use the same practices you would with non-ELs. So, let's take a closer look at what is different and what is the same about teaching language arts to English learners and to native English speakers. Picture two classrooms, side by side. In the classroom to the left is a language arts class composed of students who are not English learners, and in the classroom to the right is an ELD class made up of English learners exclusively, all at, let's say, intermediate levels of English proficiency. If you peeked in the doors, many things would look similar. You might see word banks, writing prompts, and graphic organizers. If you looked more closely at these items, you would see that they use somewhat different language, and probably different amounts of language. But if you opened the door and listened, the real differences would stand out. You'd find that the experienced ELD teacher speaks to her class using simple phrasing, pausing during natural breaks to allow students time to comprehend the language. She also checks for comprehension of her language by asking frequent questions. You might also hear her giving an explanation of an everyday term, such as a silver lining or the ninth inning. You would also hear the students struggling to find the wording to express their thoughts and opinions and the teacher eliciting and supplying language in response. These are the types of differences that the Language Arts Protocol brings into focus so teachers of EL-integrated classrooms can determine how (and in some cases if) these needs can be met in grade-level language arts lessons for all students.

Depicted in the LAP graphic (figure II.2) are the two phases and the steps that comprise the Language Arts Protocol—first an analysis phase, followed by a decision-making and action phase.

## Phase I

Because instruction in language arts/literacy for English learners involves the development of English in listening, speaking, reading, and writing, it is important to look at

FIGURE II.2
**Language Arts Protocol**

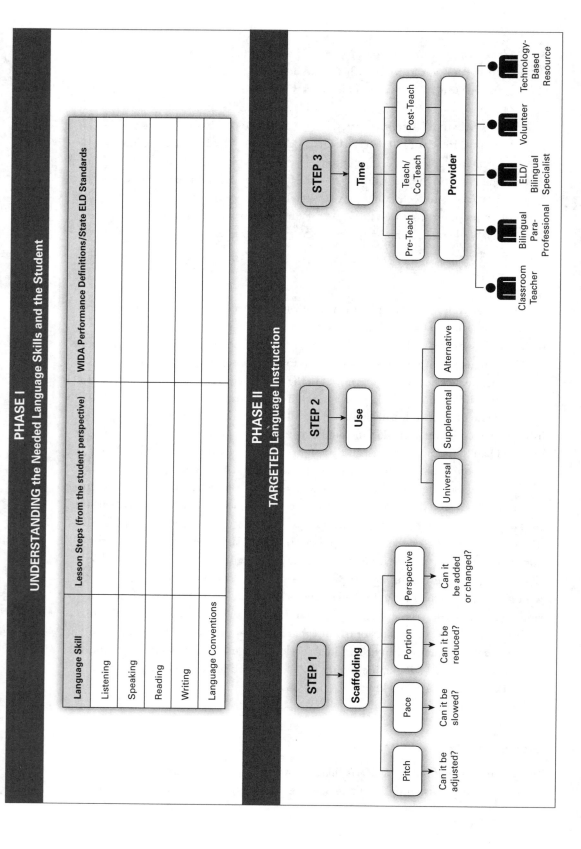

**PHASE I**
**UNDERSTANDING the Needed Language Skills and the Student**

| Language Skill | Lesson Steps (from the student perspective) | WIDA Performance Definitions/State ELD Standards |
|---|---|---|
| Listening | | |
| Speaking | | |
| Reading | | |
| Writing | | |
| Language Conventions | | |

**PHASE II**
**TARGETED Language Instruction**

STEP 1 → Scaffolding

- Pitch — Can it be adjusted?
- Pace — Can it be slowed?
- Portion — Can it be reduced?
- Perspective — Can it be added or changed?

STEP 2 → Use

- Universal
- Supplemental
- Alternative

STEP 3 → Time

- Pre-Teach
- Teach/Co-Teach
- Post-Teach

**Provider**

- Classroom Teacher
- Bilingual Para-Professional
- ELD/Bilingual Specialist
- Volunteer
- Technology-Based Resource

each language skill individually and to zoom in on each proficiency level. Therefore, we use five WIDA proficiency levels rather than clustering them into beginning, intermediate, and advanced, as we did in the ASP.[3]

Phase I of the graphic lays out the process of comparing each EL's English proficiency in listening, speaking, reading, and writing as well as their knowledge of language conventions (i.e., their WIDA or state standards levels) to the curriculum, instruction, and assessment in a language arts lesson designed at grade level.

To establish the size of the gap between the language demands and the EL student's abilities, the first task is to consider their proficiency by closely examining each cell in the WIDA Performance Definitions. Since they will be used for each lesson analysis (until the EL moves up a level in one of the language skills), we recommend teachers paste the descriptors into a table like the one in figure II.2, Phase I. It is most likely necessary to make a separate table for each EL in the class, since each student's combination of proficiency levels may be different.

The next action is to list how language will be used during the lesson *from the view of the student*. This is done first by summarizing the listening, speaking, reading, and writing elements. When comparing these tasks to the Performance Definitions, the size of the gap, if there is one, becomes evident.

## Phase II

Phase II of the LAP consists of the same three steps as in the ASP: planning the lesson adjustments, deciding their use, and deciding the appropriate time and best provider or collaborator to implement the adjustments. How to target the language arts instruction to an EL's proficiency level, however, involves a set of considerations that is quite different from those in the ASP.

**STEP 1:** Targeting language instruction to the unique needs of second language learners in an integrated classroom involves four moves, which we term the four Ps—pitch, pace, portion, and perspective.

 **KEY TERMS**

✧ **Pitch** pertains to the complexity and familiarity of the language used in the language arts classroom—by the teacher and non-EL students (spoken) and by instructional materials and media (written)—as well as the expectations for ELs' language use in classroom tasks. Pitch is considered in relationship to the English proficiency level of ELs in the class. In targeted language instruction, the language pitch is attuned to the proficiency level of the EL. Pitch consists of purely linguistic elements—in other words, what are the features of the language that is meant to be received by and is expected to be expressed by students, and does this language align with EL students' proficiency in listening, speaking, reading, and writing in English).

✦ **Pace** refers to instruction and the amount of time needed to foster and confirm ELs' comprehension, expression, and engagement.

✦ **Portion** is the amount of language content that is being taught or studied.

✦ **Perspective** deals primarily with three areas affecting language comprehension and expression for ELs in ways that are usually different from non-ELs' needs: grammar, meaning, and cultural/background knowledge.

Depending on the lesson content and the proficiency level of the English learner(s), any or all of the four Ps can be adjusted, and each P can be adjusted to a greater or lesser degree. Teachers can determine which of the four Ps is impacted by lesson elements by asking questions such as those in table II.1.

TABLE II.1
**Considerations for Adjustment of Four Ps**

| Pitch | *Teacher considerations for adjustments:*<br>• What is the linguistic difficulty used in verbal and written input (careful selection of words, sentence structures, and nonverbal connections to promote comprehension)?<br>• What are the expectations of verbal or written accuracy produced by EL students? (How complex should the language be? What errors are acceptable given the proficiency level?)<br>• Is the language used in the classroom (by the teacher, non-ELs, and instructional materials) and are expectations for the language used by ELs (speaking and writing) attuned to the ELs' current proficiency level in English? |
|---|---|
| Pace | *Teacher considerations for adjustments:*<br>• How fast should the lesson proceed? Can it be slowed down without being too slow for non-ELs?<br>• Does speech need to be slower (more pauses between phrases) during input without being too slow for non-ELs?<br>• Are any additional comprehension checks needed (these can occur during input, guided practice, or independent practice)?<br>• Is additional wait time during ask/answer or partner work beyond the "typical" time needed?<br>• Can vocabulary/phrasing introduced for/discussed with *all* students be added or further elaborated on without slowing the lesson too much for non-ELs? |
| Portion | *Teacher considerations for adjustments:*<br>• How much verbal and written input is appropriate (e.g., shortening of text or verbal explanation)?<br>• How much verbal and written output can be expected? |
| Perspective | *Teacher considerations of prerequisite understanding to participate in lesson:*<br>• Background knowledge (cultural or content)<br>• Grammar (use student's L1 for comparison, if appropriate)<br>• Vocabulary (including idioms and uncommon phrasing) that native English speakers would already know<br>• Language learning strategies (e.g., use of bilingual dictionary, cognate instruction) |

Depending on the grade level and English proficiency of the English learners, any or all of the four Ps could be the same for non-ELs and ELs, but in most cases adjustments in one or more of the four Ps is necessary for ELs. That often takes place with the teacher or a collaborator working individually or in small groups with ELs prior to, during, or after the lesson, and it also occurs in separate ELD classes for ELs at specific English proficiency levels. After determining which of the four Ps need to be adjusted so that the ELs can actively participate and build their language skills, two more decisions need to be made, which leads us to the next step in the Language Arts Protocol.

**STEP 2:** Depending on the answers to some of the questions posed in table II.1, such as whether the elaboration of vocabulary or phrasing for some English learners during whole-class instruction would slow down the lesson too much for the non-ELs (pace), indicate the use of the supportive adjustment. For example, if the additional explanation of vocabulary need not be lengthy and may even simultaneously help non-ELs who struggle with some of the vocabulary or sentence structure, the pace adjustment would be universal. If, however, there are too many words or the grammatical components of phrasing cause significant difficulty for an English learner, unpacking them would hold back the other students. In this case the teacher would need to consider adding components to teach these important pieces (supplemental use) or even identify different means altogether, providing an alternative to the grade-level instruction.

**STEP 3:** As with the ASP, the decisions made in step 3 of the LAP are directly impacted by timing and available personnel resources. Let's look at the above scenario in which the EL student requires some, but not extensive, additional unpacking of vocabulary or grammatical structures that would interrupt the flow of the lesson for the other students. To bridge this *moderate gap*, the teacher can work with the EL individually or gather other students—ELs and non-ELs who struggle with related language features and would also benefit from small-group instruction. The material can be taught adjusting the pace and portion, while the other students practice independently. Here the teacher provides the support during the teaching phase and is the provider.

When the *gaps are big*, as would be the case for beginning ELs in secondary grades, the magnitude of necessary adjustments in curriculum, instruction, and assessment to target instruction to ELs' proficiency levels, makes it less likely they can occur during a grade-level language arts lesson taught by the classroom teacher alone. Let's consider an eleventh-grade language arts lesson like distinguishing what is stated in a grade-level satirical text from what is actually meant. If the lesson used Voltaire's *Candide* as the satirical text, expectations for grade-level instruction for the non-ELs would be far from the needs of the level 1 EL who, as the WIDA Performance Definitions lay out, can process "everyday social, instructional and some content-related words and phrases, simple grammatical constructions (e.g., commands, wh- questions, declaratives), and an idea within words, phrases, or chunks of language." This student would require *instruction exclusively designed for ELs within the beginning ranges of English proficiency*. Not only would the text be inaccessible to the level 1 EL, but the discussion and unpacking of the text that the teacher and students engage in would use language that is inaccessible as well. In other words, the explanation needs an explanation. So, virtually none of the grade-level language arts instruction would be beneficial for a level 1 EL, and focusing on a small portion of the topic (e.g., the term *ridicule*) by using graphics rather than grade-level text would not be beneficial for non-ELs. Similarly, the discussion of the satirical expressions and their graphic depiction would need to be adjusted in pitch (simple phrasing of explanations and questions), pace (frequent comprehension checks), portion (limited words and expressions, with associated graphics), and perspective (possibly defining a common ironic idiom, such as *fat chance*, which most non-ELs already know means very little or no possibility). The intensity of the required instruction with this English learner would call for an alternative approach and the help of an ELD expert for the duration of the unit.

## COLLABORATION—A CALL TO ACTION

Personnel resources can vary greatly across schools within districts. Schools with large English learner populations typically have several dedicated ELD specialists and bilingual paraprofessionals. This does not mean, however, that obtaining the assistance of this staff is necessarily easier than in schools where there are fewer English learners. The larger the EL population, typically the more students there are at lower levels of English proficiency who rely on targeted individualized instruction. More so than when teaching English learners in subject areas other than language arts/literacy, substantial resources are needed to help develop their listening, speaking, reading, and writing skills. We implore teachers to actively seek others in your school who have the expertise to deliver such targeted instruction and to talk to administrators to find time for these experts to support language arts/literacy instruction that is equitable. Additionally, ask for assistance from district ELD/World Languages offices. In short, become an advocate for yourself, so that you can become the effective teacher your ELs need and deserve.

Several **essential points** may help convince other teachers and administrators to become advocates for finding the necessary personnel resources to provide the exact targeted language arts/literacy instruction English learners in an integrated general classroom need.

## Essential Points

- The **same is not enough**. To reach grade-level expectations and become college- and career-ready, English learners depend on targeted language instruction in listening, speaking, reading, and writing.
- The targets differ from EL to EL. Both *learning language* and *learning about language* are necessary, and ELs' levels of proficiency in listening, speaking, reading, and writing **differ considerably**.

- When the gap is large, a generalist **cannot provide intensive targeted** language instruction to English learners **at the same time as** delivering rigorous instruction to non-ELs.
- Teaching *language* and teaching *about language* requires substantial knowledge of grammar and second language acquisition. **Assistance from ELD specialists** in designing lessons and teaching specific components **is needed**.

## MOVING FORWARD: *BUILD* TOOLS AND TECHNIQUES

With the understanding that English language development may take place under various circumstances, we present ten English language development tools and techniques that may look quite familiar to language arts teachers who have no background in teaching ELs. This familiarity, though, might be a hindrance in targeting the tools and techniques to the needs of ELs, because there is the risk of using them the same way they are used with non-ELs (which would not be targeted). For this reason, we describe these tools and techniques in relation to their fine-tuning in pitch, pace, portion, and perspective, according to the English proficiency levels of ELs in listening, speaking, reading, and writing (language conventions are embedded into various *Build* tools and techniques). Because there is compelling research showing that targeted ELD, provided exclusively for ELs, is beneficial to ELs' achievement, the tool and technique descriptions do not include discussions of how to integrate their use into a lesson for ELs and non-ELs.[4] In the *Build* section, we focus only on ELs, describing the tools' and techniques' use with different proficiency levels. Some tools and techniques are applied very similarly with ELs and non-ELs, such as letter-sound correspondence flashcards for beginning readers, but we focus specifically on those that are widely used with ELs at different English proficiency levels, yet are employed differently than with non-ELs.

Our ten *Build* tools and techniques can be categorized in different ways, as we lay out in table II.2. First, they each emphasize a predominant language skill, so their title includes listening, speaking, reading, or writing. Second, they can also be considered in terms of whether they are primarily classroom activities or teacher practices used with individuals, and if they primarily teach language, or teach *about* language.

As you review the tools and techniques and reflect on how they may fit into your current curriculum, instruction, and assessment, we invite you to occasionally return to this description of the LAP until you feel well versed in applying (some of) the tools and techniques to support your English learners at different levels of proficiency. Additionally, we encourage you to reflect on your challenges and successes in adopting the tools and techniques.

TABLE II.2
**Taxonomy of *Build* Tools and Techniques**

| | |
|---|---|
| Tools and techniques that are **primarily whole-class or small-group activities** | • *Listening Skill Development:* Building Comprehension at Word, Sentence and Discourse Levels<br>• *Speaking Skill Development:* Learning New Language Through Songs and Poems<br>• *Reading Skill Development:* Exploring the Meaning, Form, and Relationship of Words<br>• *Reading Skill Development:* Grammatically Unpacking Sentences<br>• *Reading Skill Development:* Understanding Text Structures with Graphic Organizers<br>• *Writing Skill Development:* Grammar, Spelling, and Vocabulary Mini-Lessons<br>• *Writing Skill Development:* Planning Writing with Graphic Organizers |
| Tools and techniques that teachers use as **practice with individual** students | • *Speaking Skill Development:* Instructional Conversations<br>• *Speaking Skill Development:* EL Spoken Error Treatment<br>• *Writing Skill Development:* Responding to Sentence-Level Writing Errors |
| Tools and techniques that **primarily teach language** | • *Listening Skill Development:* Building Comprehension at Word, Sentence and Discourse Levels<br>• *Speaking Skill Development:* Instructional Conversations<br>• *Speaking Skill Development:* Learning New Language Through Songs and Poems<br>• *Writing Skill Development:* Planning Writing with Graphic Organizers |
| Tools and techniques that **primarily teach *about* language** | • *Speaking Skill Development:* EL Spoken Error Treatment<br>• *Reading Skill Development:* Exploring the Meaning, Form, and Relationship of Words<br>• *Reading Skill Development:* Grammatically Unpacking Sentences<br>• *Reading Skill Development:* Understanding Text Structures with Graphic Organizers<br>• *Writing Skill Development:* Grammar, Spelling, and Vocabulary Mini-Lessons<br>• *Writing Skill Development:* Responding to Sentence-Level Writing Errors |

## REFLECTION

At the beginning of each chapter, consider the following questions:

1. What do I know about this tool or technique?
2. How could this tool or technique help my ELs?

At the end of the chapter, consider the following questions:

1. Which of my ELs would benefit the most from this tool or technique?
2. If I had more time and resources to learn about and practice this tool or technique, whom would I ask for assistance (e.g., ELD specialist, more experienced peer)? For what purpose (e.g., planning, modeling, co-teaching)?

After you implement a tool or technique the first few times, reflect on the following questions:

1. What did I do today that helped my English learners develop stronger listening, speaking, reading, and writing skills? How do I know that instruction was targeted to their proficiency level?
2. How successful was I in facilitating all ELs' comprehension and expression of today's lesson? Were there any differences depending on ELs' proficiency levels?
3. What could I have done better to help all ELs? Do I need to consider adjusting support for ELs at specific proficiency levels?
4. How can I improve my application of this tool or technique moving forward? Are there any proficiency levels I should focus on more?

## Chapter 11

# Building Comprehension at Word, Sentence, and Discourse Levels

## DESCRIPTION

Listening skills refer to the ability of students to effectively process and understand the language they hear in social or academic contexts. Basic reception is not enough; words that are heard individually may not make sense to a learner within the context of the sentence in which they are spoken.

Focus is also an essential component of listening skills. Students must be "tuned in," ready to listen for key words, able to drown out background noise and distractions, and invested enough in the lesson to provide their full attention and put forth their best effort. They should be able to conceptualize the entire, larger picture of what the dialogue, speech, or lecture they are listening to represents. For this reason, application of the tools and techniques in this chapter is broken down into word, sentence, and discourse levels. Activities should focus on each of these separate components, as they are all required for mastery of the listening skill. Can students identify individual words? Can they process and explain the meaning of complete sentences they hear? And, finally, can students listen for the main idea of spoken text or dialogue and grasp its content as a whole?

## PURPOSE

Listening is one of the most important skills for students, as it forms the basis for all of their academic instruction in English. Without a proper grasp of what their instructors and peers are saying during their classes, students will not be able to succeed. Unlike with reading, students normally get one attempt with listening. If they did not take in what was said the first time, they typically do not get a second chance to hear the same streaming or broadcast audio, an important live presentation, or in-the-moment directions for a specific task.

In every class, English learners must be able to hear, identify, and write words they do not know, understand oral instructions for activities, and learn new concepts explained in their second language. K–12 teachers with ELs in their classes face the challenge of providing listening practice activities that adequately prepare their learners for these challenges, are diverse enough to account for the variety of English accents and dialects they may encounter, are interesting enough to keep their attention, and are at an appropriate level of difficulty–listening tasks that are too difficult may cause students to check out early and become discouraged, but ones that are too easy will lead to lapses in concentration and a failure to take the exercise seriously.

Listening with intent also allows students to home in on aspects of grammar, pronunciation, syntax, and even organizational strategies they may be having difficulty with. It is helpful for vocabulary to be heard in context, and audio of any kind— whether it be a recording or simply the instructor's own speech—serves as a model that learners follow when speaking.

## CONTEXT FOR USE

In the EL-integrated classroom, activities devoted entirely to listening may seem more challenging to implement. They might not fit into the curriculum, and in most cases these exercises are not useful for native English-speaking students. Listening skills in isolation are not often focused on in K–12 settings because many assume that such skills are an integral, inextricable aspect of standard classroom learning. When you have ELs in your classroom, however, listening as its own discrete skill cannot be neglected or taken for granted as already incorporated into the curriculum; EL students, while their academic capabilities are no less than those of their native-speaking peers, do require concerted, focused instruction in all four language skills. The question, then, becomes how to maximize the listening opportunities for ELs within your classroom.

You should always be aware, during every lesson you teach, that all of your students—both ELs and native speakers—are actively and constantly practicing and developing their listening skills throughout the school day. Additional learning strategies such as attention training, eliminating distractions, and effective note-taking will further facilitate student success in developing listening fluency.

Teachers of other content areas may use a listening activity as a means of introducing a topic, as a stimulus that attracts students' attention, or merely as a moment of entertainment for a brain break. However, only carefully designed listening activities can be enjoyable and beneficial to both native English speakers and ELs. To create such successful activities, a teacher needs to understand listening as having three levels (i.e., word, sentence, discourse) and be able to recognize learners' needs at each level.

Before and during every lesson, consider *what* you will say and *how* you will say it. Are you using words that are within the grasp of your students and words that you would like them to acquire and use? Is your speech loud and clear enough for everyone? Are you speaking at a slow enough pace for your ELs to understand, but fast enough that you still sound natural?

Listening activities have a broad range of usage. Language arts teachers can teach a lesson just focusing on listening skills, and listening components can be integrated into reading, speaking, and writing classes.

## MATERIALS AND PREPARATION

When planning to use listening activities in class, a teacher first needs to have classroom equipment with good sound quality that can be used to play audio materials, such as listening centers, CD players, and multimedia sources on a reliable computer. If visual aids are to be provided to students while they listen, a projector and a doc-cam may be necessary. Meanwhile, be mindful of the classroom environment in terms of the noise level. Recorded listening activities should happen in a quiet environment (otherwise headphones should be used), as even low-level noise can be extremely distracting and impede students' ability to focus on the listening materials.

Once a classroom is set for listening activities, selecting appropriate listening materials becomes the next step to ensure a meaningful learning experience for students. Depending on the purpose of the listening activity, a teacher may need to decide

- if it is more suitable to include authentic materials such as news, TV shows, clips, speeches (e.g., TED Talks), or tailored content materials where the speed, length, and difficulty levels of the listening material are altered based on students' level of proficiency
- if it is better to use textbook-provided supplemental audio/video, or materials self-recorded by the teacher
- if it is more effective to have students focus on the audio only, or also provide them with visual or textual aids (e.g., pictures, subtitles, transcripts, etc.)
- if any students, especially ELs, need additional scaffolded materials (e.g., word banks and vocabulary preview)
- if and how the materials can be made accessible to students after class

## THE FOUR PS OF TARGETED LANGUAGE AND LITERACY INSTRUCTION

### Pitch

Targeting the pitch of a listening activity's language to an EL's listening proficiency in English is similar in many ways to matching a reading passage to the reading comprehension level of any student. One key difference in the importance of pitch in listening comprehension, however, is the dynamic nature of some types of spoken language.

A prepared speech or a scripted dialogue can be controlled for pitch, but the type of listening required to understand a live radio weather report, follow directions given over the phone, or comprehend a class lecture involve spontaneous language use that can't be controlled for pitch. For this reason, it is important to vary the types of listening activities between those that are attuned to the EL's listening proficiency level (i.e., leveled listening tasks created for instructional purposes) and those that are not (listening tasks that use authentic language).

When English learners struggle to comprehend authentic listening tasks that use language well beyond their proficiency level, it is important to help them focus on listening for specific key information, such as whether it will rain tomorrow, rather than all the details, such as how advanced the weather radar is, what the direction and velocity of the wind will be, or if there is a small craft advisory. Being able to selectively focus on major issues, and not be overwhelmed with incomprehensible details, can help ELs develop strategies for understanding new information in a language they are still learning. And because much of what they are learning in school involves listening, helping them develop strategies for extracting key information from a lot of not-yet-comprehensible "noise" is especially important.

English speakers communicating extemporaneously don't normally adjust pitch for ELs' proficiency level unless the person addressing an EL knows to use teacher talk (chapter 5). However, when an EL listens during interactions with an English speaker, it is more likely that the EL will communicate a lack of understanding through facial expressions and even verbal requests for clarification, which makes the listening process more reciprocal.

## Pace

With listening activities, frequent comprehension checks are critical for ELs. Checking for listening comprehension involves more than just watching facial expressions to see if students are "with you." It is important to intersperse questions that are appropriate to their listening proficiency (see chapter 6) rather than assume that they comprehend if they don't ask any questions.

Pacing speech to the level of English learners involves a number of options. Teachers can pronounce words or a word more slowly, pause between words, pause between phrases (or what some might call natural breaks), pause after sentences or after a couple sentences to allow for processing or dramatic effect, or pause after paragraphs to allow for reflection on the main points. Professional speakers (broadcast journalists, public speakers, etc.) often slow their pace of speech by pausing between phrases.

## Portion

Portion control is very important when practicing and developing listening skills. The more attuned the pitch is to the EL's proficiency level, the more listening content can be processed. When the content is well outside of the targeted area of language instruction for an EL, it becomes very difficult to catch even a few key details because the amount of noise (incomprehensible language) overwhelms the ability to isolate the signal that *is* comprehensible (e.g., key words). Also, after ELs listen to extemporaneous or recorded spoken language, unpacking challenging or incomprehensible parts takes considerable time, so when using listening activities well beyond an EL's English proficiency level, it is important to work with small chunks at a time.

## Perspective

Several aspects of listening skill development are similar for EL and non–EL students, such as the ability to listen for specific words, ignore distractions, and remain attentive during an aural activity, but ELs have specific needs for comprehension.

Different accents or dialects can be confusing to ELs, as can different registers of spoken language, such as slang or academic language. If the EL has learned some English through formal study in their home country, they many have difficulty comprehending slang like *gonna*. The disfluencies of spoken language, with statements whose word order begins one way, then stops because that word order won't work for what they want to say, and then goes in another direction ("The person that I work with's daughter . . ."—pause—"I work with a person, and her daughter . . ."), can also be confusing to an EL who knows only "textbook" English that uses perfectly formed sentences. Additionally, if someone uses nonstandard grammar in informal speech, such as "I coulda went to the party" instead of "I could have gone to the party," the standard form, an EL can become confused. For all types of language registers, the perception of sounds that affect meaning is an area of challenge for ELs. For example, it is often difficult for ELs to perceive the difference between *can* and *can't* because most speakers of American English don't fully pronounce the final /t/.

| APPLICATION IN PRE-TEACHING, TEACHING/CO-TEACHING, AND POST-TEACHING | |
| --- | --- |
| **Elementary Grades** | **Secondary Grades** |
| *Word-Level Activity Using Songs* Students identify missing words in a fill-in-the-blank passage of song lyrics by listening to the song. <br><br> Select a song that has a slow beat and uses repetition. Transcribe the song lyrics, then delete key nouns and verbs, approximately one per sentence. <br><br> <u>Example:</u> <br><br> "This Old Man" <br><br> This old _____, he played one <br><br> He _____ knick-knack on my thumb <br><br> _____ a knick-knack paddy whack <br><br> Give a _____ a bone <br><br> This old man _____ rolling home. | Generally, listening activities for ELs progress from word to sentence to discourse with ELs' growth from beginning through advanced levels of English proficiency. <br><br> *Word-Level Activity* <br><br> Misunderstanding a key word can cause ELs to misunderstand a key subject. Two words that ELs often can't hear the difference between are *can* and *can't*. American English speakers do not normally pronounce the final /t/ sound in *can't*, and the way native speakers tell the difference is that the sound prior to the /t/ in *can't* is extended and less abrupt, versus the word *can* (try saying both naturally, as you would in conversation, and see how *can't* sounds more abrupt). Also, the vowel in *can* is often switched to a short *i* /I/ or short *u* /ə/ sound when the word *can* is not stressed in a sentence. There are many online resources to help ELs listen for this distinction. For instance, you can search for "CAN and CAN'T—hearing the difference (ESL practice) Barry Lank" and use his YouTube tutorial and examples to help students learn to distinguish the sounds. |

| Elementary Grades | Secondary Grades |
|---|---|
| *Procedures*<br><br>1. Ask class to listen while you play the song through to the end.<br><br>2. Pass out the fill-in-the-blank activity. Tell students to listen for the missing word and to write it (they can do this phonetically or with inventive spelling if appropriate to their level). When preparing the handout(s), remember that the higher the level, the more deletions you should make.<br><br>3. Play the song while students write.<br><br>4. Play the song again.<br><br>5. Read the lyrics aloud and ask for volunteers to identify the missing word in each line.<br><br>6. Show the full lyrics and ask students to check their spelling against the correct spelling.<br><br>7. Discuss meaning, such as asking students who or what it is about.<br><br>8. When discussing new vocabulary (for example, *bone*), you can use what we call the three-step vocabulary instruction formula for ELs: start with a visual (real object or illustration), then say the word, and then show the printed word. The sequence can be varied, but linking all three elements helps ELs learn new words by seeing the object/image and hearing and seeing the word.<br><br> 🦴 → "bone" → *bone* <br>etc.<br><br>Another word-level listening activity with songs begins with writing a few key words from the song lyrics on the board, and then telling students to stand or raise their hands whenever one of the words is sung. For example, for "This Old Man," you could write half of the numbers from 1 to 10 on the board and some of the words that change in each stanza (thumb, knee, hive, etc.); students can raise their hands for the numbers and stand up for the other words.<br><br>*Beginning Listening Activity for Students Who Already Know Basic Addition and Subtraction*<br><br>Count from 1 to 10 while everyone listens.<br><br>Write the numbers 1 through 10 while counting.<br><br>Write and say + (plus) and − (minus). | A similar type of listening activity can be used to help ELs distinguish /p/ and /b/ (a difference that speakers of Arabic struggle to perceive), such as *park* and *bark*, or /r/ and /l/ in *rip* and *lip* (difficult for Japanese speakers), by stating pairs of words that are the same except for the sound they are representing. This is referred to as a minimal pair activity.<br><br>*Sentence-Level Activity*<br><br>As students are learning about climate change, a listening activity could include statements about facts from a news broadcast and from a podcast commentary about opinions. For example, if students have been learning the passive voice, they could listen to sentences such as "Rising ocean levels are caused primarily by climate change," and then choose the answer that means the same as the sentence:<br><br>1. Climate change is increasing.<br><br>2. Climate change is decreasing.<br><br>3. Climate change is causing ocean levels to rise.<br><br>4. Climate change is caused by rising ocean levels.<br><br>An alternative to verbal multiple-choice answers would be to allow them to identify a diagram that illustrates the correct statement or write their own statement in English.<br><br>*Discourse-Level Activity*<br><br>The same podcasts used to isolate sentences for listening activities can be used with longer passages that ELs listen to. There are many free websites with listening passages and even follow-up comprehension questions that teachers can use (see Additional Information and Resources).<br><br>For listening passages that are longer than individual sentences, it is helpful to develop activities to use before, during, and after listening. The before-listening activities might include a preview of new vocabulary or specific information to listen for (focused listening). Gauging students' cultural/background knowledge in the topic of the listening passage is also useful, such as asking them questions about the traditional food eaten at Thanksgiving. During-listening activities can include note-taking or filling in a form with details from the listening passage. Common after-listening activities are multiple-choice quizzes or oral re-tells. |

| Elementary Grades | Secondary Grades |
|---|---|
| Model and tell students you will give them a math problem, and they will write the problem and the answer on their individual whiteboards. | When using a listening passage intended for English learners, such as those on *News in Slow English* (search these terms for the website), pre-listening can be reduced, and the length of the passage can be increased. If using an authentic listening passage (one not made for English instruction purposes), such as a TED Talk, the lower the level of English proficiency, the shorter the passages should be, and the more pre-listening should occur. With beginning-level ELs, if using authentic listening materials, ample pre-listening instruction, short passages (30–60 seconds), unpacking complex grammatical constructions and teaching new vocabulary, and frequent comprehension checks are critical. |

3 + 4 = (students write the equation
            and the answer, 7)

10 – 5 =

8 – 6 =

1 + 1 =

etc.

Have students hold up their whiteboards after each answer to check for comprehension. After 1–10 are learned, go on to 20 and beyond.

**Proficiency Level Differentiation**

Certain listening activities can be differentiated for ELs learning alongside non-ELs. For example, if the whole class is doing a listening activity where they take notes on a presentation and then turn in their notes as an assignment, depending on ELs' proficiency levels, they can be given an outline with different amounts of missing text for them to fill in. Alternatively, they could turn in notes in English or their native language (if there is a bilingual aide) and the student's amount of intake could be assessed.

## SUGGESTIONS FOR SUCCESS IN THE EL-INTEGRATED CLASSROOM

Teachers who use word, sentence, and discourse listening activities successfully have shared the following pointers.

### Pre-teaching, Teaching/Co-teaching, and Post-teaching Variations

By and large, effective *pre-listening* activities should fulfill the purposes of increasing students' motivation for listening, contextualizing the material, and/or preparing students for specific vocabulary and expressions that are key to understanding the spoken language. Then, the *while-listening* activities may vary depending on the goal of the lesson. It is also in this phase that teachers should consider how to balance the learning needs of the ELs and non-ELs. A teacher may need to work out two versions of supplementary worksheets, one for native English speakers and one for ELs, that contain the same main tasks but with more word-level and sentence-level exercises in the EL version. Listening materials may need to be played in class more than once for the students to fully digest the texts and successfully participate in the activities. Last, meaningful post-listening activities usually invite students to react to the text or lead students to analyze the language.

## Informal Assessment

Listening provides constant opportunities for informal assessment. One of the most direct methods of assessment involves note-taking. By examining students' notes, teachers can gain insights into students' attention level while listening (e.g., did students stay focused throughout listening or lose concentration halfway through?). More importantly-, note-taking can be used to assess students' listening strategy use. For example, if a student's notes were a collection of unrelated words, the student may have captured information only at the word level, rather than at a sentence or discourse level. If a student's notes resemble an outline of listening material with key concepts clearly identified, the student will likely have gained a fair understanding of the content as well as the structure of the listening material.

Instead of, or on top of, using note-taking as informal assessment, for students with lower level English proficiency who are still developing word-level listening skills, dictation may be an effective method to test students' vocabulary, spelling, and phonological awareness. As for students who are able to listen and comprehend at a sentence level or discourse level, comprehension questions and/or oral recount activities based on the listening material are additional means of verifying whether students understood the concepts.

## ADDITIONAL INFORMATION AND RESOURCES

1. Listen Wise. listenwise.com.

   This website offers teachers free access (but you must sign up) to public radio stories and podcasts, as well as materials emphasizing current events and other content areas. These resources can be particularly helpful for EL students because they comprise interactive transcripts, tiered vocabulary lists, graphic organizers for active listening, and reduced-speed audio that facilitate teachers' scaffolding as well as their assessment of listening skills development according to students' grade level. A free account is required to access the podcasts.

2. ESL-Lab. "Randall's ESL Cyber Listening Lab." www.esl-lab.com.

   This website provides free online listening activities for teachers and students.

3. Sperling, Dave. "Dave's ESL Café." www.eslcafe.com.

   This website has a plethora of teaching resources, including lesson plans, quizzes, and activities.

4. Voice of America News. learningenglish.voanews.com.

   This website provides podcasts for English learners that use slower speech and simpler terms and sentence structures.

5. Podcasts in English. podcastsinenglish.com.

   This site contains free access to podcasts featuring listening activities for English learners and teachers. Paid members also have access to worksheets, webcasts, and transcripts that provide lessons to support student learning at differing levels of English proficiency.

6. English Listening Lesson Library Online (ELLLO). www.elllo.org.

   Select from over 2,500 free ESL lessons with audio and video to support teaching specific skills (e.g., grammar) to students at varying language proficiency levels.

7. News in Slow English. www.newsinslowenglish.com.

   On this website, you will find a comprehensive catalog of grammar and expressions lessons, from beginning to intermediate English. When the translation function is chosen, important vocabulary or phrases can be read in Arabic, Mandarin, Russian, or Spanish when the curser hovers over them.

## Chapter 12

# Instructional Conversations

## DESCRIPTION

According to Claude Goldenberg, instructional conversations are "discussion-based lessons geared toward creating richly textured opportunities for students' conceptual and linguistic development."[1] They incorporate both instructional and conversational elements, focusing on a theme of instruction that allows elicitation of reasoning and connected discourse.

## PURPOSE

Instructional conversations help students learn to sustain discourse about a theme or issue and to discuss its details thoughtfully, with extended expression and conversational moves that are appropriate for the discourse type (e.g., scientific debate, literature analysis). Teachers lead instructional conversations both to engage the class or groups of students in discussion and to model critical thinking and the language used to engage with others, in discourse that elicits and considers others' positions, and that expresses and further develops one's own.

If instructional conversations are used with ELs exclusively, they can include an instructional focus on the language they use during discussion, which targets language arts instruction to their English developmental level. This might involve the teacher's keeping note of a frequent grammatical error that can be brought up for analysis at the end of the discussion, or it could involve a discussion of wording for requesting or taking the floor, and cultural differences in interjecting a point during a conversation.

Instructional conversations may incorporate facets of other oral-language-oriented tools and techniques, such as teacher talk for ELs, leveled questioning, and EL spoken error correction, but their purpose is to lead English learners in extended discourse and to use that discourse to teach language that is appropriate to their levels.

## CONTEXT FOR USE

Instructional conversations in the EL-integrated classroom can be inclusive of English learners, especially those at the upper levels of English proficiency, but their greatest benefit to ELs comes from targeting the discussion to ELs' proficiency levels and potential for growth. Additionally, if ELs at intermediate levels and beyond have the opportunity to participate in small-group instructional conversations that are focused on their needs, this extra practice and support prepares them to participate in class discussions that might otherwise be dominated by non-ELs.

Although instructional conversations are language development activities, the topic of conversation can include any subject area, such as contemporary literature, world history, earth science, or geometry. The objective is to make participants' critical thinking apparent and to enable them to express their reasoning with appropriate language, in dialogue with others learning the same concepts. All participants should be asking and answering questions that elicit deep thinking.

## MATERIALS AND PREPARATION

- Realia (objects) in the classroom that students can touch and interact with in order to facilitate the production of descriptive or opinion-based language (examples could include figurines, stuffed animals, toys, photographs, drawings, etc.)
- Dialogue and sentence frames with word banks that students at lower levels can use to help formulate their answer
- Posters around the classroom (particularly at elementary levels) that remind students of their wh- question words, adding details, and other strategies
- Socratic questioning resources (e.g., a list of procedures students follow before, during, and after a Socratic seminar), which can be helpful for academic discussions

For lower-level students, expressing themselves in English might require word cards and pictures to help them access the vocabulary they need; it is also useful to write what they say to demonstrate that they have successfully produced a sentence or paragraph in English and tie the speaking skill in with reading and writing.

## THE FOUR PS OF TARGETED LANGUAGE AND LITERACY INSTRUCTION

### Pitch

Instructional conversations are sensitive to pitch, in both the language used with ELs (e.g., teacher and peer talk, instructional media and materials used to spur discussion) and the language expected of ELs (their talk). According to English proficiency level, specifically listening and speaking skills, English learners can engage in meaningful conversations, but if they are at beginning levels during a whole-class discussion, they will gain little from the experience. More advanced ELs will benefit from hearing how others express agreement, disagreement, and evidence for a particular stance, for example, but they may not feel comfortable expressing their ideas if they know that they make grammatical errors, lack vocabulary, or can only begin expressing a thought but are unable to phrase it comprehensibly and state it fully. Instructional conversations that are most helpful to ELs elicit language that they are capable of expressing with support, and analyze the language they produce, which is a form of instructed second language acquisition.

## Pace

The pacing of instructional conversations conducted with ELs at similar proficiency levels will be markedly different from those with non-ELs. Because the exchanges promote expression of ideas and open communication, ELs are encouraged to ask for clarification if an unfamiliar concept or phrase is used. Teachers will also build in frequent comprehension checks as part of the discourse, ensuring that all ELs are following the discussion and are contributing their thoughts and ideas. This may also require additional think time, as ELs may struggle in composing and expressing their thoughts in English. Although addressing some language-focused aspects of the conversation, such as a grammatical structure that students struggled with, may be delayed until the end of the conversation, in other cases it may be most appropriate to bring up an issue mid-discussion. This would also slow the pace of the conversation.

## Portion

Portion is less of an issue for instructional conversations than the other language and instructional factors for ELs (pitch, pace, and perspective). While English learners will likely produce less language than native speakers in the same time period, the volume of language isn't the main concern; rather, the ability to participate in extended discourse and to articulate critical thinking, while reflecting on the language used, is key.

## Perspective

Because the discussion topic's content and language are not predetermined or highly structured, instructional conversations can lead to any number of areas where English learners require explanation of meaning, grammar, or cultural/background knowledge that non-ELs would not need. And because for English learners, comprehending and using language is as important as the concept or theme being addressed, there is a necessary focus on vocabulary and grammatical structures they can learn to improve oral language proficiency in English. This means that unfamiliar terms need to be defined, grammar rules pointed out, and cultural references explained.

## APPLICATION IN PRE-TEACHING, TEACHING/CO-TEACHING, AND POST-TEACHING

### INSTRUCTIONAL CONVERSATION

After the teacher reads the class *One Green Apple*, a story about an immigrant student who initially felt out of place in her new school, he directs non-EL students to work in groups. He then gathers English learners from levels 3 and above and leads them in an instructional conversation.

The theme of the conversation is *belonging*, and the teacher begins the discussion by asking, "What does it mean to belong?" He asks the students to think quietly for a few seconds before volunteering an answer. When the teacher gives the signal, three of the six students raise their hands. He calls on the first student who did (a level 3).

The student replies, "It mean you go with other . . . other people. They like you."

The teacher nods and looks at everyone in the group. "So, you said it mean**s** you go with other people; you are **together** with other people, right? You also said they like you. Do other people **have to** like you for you to belong?"

"I think," responded the student.

The teacher followed up, "Can you give an example where this is true?"

"OK, so like my friend, I have a lot of friend . . ." the student trailed off.

"Keep going. Tell me more," encouraged the teacher.

"I belong to my friend. They like me."

"Hmmm. You have a lot of friend**s**, and you feel you belong in your group of friends because they like you. This is evidence for your opinion, you're right. You feel like you are a part of the group, like you belong."

The teacher writes, "Belonging means people in a group like you, and they want you to be part of their group" on the whiteboard and continues questioning the student.

"Can you think of a counterexample—an example where your point is not true?"

The student looked down toward the floor and shook her head no.

"Who can help her with an example?" the teacher inquired.

No hands went up. The teacher elaborated on the question.

"Is it possible to belong to a group, and it doesn't matter if they like you or not?"

"Maybe my family?" blurted out another student (level 5). "My uncle makes everyone crazy, but he still belongs in our family." Everyone laughed.

"Oh yeah, family is a good example of belonging to a group whose members don't all like each other! What other types of groups might be the same?" continued the teacher.

"I guess like a class or a school," the student offered. "If you think you are like other people, even if you don't like them or they don't like you, you can feel that you belong. And maybe if you are not like them in every way, they can still accept you in their group."

"Yes, feeling accepted is the most important part of belonging. Every student is accepted as a member of *this* class, and every student belongs here." The teacher wrote, "Feeling that you are accepted makes you feel that you belong" on the board, and he drew a circle with *belong* in the middle and drew a line and another circle with *accept* in the middle.

"I also noticed that you used *like* two ways in how you described belonging," commented the teacher as he wrote *like* twice on the board. "You used *like* to mean that somebody likes you, that they have positive feelings about you. You also said that people *are* like you, that they are similar to you in some way. That word *like* has two meanings, but both of them are connected to our definition so far of belonging," noted the teacher as he wrote each phrase next to the word *like*.

"Now think for a minute everyone," continued the teacher. "We said that you can belong to a class because the people in the class are students like you. If you saw someone in your class who was being treated like she didn't belong, would you say or do anything? If yes, what would you do and why would you do it? Turn to your partner and discuss your thoughts, then write your key points, in your own words, on your whiteboard."

The teacher paired students at different levels, with level 5 students working with levels 3 or 4, and so on.

---

**INSTRUCTIONAL CONVERSATION**

When the group reconvened, the teacher began by focusing on argumentation and fluency, keeping the conversation flowing, asking probing questions, and eliciting more details. As he listened to the students' responses, he noticed variation in the correct use of the conditional phrasing, If _____ happened, I would _____. A number of students, especially those at levels 3 and 4, made grammatical errors with this sentence pattern. For example, a level 4 student said, "If I am seeing someone who treat like they don't belong, I speak up and tell others to be kind."

The teacher jots a few notes while the students speak, and once everyone has had their say, he states that he noticed a common grammatical error, writing the level 4 example from before on the board. "Look at this sentence," he motioned to the board. How can we improve this sentence?"

A level 5 student says, "If I **saw** someone who **was treated** like they don't belong, I **would** speak up and tell others to be kind."

"Excellent suggestion for improving the sentence's grammar!" the teacher exclaimed as he wrote the students' answer under the original version. "Let's look at what we added and what we changed to make the grammar correct." The teacher continued to point out the word forms and sentence structure in the original sentence compared to the corrected one, asking students to describe the rule for each correct item (e.g., use the past tense for the main verb after "If I . . ." if you are talking about something hypothetical or imaginary).

After the grammar discussion, the teacher asked students to write the rule in their grammar notebooks and gave them an assignment to look for other examples of conditional statements as they work on other subjects and assignments. Once the small-group discussion wrapped up, the teacher brought the class back together to share what they discussed in their groups and continued with a whole-class instructional conversation, asking what it is like to feel that you don't belong and what everyone in the class can do to help all students feel that they belong.

**Proficiency Level Differentiation**

If this type of instructional conversation took place with beginning to intermediate ELs, sentence frames, word banks, and first-language support could be offered to enable conversation and expression of complex, critical thinking. Concepts and language could be broken down into smaller parts so they can be explained and translated, and more frequent comprehension checks would be added.

## SUGGESTIONS FOR SUCCESS IN THE EL-INTEGRATED CLASSROOM

Teachers who use instructional conversations successfully have shared the following pointers.

### Universal, Supplemental, and Alternative Applications

During whole-class instructional conversations, each student will have particular struggles and strengths. English learners, however, will need extra support where possible. If support for ELs is not provided, intermediate ELs can gain from listening to others' discussion of the topic but may not readily participate. Advanced ELs should be able to participate without extra support, but it would be helpful to provide briefer versions of some of the supports that are appropriate for intermediate ELs, such as templates, sentence starters, and sentence frames (chapter 10), on an as-needed basis. Beginning ELs won't likely gain much from a whole-class instructional conversation, but if some visual support is used, they can acquire new vocabulary at the least.

Instructional conversations for ELs work best when a small group of ELs at similar English proficiency levels can be assembled, led by the classroom teacher or collaborator during small-group activities that non-EL students are participating in, or conducted before or after a lesson in an ELD setting. This is especially helpful for lower-level students because teachers can use WIDA performance levels to adjust their own language so the student will be able to understand and respond.

## Collaborative Practices

The language focus could continue with the collaborating ELD teacher facilitating a mini-lesson about the phrasing of hypothetical statements, giving EL students sample sentence templates and sentence completion exercises to practice the correct form. Beginning ELs could work with the ELD teacher while the class is engaged in instructional conversations.

## Informal Assessment

Informal assessment during participation in a group discussion or debate or a one-on-one conversation may require students to provide appropriate answers—and follow-up answers—to the questions the teacher asks them. This is a particularly effective way to assess ELs, as well as to prepare them for language proficiency testing (e.g., WIDA ACCESS) at the end of the year. Rubrics focusing on listening, speaking, and discourse moves can be used for dynamic assessment of students' participation in instructional conversations.

## ADDITIONAL INFORMATION AND RESOURCES

1. Lavery, Clare. "Fluency Activities for Lower Levels." 2011. British Council/BBC. www.teachingenglish.org.uk.

   Read this article for scaffolding tips and examples of how to incorporate activities that encourage English learners to speak.

2. Lavery, Clare. "Fluency Activities for Higher Levels." 2011. British Council/BBC. www.teachingenglish.org.uk.

   This article describes four activities that can be applied to different topics in which students have to speak at some length.

3. One Stop English. "Speaking Lesson Plans." www.onestopenglish.com.

   This website by Macmillan Education includes free lesson plans devoted to teaching various areas of speaking, including controlled speaking, storytelling, discussion, pronunciation, and role play, as well as accompanying worksheets. Searches can be filtered by language focus, age group, proficiency level, etc.

4. ThoughtCo. "Resources for ESL Teachers." www.thoughtco.com.

   On this website you will find many articles and mini-lessons about how to help students to develop speaking (including pronunciation), writing, reading, vocabulary, and grammar skills.

5. Boggles World ESL. "Lanternfish." bogglesworldesl.com.

   This website contains a variety of resources, lesson plans, and worksheets, many of which are dedicated to speaking activities.

6. English Club. "Conversation Worksheets." www.englishclub.com.

   Each conversation worksheet comes in a student version that gives discussion points, questions, and vocabulary to be used for different speaking activities, in addition to a teacher's notes version that lays out the individual steps of the activities.

7. Teacher, Diane. "12 Fun Speaking Games for Language Learners." Edutopia. 2015. www.edutopia.com.

   The twelve activities described in this article are for intermediate-level English learners.

8. Verner, Susan. "Speak Up: 6 Fabulous Games to Get Your Students Speaking." Busy Teacher. busyteacher.org.

   The games described in this brief article can be used as quick warm-ups or as bridge activities. Some activities are variations of commonly known games such as Bingo or Hot Potato.

## Chapter 13

# Learning New Language through Songs and Poems

## DESCRIPTION

Songs and poems are no strangers to K–12 language arts teachers. As natural ways for students to have fun, rich language experiences, they not only play key roles in first language development, but also are powerful tools in second language learning. Music and rhythmic texts typically engage learners in an interactive, enjoyable, and social process, helping learners gain confidence and literacy skills as well as cultural knowledge.

## PURPOSE

As authentic materials, songs and poems can be easily incorporated in various activities to develop students' proficiency. The repetitiveness of the texts also helps ELs acquire new grammatical patterns and promotes vocabulary learning. Additionally, music and songs are an amusing and effective means of increasing listening skills. Engaging students in reciting or chanting rhymes/poems or singing activities supports phonetic development in oral language as well as literacy. English learners can pronounce and repeat new sentence patterns and words in a low-risk activity, and this exposure to new vocabulary and grammar enables them to produce the example and then use it in real communication.

Music and poems are used all over the world for young children to acquire their first languages, remember stories, and learn about the world. Therefore, whether students are native English speakers or ELs, they've most likely had experience learning language via these activities. Moreover, even if English learners do not fully understand the text, the rhythm and melody naturally yield positive feelings and make new words and phrases easier to remember.

Songs and poems are also holistic approaches to intercultural language learning. Because songs and poems are essential elements of each culture, they provide windows and contexts for language learners to learn parts of a foreign culture and make comparisons with their native culture. Using songs and poems from different cultures is a great way to broaden the cultural knowledge of your EL and non-EL students.

## CONTEXT FOR USE

Songs and poems can be used under various circumstances in a language arts classroom, engaging both native English-speaking students and ELs. For general classroom usage, they can be presented at the beginning of a class in warm-up communicative speaking activities to create atmosphere, introduce a topic, and arouse interest. Where relevant, they can also be used as cultural references or to inspire cultural discussions.

In reading and writing classrooms, songs and poems can be both the content and the approach to strengthen students' skills of understanding and appreciating theme, textual structure, and genre in English. Especially for students in higher grade levels or with higher English proficiency, creative writing activities such as poem or song writing can be employed afterward, thereby allowing students to apply the knowledge and skills they have learned through critical appreciation of poems and songs.

Poems and songs that have texts/lyrics can be used for aural discrimination and pronunciation training. As students are gaining a better sense of rhythm in the spoken language through reciting chants or poems or singing songs, their intonation and pace of speech are likely to improve. Other communicative tasks can be either free discussions about a certain song or rhyme, or more structured activities like presentations or recitals.

## MATERIALS AND PREPARATION

An abundance of song and rhyme collections is available in public libraries or online. Teachers need to exercise careful planning before selecting and adapting appropriate materials to suit their students' needs, interests, and language proficiency.

When selecting materials, consider the length and the language difficulty level as well as the theme. When finding materials online, the teacher may consider specifying their search terms to find suitable materials more efficiently. For example, instead of generally searching "songs for teaching," one may consider specific searching terms such as "finger play songs," "counting songs," "spelling songs," "drop-a-word songs," or "role-play songs."

General preparation for teaching songs, poems, and chants frequently includes assembling a CD player, visual aids such as music videos or pictures, printouts of the texts or lyrics, and student worksheets.

## THE FOUR PS OF TARGETED LANGUAGE AND LITERACY INSTRUCTION

### Pitch

Songs and poems can have extremely simple, repetitive styles; complex, dense, and esoteric styles; or anything and everything in between. In other words, their pitch runs the gamut from simple rhymes about everyday items to lengthy sonnets using archaic language and historical references. The language used in elucidating the content of songs and poems can be adjusted to the level of English learners, but doing so requires adjustment in pace and portion. If it is critical to use original, grade-level poems for all students to recite and analyze, then only key lines should be the focus of extensive unpacking, attending to vocabulary, literary phrasing, and cultural/background knowledge.

## Pace

Because English learners' takeaways from songs and poems may be different from those of non-ELs, the pace of recitation and explanation will be markedly slower. Learning the articulation of new and unfamiliar sounds (e.g., the sounds represented by *th*) requires a slowing down of recitation, where the teacher exaggerates the sounds and solicits choral repetition. Whereas choral repetition may be used to promote reading skills for non-ELs, with ELs it serves a dual purpose. In addition to articulation of sounds and combined sounds, recitation and chanting provide practice in intonation, which is exaggerated by the rhythm or melody. EL students may want or need to repeat each line many more times than non-ELs to begin to feel comfortable using new sounds and sentence patterns.

## Portion

In general, the lower the level of proficiency, the shorter and more repetitive the song or poem should be. Reciting short, repetitive songs and poems allows ELs at beginning levels to take in new language sounds, phrasing patterns, and words and remember and produce them in chunks. If the lesson objective is to analyze the use of figurative language in a poem or song written for adults, then only a couple sentences or phrases would be appropriate to teach the poem to an EL who has yet to reach intermediate level because so many aspects of the language and background knowledge needed to understand the meaning would have to be unpacked.

## Perspective

English learners who enter school not having heard English nursery rhymes in preschool would need explanation of many uncommon words that non-EL children would likely have been exposed to; for example, the word *king* in Humpty Dumpty. Because poems often use unusual language, there will be words that need definition for ELs and non-ELs, and the grammatical structures used in poems, such as the subjunctive mood ("Had we but world enough, and time . . .") likely will need explanation for ELs. Cultural/background knowledge might be the most prominent difference in perspective that ELs need when learning songs and poems. Not only academic information, such as British history, would affect English learners' understanding, but also elements of popular culture, such as idioms in song lyrics—for example, "He can't read my poker face."

## APPLICATION IN PRE-TEACHING, TEACHING/CO-TEACHING, AND POST-TEACHING

### POEM ACTIVITY

The following poem activity works well for beginning English proficiency levels, whether at elementary or secondary levels, because it uses simple present tense in each line. If used in primary grades, it could be a whole-class activity with ELs and non-ELs. For upper grades, where the language used and expected is more complex, this poem activity could be provided by an ELD teacher in a small-group activity exclusive to beginning ELs.

FLINT[1]

*by Christina Rossetti*

An emerald is <u>as green as</u> grass,
A ruby red as blood;
A sapphire shines <u>as blue as</u> heaven;
A flint lies in the mud.
A diamond is a brilliant stone,
To catch the world's desire;
An opal holds a fiery spark;
But a flint holds fire.

**Vocabulary**

Emerald

Ruby

Sapphire

Flint

Diamond

Opal

Fiery Spark

The teacher begins by reading the poem aloud, tapping the beat with her hand on the table. "An emerald is . . . as green as grass . . ."

She rereads the poem, this time pointing to each written word as she says it.

Next, she pronounces key words from the poem, pointing to their picture in the vocabulary list—"Em'-uh-ruhld, roo'-bee . . ."—and pronouncing and explaining any other words that might be unfamiliar (e.g., *fiery*).

Then she invites the class to read aloud with her once.

After the whole class reads aloud, she writes an A to the left of the first, third, fifth, and seventh lines, and a B to the left of the others. Then she points to the left side of the class and tells them they will recite the A side; she points to the right side and tells them they will recite the B side. The teacher leads the class like a conductor leads an orchestra, pointing to the line and group, then alternating to the next line and group, as she says each line with them.

At this point, the teacher pairs students, giving each an A or B ticket. The students take turns reading each assigned line until they recite the entire poem; then they switch tickets and read the poem once more.

Now that the class has recited the poem rhythmically together and individually, the teacher focuses line by line on the meaning. "An emerald is as green as grass. What does that mean?" she asks. "Emeralds are green, like grass," replies a non-EL. The teacher continues, pointing to pictures and gesturing when defining vocabulary such as *blood, heaven,* and *mud.*

After the teacher has confirmed comprehension line by line, she leads a brief discussion of the poem's overall meaning, eliciting from students the qualities of each stone, and noting that the plain, grey flint can do something that all the other colorful stones cannot. "What can a flint do?" she ponders aloud. "Make fire!" a few students reply in unison, and they gesture using flints to create a spark. "Is this poem talking only about stones?" she follows up, and the discussion turns to the concept of *metaphor* that the class had learned previously. "What did the author say about stones that is also true about other things?" She asks students to discuss in pairs. "What other people, places, or things are like gems or like flints?" The pairs complete graphic organizers categorizing the qualities and examples as they discuss, and afterward put their completed forms in the assignment basket.

Once the discussion concludes, the teacher directs attention to the first stanza of the poem and the *as + adjective + as* phrases she underlined:

An emerald is as green as grass.

A sapphire shines as blue as heaven.

She points out that we can describe something in English by comparing it to something that has similar qualities. When we do this, we follow a pattern:

A person/place/thing/idea + Verb + *as* + Adjective + *as* + a person/place/thing/idea.

She writes, "A pencil is as _____ as _____," and asks someone to suggest the missing words.

"A pencil is as *thin* as *spaghetti*!" one student shouts, and the teacher praises the creative response and writes it on the board.

"Now I want each of you to find five objects in the classroom that you will write '*as* _____ *as*' sentences about," and she handed her beginning ELs a vocabulary list with pictures for extra support.

## Proficiency Level Differentiation

More linguistically complex poems can be used with WIDA level 3 and above students, for example, "The Road Not Taken," by grammatically unpacking (chapter 16) each line.

## SUGGESTIONS FOR SUCCESS IN THE EL-INTEGRATED CLASSROOM

Teachers who use songs and poems successfully have shared the following pointer.

### Informal Assessment

Students can be asked to respond to the imaginative ideas and moods expressed in poems, songs, or chants through written, oral, and performance means. For speaking-related assessment, individual/group presentations, role plays, student interviews, and video-taping or live performance of a song, poem, or rhyme are tried and tested ways of informal assessment.

## ADDITIONAL INFORMATION AND RESOURCES

1. English Language Education Section Curriculum Development Institute. *Learning English Through Poems and Songs.* Hong Kong: Hong Kong Special Administrative Region, 2010.

   This free online resource package for high school students is full of songs and poems and their matching worksheets/teaching plans ready for use or adaptation. The package also offers great teaching ideas and tips for differentiation (called "catering for learner diversity"). Examples for teaching songs and poems are:

   – Tips on Reciting Poems (page T77)
   – Song Lyrics Reading and Writing (page T51)
   – Planning and Organising Your Presentation (page T67)

2. Robertson, Kristina. "Introducing and Reading Poetry with English Language Learners." Colorín Colorado. www.colorincolorado.org.

   Read this article to learn about the benefits of using poetry with English learners, how to introduce poetry, and how to use it to develop reading and oral language skills.

3. ESOL Courses. "Learn English with Songs." www.esolcourses.com.

   This website offers free, self-paced grammar and listening lessons through songs by artists ranging from the Beatles to Michael Jackson to Adele. While the lessons are designed to improve listening comprehension, students will want to sing along, thus improving their speaking skills.

4. Hoskins Sakamoto, Barbara. "How to Create a Jazz Chant by Carolyn Graham." Teaching Village. 2010. www.teachingvillage.org.

   This video shows an ESL specialist demonstrate how to make a jazz chant that teaches both vocabulary and grammar with just a few words and phrases.

5. Lyrics Training. This is a free app that features popular songs in multiple languages. Users can select song videos and type of activity (multiple choice or karaoke). For the multiple-choice activity, there are four proficiency levels (beginning, intermediate, advanced, and expert). Access Lyricstraining.com to sign up for a free account.

## Chapter 14

# EL Spoken Error Treatment

## DESCRIPTION

Teachers are placed in quite a difficult position when it comes to deciding when and how to correct the various forms of spoken errors their ELs and native-speaking students produce. In general education classes of any subject, all learners use English when answering questions, giving presentations, working with their classmates in partners or groups, or asking their own questions and communicating their concerns to the teacher. While no teacher wants their students to become discouraged or demotivated due to overly frequent corrections, not acknowledging or correcting mistakes that students make repeatedly could cause them to turn into persistent errors in language production. Once an error has become chronic, it will become more difficult to remedy over time, possibly leading students to become frustrated and confused as they continue to perform poorly at something without knowing why.

In contrast to written error correction, which is a form of delayed feedback provided hours or even days after a mistake is made, oral corrective feedback is an immediate response by the teacher to student-produced mistakes. Students of all ages and English proficiency levels in classes of all types need their mistakes corrected in one form or another, making effective oral corrective feedback one of the most important skills any teacher needs to master. Teachers should think of students' spoken errors as opportunities for correction or expansion, deliberately responding when appropriate so no opportunities for language development are lost. Error correction is an important facet in instructed second language acquisition. It can be made explicitly or implicitly.

**Explicit** feedback involves pointing out that an error has been made, followed by either providing the correct answer or indicating the general type of error to the student, who can then employ metacognitive techniques to fix the mistake herself. This use of error correction encourages students to more deeply understand their error and how to avoid it again in the future.

**Implicit** feedback is more indirect and involves asking the student to say something again, repeating the mistake in the form of a subtle question (e.g., "*A* [placing emphasis on the error] underlying issue?"), or repeating what the student said but in proper form (e.g., "An underlying issue is _____.") in what is called a *recast* of the student's utterance. However you decide to correct your students' oral language, make sure your class understands that errors are a necessary part of learning and are welcome in your classroom.

## PURPOSE

The purpose of all forms of error correction, whether written or oral, should be to help the students produce more accurate speech and to facilitate your lesson. The goal is not to punish or embarrass students in any way. The focus of this technique obviously is the development of speaking accuracy in word choice, grammar, or discourse organization. However, when English learners become aware of their spoken errors and learn how to avoid them, they are able to transfer the gained skill to their written language production.

## CONTEXT FOR USE

Spoken error correction can be addressed by teachers universally, since even native English speakers can encounter difficulties with correct grammar and pronunciation. Although you need not be as concerned with rectifying mistakes by non-ELs that do not interfere with their overall message as you are with the ELs, all students can benefit from your comments. During whole-class instruction, to create a more equitable atmosphere, try not to draw unfair attention to mistakes made by students at lower proficiency levels, and instead work on identifying errors of various types across all the students in your class. If you are able to pull EL students into small groups or one-on-one, or if the ELD expert can be brought in for more individualized error correction, this can be a supplemental and focused tool to target more specific language-based problems.

Speaking errors are most commonly corrected when students have been asked by the teacher to produce a target language structure to complete an instructional goal. This may mean answering a question, sharing work or a presentation with the class, performing a dialogue with another student, reading out loud, or giving a speech; whenever the students are producing oral language upon your request, you should be alert and ready to provide correction if you deem it appropriate. Each time you do not grab the opportunity to correct errors, the students miss out on a chance to develop accuracy and, subsequently, fluency in speaking English. Consider the following questions as you develop a plan for spoken error correction in your classes:

1. Do you know the specific grammar and/or pronunciation rule well enough to explain *why* something is wrong and *how* it should be corrected on the spot?
2. Is it within the realm of knowledge you can reasonably expect them to have at their level of proficiency?

3. Does your correction rectify a problem that is impeding a student's performance on the targeted task or production of a specific language structure, or could it possibly be saved for later? If so, could you create a separate lesson on this type of spoken error that may benefit the entire class without targeting just one student?

4. Is there a pattern of errors you can see in the language production of that particular student, and does it extend to other ELs or even native speakers in your class?

5. Do you know each EL student's preference for error correction? Some students only want correction of errors that impede intelligibility, but other students want correction of all errors. You can take students' preferences into account when deciding how to treat spoken errors.

The answer to these questions will help you decide your error correction strategy, taking into consideration your general classroom environment, the personality of your class as a whole, and that of individual students.[1]

## MATERIALS AND PREPARATION

Spoken error correction does not require any specific materials. However, it is helpful to keep a notebook with a brief description of your daily lesson and the most common spoken errors you heard throughout the class. Categorize them into broader types and consider using these notes when planning or coplanning future grammar and pronunciation lessons. You can even create reference sheets based around these errors and provide them to students who need them to keep in their folders/binders.

Try to anticipate problem areas that both your ELs and non-ELs may face as you prepare your lessons. Are there words that are difficult to pronounce or that break common sounding-out and spelling rules? Are there sentence structures, constructions, or verb tenses in the lesson that might cause students to misuse language? Keeping sample sentence frames (chapter 10) on hand can facilitate a quick explanation and practice if a number of ELs and non-ELs make anticipated errors.

## THE FOUR PS OF TARGETED LANGUAGE AND LITERACY INSTRUCTION

### Pitch

In targeting spoken error correction to ELs' proficiency levels, it is important to pay attention to persistent grammatical errors. An example of a persistent grammatical error is "Did she went to the movie?" These types of errors indicate stages in the second language development continuum, and research shows that ELs, especially those who are beyond the primary grades, are more likely to move past these errors to the correct forms if they receive strategic feedback.[2]

Some language errors are less sensitive to level, and therefore teachers' responses don't need to give first consideration to whether they are developmental and if they should be corrected. An example of this type of nondevelopmental error is using a word to mean something different from its dictionary meaning, such as calling a lifeguard a security guard.

## Pace

The way the teacher addresses errors affects pacing. For example, simply pointing out the error and then stating the correct form, which might be the approach taken when correcting a student for the second or third time, takes seconds. However, if the teacher wants the student to reflect on the error and the proper form, she may lead the student through a process of deriving the rule. This might be an approach the teacher takes the first time the error occurs. If the student said, "Did she went to the movie?" the teacher might write "Did she went . . ." and ask the student about questions referring to actions in the past and which word(s) need to change to show that.

## Portion

When English learners speak, they often make errors. It's important to be judicious in selecting which errors to focus on. This is true not only because pointing out all errors would be overwhelming, but also because certain errors are more prone to improvement at that point in the EL's language development. And because, unlike writing, speech is an immediate form of communication, it's difficult to isolate errors as they are spoken within conversation or discussion without damaging the flow of thoughts and ideas.

## Perspective

The EL's perspective on errors might be very different from that of a non-EL. While both might make errors in subject-verb agreement, such as "There's a lot of books in the new library," English learners are likely to make subject-verb errors such as "Many moneys is in his wallet," making the subject *money* plural and its verb *be* singular.

Errors in meaning occur frequently with ELs. An example is an advanced EL who said, "It was like taking candy from a baby" and meant that what he did made someone cry rather than simply being very easy to do. Another advanced EL said she was "dead set on going to graduation" and meant that she was not going because she thought that being dead to something means you won't do it. Cultural/background knowledge also comes into play with spoken errors. An EL who doesn't know that "getting to first base" has cultural meanings other than making it to the first stop in a journey could express something very different from what she intended!

# APPLICATION IN PRE-TEACHING, TEACHING/CO-TEACHING, AND POST-TEACHING

## TREATING SPOKEN ERRORS

### Elementary Grades

An example of an elementary application of implicit spoken error correction is a small group of level 1 and 2 ELs working with the classroom teacher while the other students work in groups. The objective is to discuss a story's plot, and the teacher has prepared a story map to refer to and has sentence starters and a word bank on hand for support.

The teacher asks, "What happened first?" and the level 2 EL responds, "Farah go to school." The teacher acknowledges the correct content of the answer and recasts it with correct language: "Yes! Farah went to school," stressing the word *went*. "She went to her new school," the teacher continues, expanding the sentence with more detail. In this example, the recast and expansion are appropriate correction types for the early grades and serve as a model for ELs to acquire.

An example of explicit correction is when the teacher stops by the desk of a level 3 EL and asks if his cousin rides the bus to school. The student responds, "No, my cousin, he walk to school," and the teacher says, "Remember, always pronounce the *s* that you add to the end of the verb when you are talking about what one person or thing does. He walks to school." Then the teacher says, "Let's say that together, 'He walks [they exaggerate the articulation of the *k* and *s* sounds] to school,'" and the teacher continues to point out when the student makes the same error, by repeating what the student said ["She speak two languages?"] and asking what is missing.

### Secondary Grades

In a flipped, EL-integrated classroom, the teacher assigns a documentary video on climate change for homework. Two periods before class discussion of the video, the ELD teacher meets with the ELs from the class, who are at levels 2 and 3. They practice cause-and-effect sentence patterns because the classroom teacher shared her questions with the ELD teacher (her collaborator), and the questions primarily focused on causes and effects, such as, "How is sunlight absorption affected by greenhouse gas molecules?"

The ELD teacher begins by showing a sentence starter, "If carbon emissions increase, _____," and asks "What happens if carbon emissions increase?" A level 3 EL replies, "The Earth get hot." The teacher responds, "You said, 'If carbon emissions increase, the Earth get hot.' How can we improve this sentence? Another level 3 EL replies, "The Earth gets hot." The teacher answers, "Yes, we need the *s* at the end of the verb if we are talking about the Earth. Good catch! But here we are saying that if one thing happens, another will happen after. The student replies, "The Earth will get hot." "Yes, that's correct," confirms the ELD teacher. "The grammar is correct now. 'If carbon emissions increase, the Earth will get hot.' Let's take a minute to think how we can make this language more academic." After a pause, a student volunteers, "If carbon emissions increase, the temperature of the Earth will rise." The teacher praises this answer, writes it verbatim on the portable whiteboard, and everyone copies in it their science journal.

Afterward, the ELD teacher gives a note to the classroom teacher with the questions and sentence frames that the ELs are ready to answer during the whole-class lesson. Now the classroom teacher knows to call on her ELs during questioning, confident they are prepared to phrase their answers without hesitation.

### Proficiency Level Differentiation

Although pronunciation can be corrected at any level, for level 1 students, it's helpful to correct pronunciation if the word is unintelligible, such as saying *category* with the stress on the *e* (pronouncing it *ca-TEH-go-ree* instead of *CAT-eh-GOR-ee*) or pronounced as another word, such as saying "beard" for "bird" in the sentence, "I see a [beard] in the sky." Wrong word choice, such as calling a desk a table, is also helpful to correct for level 1 students. They are typically able to note the correction and pronounce or use the word correctly from then on.

With level 4 and 5 students, it's important to address persistent grammatical errors at the sentence level, such as, "I don't know why couldn't she come to class on time." In these cases, it may be preferable for the classroom teacher to keep a log of spoken (and written) errors she notices, and to pass them along to the ELD teacher for individualized grammar mini-lessons (chapter 10).

## SUGGESTIONS FOR SUCCESS IN THE EL-INTEGRATED CLASSROOM

Teachers who treat EL spoken errors successfully have shared the following pointer.

### Informal Assessment

Keeping track of errors that your students make during class—even if only once or twice a week—is one way to map the progress of ELs as you attempt to focus your corrections on areas that need improvement. In a broader sense, oral feedback as a cooperative classroom exercise can also be added as a requirement for class discussions and presentations. For instance, perhaps each student must make at least one comment in response to a peer's work that includes a helpful suggestion or note for improvement. While these comments may not be specifically focused on errors in language production, they sometimes will be; this would also give you a chance to assess the attention level of the rest of the class. Small-group academic discussions can include speaking rubrics for group members to fill out for one another, and these types of informal feedback, as well as teacher notes of persistent errors, can be compiled in a language arts portfolio to track progress over time. On a certain schedule, you could also review common errors that your students have made as a whole in the form of mini-review lessons. Their response to these lessons will be a good indicator of their level of understanding.

## ADDITIONAL INFORMATION AND RESOURCES

1. Teaching English. "Error Correction." British Council/BBC. 2015. www.teaching english.org.uk.

   This article outlines some very useful ways for teachers to decide how to orally correct errors in their classrooms, including the "stoplight" suggestion.

2. Languages International. *ETS TaskBook*. Self-published. 2009. akoaotearoa.ac.nz.

   This professional development resource consists of five units and forty tasks that address different facets of teaching English learners. Read "Correcting spoken errors: Unit 2g" of this valuable resource to recognize the types of errors learners make, learn about correction techniques, make a plan for correcting errors, reflect on how to correct them, and review example-based practice activities in different classroom situations that would require oral corrective feedback.

3. Ferlazzo, Larry. "The Best Resources On ESL/EFL/ELL Error Correction." 2011. larryferlazzo.edublogs.org.

   In this list Larry Ferlazzo shares links to research on error correction and teaching tips for error correction from practitioners.

4. Roberts, Rachael. "Tips and Techniques for Correcting Spoken Errors." elt-resourceful. 2016. elt-resourceful.com.

   In this last of three articles on oral error correction, the author provides practical tips for correcting errors, including the use of gestures for drawing students' attention to commonly made errors.

## Chapter 15

# Exploring the Meaning, Form, and Relationships of Words

## DESCRIPTION

Studying word meaning (semantic features), word parts (morphemes), and word relationships (both semantic and morphemic features) are three helpful ways to build native English-speaking students' lexicon and accelerate the growth of receptive and productive vocabulary skills in English learners.

**Semantic analysis** shows similarities and differences in meaning among groups of words and how the words relate to one another. They thus enable English learners to focus on meanings of words.

**Morpheme analysis**, more specifically derivational morpheme analysis, examines the prefixes or suffixes used in English to create new words by changing the meaning of an existing word (e.g., prefix *un-* + *happy* = *unhappy*), or change the part of speech of a word (e.g., adjective *happy* + suffix *-ly* = adverb *happily*).

**Cognate analysis** focuses on words from different languages that have similar pronunciations/spelling and meanings, such as *person* in English and *persona* in Spanish. False cognates exist where pronunciations or spellings are similar but meanings differ, such as *carpeta* in Spanish, which means *folder*, not *carpet*, in English.

## PURPOSE

An extensive vocabulary and solid understanding of everyday and academic words are predictive of success in reading comprehension as well as writing. While all students need to master increasingly large and complex academic words as they progress through the preK–12 grade continuum, English learners, especially at the beginning and intermediate levels, have to acquire everyday words at the same time.

The purpose of using **semantic analysis** is to focus on the meaning of words. It can be used to assist all learners to make connections between and among words and to discover variations in their use. English learners benefit from semantic analysis when they recognize similarities and differences between their native language and English.

The purpose of teaching **morpheme analysis** is to demonstrate how words are constructed. By breaking up words into smaller, already known units, all students can understand meanings of unfamiliar words. Morpheme analysis that includes the English learner's native language builds on their linguistic assets. For example, once a French speaker has learned that the English suffix *-er* added to a verb carries the meaning of the French suffix *-eur* when added to a verb (e.g., *doer, maker, thinker*), she can apply that knowledge moving forward.

The purpose of **cognate exploration** is to engage English learners in searching for known words or terms, which may help them comprehend portions of a text, reading passage, or story. When ELs encounter unknown words in English that look similar to words in their native language, their confidence is immediately lifted and they are more motivated to continue reading.

## CONTEXT FOR USE

Explicit analysis and exploration of word meaning, form, and relationships between words should not be considered exclusive to language arts and literacy instruction. Semantic, morpheme, and cognate analyses can easily become part of a regular vocabulary lesson before or during a unit. They can also be implemented as a systematic study of words over a longer period of time. In math, for example, these tools help learners understand the similarities and relationships among words such as *add*, *sum*, or *more* (semantic analysis), which are often used in directions on assessments. In social studies, where larger units of information are conveyed through text, semantic analysis can be used before reading passages to focus on the differences in meanings of polysemous words (i.e., words that have multiple meanings, such as *lobby* in a building vs. a political *lobby*), and derivational morpheme study can be incorporated during reading to understand words through context based on their individual parts. Cognate exploration can be useful when introducing any new concept or text to allow English learners to identify similar words in their native language.

Rather than occasionally using these tools as instructional strategies to change up vocabulary study, teachers who systematically apply semantic, morpheme, and cognate explorations equip their students to become self-sufficient learners. Once students become comfortable users of these tools, they can apply them to understand directions, concepts, and basic words in any context. Second language teachers have developed many innovative hands-on activities that make breaking down and analyzing words and their meanings fun and engaging for all students in every content area.

## MATERIALS AND PREPARATION

Semantic analysis, derivational morpheme study, and cognate explorations lend themselves to hands-on activities. In addition to grade-specific vocabulary lists and lists of prefixes and suffixes, teachers typically have the necessary materials in the classroom already: grids with pictures of the items in each category, realia, graphic organizers that show relationships (e.g., bubble map), chart paper, pocket chart, index cards for sorting, pencil, and paper.

## THE FOUR PS OF TARGETED LANGUAGE AND LITERACY INSTRUCTION

### Pitch

Exploration of word meaning, form, and relationships is less sensitive to English proficiency level (pitch) than many other *Build* tools and techniques. This means that, in general, word exploration can be part of whole-class activities that help all students, including English learners, build receptive and productive vocabulary.

In terms of English learners' readiness to acquire new language elements, individual words and word families present fewer developmental constraints than would grammatical word endings (e.g., the past tense *-ed* added to verbs) or word sequence in phrases or sentences (e.g., asking a question in the past tense: "Did she like the movie?"). In addition, words that are typically taught in specific grades might be missing from an EL's English vocabulary, but the EL may know the concept in their first language and would simply need to acquire the English term rather than relearn the whole notion. For example, for a beginning English learner in middle school to learn the English word *divide*, he would not have to learn the word *subtract* in English first.

Also, words that are considered to be more academic in English are not necessarily more difficult for ELs than their less academic synonyms. Learning the form and meaning of the word *intractable*, for instance, would not be more difficult than learning the form and meaning of *stubborn*, and depending on the ELs' experience in English-speaking environments and their native language (the Italian word for *stubborn* is *intrattabile*, for example), it is possible that they might learn *intractable* before *stubborn*.

### Pace

The pacing of instruction can be adjusted to check for understanding, especially when English terms are used to define other English terms (e.g., explaining the meaning of *conspicuous* by referring to the synonym *obvious*). Taking an extra moment to confirm that the ELs have understood the new term, either by looking it up in their first language or in a visual dictionary, for example, will make a difference in their vocabulary growth.

## Portion

Because ELs have likely had less incidental exposure to the new English words of focus in a lesson than non-ELs have, it may be more difficult for them to acquire as many new words in the same lesson as non-ELs. Depending on the ELs' levels of proficiency, it may be better to select a subset of the new words of focus for them to learn and be assessed on.

## Perspective

The main difference in targeted vocabulary activities for English learners is in perspective, in terms of the vocabulary chosen and the definitions and explanations provided.

English learners may acquire new words for similar items without understanding the nuances that native speakers have picked up over time. For example, an English learner may have learned that *plate* and *dish* can mean the same thing (a shallow container on which food is served, such as a paper plate) but might not know that *dish* can also refer to the meal it contains (e.g., a delicious dish was served). An English learner may ask something like, "What is your favorite traditional plate?" to inquire about preferred meals. In addition, each of these two examples has other meanings (e.g., a license *plate*, a satellite *dish*) that may be mentioned and defined to allay any confusion regarding these polysemic terms. To help English learners understand these differences, teachers should break down the elements of meaning for ELs in an explicit way (semantic analysis with a grid or differential is a useful tool for explicit instruction of elements of meaning), as shown in the following section.

Cultural elements of meaning are a key dimension of perspective. For example, English learners' mental images of fruit might be different based on their native country, such as thinking of tropical fruit when others are thinking of apples. Different experiences and environments can mean that a listener's mental image won't match that of the speaker.

Another contrast in perspective is the multiple meanings a word can have in one language, but not its counterpart in another language. For example, the word *realize* has two major meanings in English, to become aware of something or to accomplish something, but in Italian *realizzare* only denotes accomplishing something. Consequently, translating a word from English to the native language is not always sufficient to establish the full meaning of the new English word.

# APPLICATION IN PRE-TEACHING, TEACHING/CO-TEACHING, AND POST-TEACHING

## SEMANTIC FEATURES ANALYSIS

### Elementary Grades—Semantic Features Diagram

To show that related words cannot be used interchangeably, draw a graphic organizer with three or four terms on the smartboard. List the features that describe them as students call them out. Discuss which features go with the individual terms, and move/copy them. The resulting diagram can be printed out and hung on the wall, or you can continue with the exploration the next day by asking the students to devise a Venn diagram in which they compare and contrast the terms and features.

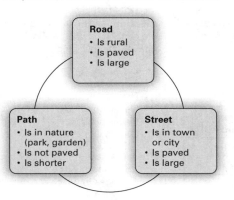

### Secondary Grades—Semantic Features Grid

To visually present the features of abstract general academic vocabulary, select the terms of an upcoming unit of study. Reserve as many columns as needed for features, but leave the labels empty. Tell students to write in a feature when they come to it in the lesson and put a + in the box where the feature exists and a – where it does not. The grid grows little by little as the unit progresses.

| Type of Government | Features | | |
|---|---|---|---|
| | *Single Entity* | *Centralized* | *Authoritarian* |
| Democracy | – | + or – | – |
| Dictatorship | + | + | + |
| Monarchy | + | + | + |
| Oligarchy | + | + | + or – |
| Republic | – | – | + or – |
| Plutocracy | + | + or – | + or – |

### Proficiency Level Differentiation

Level 4 and above English learners should be able to actively contribute to the completion of the grid, whereas you may need to reduce the portion for lower-level ELs by giving a grid with fewer features to be analyzed.

If translations of the terms are provided for level 1 and level 2 ELs through modified texts during student research or reading, include them in the grid as well to reinforce the linguistic benefits of biliteracy.

## SEMANTIC GRADIENT (ELEMENTARY AND SECONDARY GRADES)

To negotiate the variation of the word meanings with one another, give students cards with the adjectives that indicate gradients. The students may self-select where to stand or be directed by their peers and explain their placement. Once agreed upon the placements, insert the cards into the pockets of a pocket chart. Repeat the activity the following week with another set of adjectives. Change out when the chart is full.

| Frigid cold | Cold | Tepid | Lukewarm | Warm | Torrid hot |
|---|---|---|---|---|---|

### Proficiency Level Differentiation

WIDA level 1 and 2 English learners likely require translated terms and, if possible, a more advanced language peer who can translate the reasoning of the group to the EL or the EL's thoughts to the group. You can further challenge level 3 and above ELs by giving them nouns that go together, or collocate, with certain adjectives, such as lukewarm + water and torrid + affair.

# MORPHEME ANALYSIS

## Elementary Grades

To co-construct the table with the class, write a number of words that have the same prefix or suffix on the board. Ask what these words have in common, underlining the prefix/suffix and the root word with different colors based on the students' answers. Display the grid with the prefix or suffix and your original words completed, then ask the students what these words have in common in terms of the meaning. Finally, tell the students to write down as many (real) words as they can using the prefix in one minute. Select a few additional examples for the table after debriefing.

| Prefix | Meaning | Original Word | New Word |
|--------|---------|---------------|----------|
| pre- | before | game | pregame |
| | | arrange | prearrange |
| inter- | between | national | international |
| | | state | interstate |

Display the table as an anchor chart. The next day, students share sentences in which the words are used with a partner. Moving forward, ask students to scan a text for words with the taught prefixes prior to reading to reinforce the vocabulary learning strategy. Students can earn points for adding them to the grid.

It is beneficial to point out the part of speech of words when teaching suffixes because many change the part of speech when added.

| Original Word and POS | Suffix | Meaning | New Word and POS |
|-----------------------|--------|---------|------------------|
| help—verb | -ful | full of | helpful—adjective |
| thought—verb | | | thoughtful—adjective |
| kind—noun | -ness | state of being something | kindness—noun |
| good—adjective | | | goodness—noun |

If the word is not abstract, students can also draw a picture as they write the words in a sentence.

## Secondary Grades

Generate excitement to explore derivational morphemes by putting students in teams. Announcing a friendly competition creates additional buy-in.

Generate stacks of derivational suffixes for each pair or small group. Write a verb, such as *develop*, on the board and instruct the students to select the suffixes with which a derived word can be created. The first sort may look like this:

Develop
-ment
-able
-ing

For the second round, ask the students to find additional suffixes that they can add to words already created. The students should come up with the following list:

Develop
Development
Developmental
Developmentally
Developable
Developing

In the next step, the students should create their own definitions or sentences in which the derived words are used. They may use words created by others as well. The group with the most words and correct definitions wins a small prize or bragging rights.

## Proficiency Level Differentiation

Level 4 and above English learners should be able to fully contribute to the activities. Lower-level ELs should be allowed to generate fewer new words, as their lexicon of root words to which prefixes and suffixes are added is smaller.

## Cognate Analysis (Elementary and Secondary Grades)

As stated, cognate analysis is a tool that is particularly well suited for English learners, since it connects terms in the EL's native language to English. As the example below illustrates, cognates sometimes exist across languages that are not in the same family.

To begin the process of identifying cognates, tell the learners to skim a passage or story and highlight words that look similar in their native language. Then, have them write the similar word in their native language above the words. Using Google translate, check whether it is a true or false cognate. If it is a true cognate, the teacher and learners can create a word wall of the words in English and the learners' native languages.

### Selected Cognates in English, Spanish, Arabic, and Kreyol

| English | Spanish | Arabic | Haitian Kreyol |
|---------|---------|--------|----------------|
| gazelle | gacela | غزالة (ghazaalah) | gazèl |
| orange | naranja | نارنج (naarinj) | zoranj |

## Proficiency Level Differentiation

No differentiation is needed. This tool can be introduced at the very beginning of WIDA level 1.

## SUGGESTIONS FOR SUCCESS IN THE EL-INTEGRATED CLASSROOM

Teachers who explore the meaning, form, and relationship of words successfully have shared the following pointers.

### Universal, Supplemental, and Alternative Applications

Because native English speakers also have to learn academic vocabulary, semantic features analysis and morpheme study can easily be done as a whole-class activity. During these instructional events, native English speakers and advanced ELs acquire new vocabulary words and may also add specificity to their already existing vocabulary knowledge. In this setting the tools are implemented universally.

To differentiate for English proficiency during whole-class instruction, teachers can add pictures, provide translations and the names of the items, or point out cognates in the ELs' native language as a supplemental support.

Some teachers create alternative vocabulary-building instructional opportunities when they know that English learners lack the vocabulary necessary to understand a future text.

Cognate analysis is a suitable alternative tool because it facilitates the building of background knowledge that native English speakers would not typically need.

### Pre-teaching, Teaching/Co-teaching, and Post-teaching Variations

When checking on the depth of understanding of the vocabulary exploration or practice, teachers can ask ELs to explain their thinking while looking at the product from the lesson (e.g., semantic features grid or semantic gradient). Higher proficiency level English learners can be asked to describe what they did and why with little prompting.

For English learners at levels 1 through 4 the teacher should engage the students in leveled questioning (see chapter 6), adjusting the length and complexity of the question to the EL's proficiency level, and accepting responses that are representative of the student's current ability to express herself in words, phrases, or sentences.

### Collaborative Practices

The EL-specific aspects discussed in the four Ps sections can be addressed in advance or after the semantic/morpheme/cognate analysis activity by an ELD specialist or assistant. A bilingual assistant can help with possible cognates/false cognates and with pointing out different nuances in meaning between a translated word and its English counterpart.

### Informal Assessment

Once students have participated in a teacher-led activity using one of the word meaning, form, or relationships analysis tools, they can complete their own grids, gradients, or maps to assess their attainment of the activity's objective. For beginning and intermediate ELs, providing support materials, such as handouts with additional visuals or word banks to search for examples, can enable them to complete the assessment task.

## ADDITIONAL INFORMATION AND RESOURCES

1. Ebbers, Susan M. "Linking the Language: A Cross-Disciplinary Vocabulary Approach." Reading Rockets. 2008. www.readingrockets.org.

   This article shows how to plan for and execute morphology study in vocabulary teaching across different subjects.

2. McEwan, Elaine K. "Root Words, Roots and Affixes." Reading Rockets. www.readingrockets.org.

   In this excerpt from her book *The Reading Puzzle: Word Analysis*, the author offers downloadable lists of common Latin and Greek root words as well as prefixes and suffixes. All tables contain the root or affix under analysis, a definition, and examples of their use in words.

3. Reading Rockets. "Semantic Gradients." www.readingrockets.org.

   This article presents different ways to teach semantic gradients and provides examples for different subject areas at elementary and middle school grade levels. A video of students constructing a gradient is also included.

4. Reading Rockets. "Semantic Features Analysis." www.readingrockets.org.

   The article on this page shares examples of semantic feature analysis from language arts, math, science, and social studies, and provides tips for differentiating analysis instruction. Two videos of teaching compare-contrast are also included.

5. Beck, Isabel, Margaret McKeown, and Linda Kucan. "Choosing Words to Teach." Reading Rockets. www.readingrockets.org.

   In this excerpt from their book on robust vocabulary instruction, the authors explain, with specific examples for both younger and older learners, how to select tier II vocabulary, how to decide which words to include in a lesson, and considerations beyond tier II words.

6. Florida Center for Reading Research. Florida State University. www.fcrr.org.

   This site's resources collection contains activity descriptions, games, and copy materials for roots and suffixes that are designed to support language and literacy learning for both developing and struggling readers.

7. Cognate Linguistics. "ELT Though Cognates." cognates.org.

   This website offers a wide range of resources related to cognates, such as English-Spanish-French-Portuguese cognates, as well as free cognate identification and highlighting technology tools.

## Chapter 16

# Grammatically Unpacking Sentences

## DESCRIPTION

Analyzing sentences and grammatically unpacking them is a tool used to deconstruct complex sentences in academic text into smaller sentences or sentence chunks to make them more comprehensible for readers. The tool adds to the skill set of independent readers while also teaching grammatical understanding of how English sentences are constructed. English learners whose first language is similar in structure to English have fewer difficulties comprehending how to deconstruct complex sentences and repack the information in simpler, shorter sentences. If, on the other hand, the native language differs from English, unpacking sentences becomes more challenging and will require more support when connecting the elements of a sentence to arrive at its meaning.

In addition to learning about phrase-level grammatical structures, EL students benefit from the naturally incorporated review of English sentence structure S-V-O (subject, verb, object, as in *I eat chocolate*). This tool thus enhances future language development in addition to helping ELs become self-sufficient readers.

## PURPOSE

The primary purpose of grammatically unpacking sentences is to make the author's core message accessible by breaking down longer, more complex sentences that are difficult to understand into shorter, less complex phrases. Through this tool students improve reading comprehension because they develop awareness of the relationships of words and sentence construction. Grammatically unpacking sentences builds language control and accuracy, which are important components of the Common Core State Standards. Students who become strategic users of this tool eventually transfer their grammatical understanding from reading to writing, creating a cycle where reading comprehension helps support writing and more writing supports reading comprehension.

## CONTEXT FOR USE

Grammatically unpacking sentences has traditionally been employed in second language courses and with fictional text or literary works. However, texts from all content areas, even word problems, lend themselves to this tool, and *all* students further their reading comprehension with it. Academic texts often contain many complex sentences composed of a variety of phrases, clauses, and content words that can be linguistically burdensome for readers and may negatively affect reading comprehension. English learners can quickly become lost amid the many words used and ultimately lose track of the sentence's meaning. Knowing how to chunk words into phrases and clauses reduces the need to translate every word, which, in turn, reduces frustration. Table 16.1 provides a user-friendly definition and examples of the most commonly used terms when teaching how to grammatically unpack sentences.

## MATERIALS AND PREPARATION

Since grammatically unpacking sentences can be taught using any content-area text, teachers can use their classroom textbooks or other passages they read with their students. Other materials include chart paper, markers, highlighters, paper, and scissors.

Because explicit teaching through modeling is paramount with this tool, we recommend you write the first two sentences of a selected text on chart paper or a sheet of paper that you will project on a screen. Prepare sentence strips of the constituents of these sentence(s) to visually show how the sentences are composed. Type a few sentences of the text with sufficient line spacing for the students to cut them into sentence strips during individual or collaborative group practice. You can also show sentences from books to the class for unpacking, projecting them for the class with a document camera on a whiteboard and then writing on the whiteboard with markers to separate constituents and unpack their meaning.

## THE FOUR PS OF TARGETED LANGUAGE AND LITERACY INSTRUCTION

### Pitch

Newcomer ELs and those with very low proficiency levels do not benefit from participating in grammatically unpacking sentence activities because their immediate focus is on building vocabulary and understanding repetitive phrasing.[1] They are better served completing an alternative activity parallel to or done during the time they spend with the ELD specialist.

When grammatically unpacking sentences with the entire class, an adjustment of pitch you should consider is the need for leveled text for level 2 ELs whose current language proficiency level does not yet include complex sentences. The text simplification for level 3 ELs does not need to be substantial. A reduction of the number of adjectives and adverbs that don't contribute significantly to the understanding of the text is likely sufficient. Discourse markers (e.g., *in fact*, *indeed*) can also be removed because the focus of the tool is on reducing grammatical complexity rather than larger text organization. Since the end result of the lesson is for students to be able to repack text into shorter and simpler sentences and level 2 and 3 ELs will base their sentences on already

TABLE 16.1

**Terms for Teaching How to Grammatically Unpack Sentences**

| Term | Definition | Example |
|---|---|---|
| *English word order* | Subject – Verb – Object | *Joe* (S) *caught* (V) *the ball* (O) |
| *Constituents* | A word or group of words that are part of a larger unit within a sentence. | *The woman with the cute puppy* adopted it from the shelter.<br><br>*The woman* (NP) *with the cute puppy* (PP) *adopted it today* (VP).* |
| *Noun phrase (NP)* | Must include a noun or pronoun as its head but may include premodifiers (words before the noun) or post modifiers (words after the noun). | **Premodifier**<br>The tall boy went to the store.<br>*The* (determiner that modifies boy)<br>*Tall* (adjective that modifies boy)<br><br>**Postmodifier**<br>The boy reading a book laughed at the joke.<br>*Reading a book* (*reading a book* modifies *boy*) |
| *Verb phrase (VP)* | Contains a verb at its head and may include a main verb, linking verb, or a helping verb. | They danced.<br>*Danced* (main verb)<br>Jack is kind.<br>*Is* (linking verb)<br>Joe can study.<br>*Can* (helping verb) |
| *Prepositional phrase (PP)* | These phrases modify nouns or verbs in sentences. | The box by the window broke into many pieces.<br>*By the window* (prepositional phrase) that modifies *box*, a noun)<br>*Into many pieces* (prepositional phrase) that modifies *broke*, a verb) |
| *Clause* | There are many clauses in the English language. They can be dependent or independent sentences that contain a subject or predicate. | She traveled to another country because she was sad.<br>*She traveled to another country.* (independent clause—this clause can stand on its own as a sentence)<br>*because she was sad* (dependent clause—this clause cannot stand alone as a sentence. It needs to link with an independent clause to form a sentence.) |
| *Nominalization* | During nominalization, verbs and adjectives are changed into nouns by adding suffixes. | *Discriminate* (verb); *discrimination* (noun)<br>*Sad* (adjective); *sadness* (noun) |
| *Conjunctions* | There are two types of conjunctions in English: coordinating and subordinating.<br><br>Coordinating conjunction: connects words, phrases, or clauses that function as the same part of speech.<br><br>Subordinating conjunction: connects subordinate (dependent) and main (independent) clauses. | *Jodie wrote and read the letters.*<br>*Wrote* (verb) *and* (coordinating conjunction) *read* (verb)<br>*After they studied, they rested.*<br>*After they studied* (subordinate clause)<br>*they rested* (main clause). |

* NP, noun phrase; VP, verb phrase; PP, prepositional phrase.

simplified text, expectation adjustments for grammatical accuracy of their repacked sentences are minimal. Some allowances for grammatical accuracy should be made for ELs at levels 4 through 6 who work with the original text. The focus should be on retaining the meaning.

### Pace

Minor pace adjustments to how quickly the lesson proceeds can be made without impacting the non-EL students in the class. When English learners whose listening scores fall within proficiency levels 2 through 4 are present, you should deliberately point to the individual sentence constituent and briefly pause between each one as you model the tool or discuss the sample sentences produced by the class. This affords the ELs time to connect what they hear and read in the text. Some allowances need to be made for wait time when asking them to identify the different phrases, but these pauses do not greatly impact the overall pace of the lesson.

### Portion

Portion is the most level-sensitive component of the four Ps with this technique. Consider how many sentences the ELs can realistically be expected to work on in groups or independently. We feel two to three sentences are reasonable for the beginning level when a paragraph of grade-level difficulty is chosen. As a rule of thumb, English learners can be given one to two additional sentences for each of the next proficiency levels, with level 5 and 6 learners being able to identify and unpack close to if not as many sentences as native English speakers.

### Perspective

For English learners at varying proficiency levels, selecting key vocabulary necessary to understand the text is central to using this tool effectively. If too many words are unfamiliar, an English learner will try to translate every word to assemble the sentence(s) instead of focusing on identifying constituents. ELs at levels 2 through 5, as well as struggling readers who are not English learners, likely won't understand some words within the passage, such as the adjective *massive*. If these words are few and not very abstract, you can incorporate them at the beginning of the instructional time or as they show up in the text. However, level 2 English learners may also need to acquire the adjective *greater* and its synonyms as applied to size and force (e.g., *big* or *large* and *strong*) in order to understand *massive*. The number and complexity of vocabulary words in the passage would determine whether teaching tier I (everyday words), tier II (words used across the content areas, such as *summarize* or *exclude*), or tier III (content-specific vocabulary, such as *hypotenuse*, *moraine*, or *feudalism*) terms can be done during whole-class instruction, or whether some students need a separate vocabulary lesson prior to the class lesson.[2]

To engage in the process of unpacking complex sentences, it is important to review or point out certain grammatical concepts. This can easily and quickly be done during the lesson. If the necessary terms or concepts are novel to some of your English learners, however, you would need to consider adding a grammar mini-lesson (chapter 18) to build background knowledge prior to using this technique.

## APPLICATION IN PRE-TEACHING, TEACHING/CO-TEACHING, AND POST-TEACHING

| Elementary Grades | Secondary Grades |
|---|---|
| *Complex to simple sentences activity:* | *Complex to simple sentences activity:* |

**Elementary Grades**

*Complex to simple sentences activity:*

- Read a short paragraph or opening sentence(s) of a passage, underlining or highlighting complex sentences.
- Use previously prepared sentence strips of the deconstructed or unpacked sentences to serve as a model when using the technique with students. Tape each strip to the chart paper as you make connections between the complex sentences and the unpacked sentence strips.
- Rewrite the complex sentences in simple-sentence format. Note: Since the passive voice is often used in academic text, which makes the sentences more challenging to understand for ELs, the simpler sentences should be written in the active voice.[3]
- Tell students to do the same with the rest of the passage. This can be done in pairs or small groups.

*Simple to complex sentences activity (also appropriate for secondary grades and with fiction or literary texts):*

- Display a diagram of a content-area concept recently covered (e.g., water cycle, photosynthesis). Hand out one copy per group.
- Model writing a few short, simple sentences (e.g., The water flows underground) that describe the diagram and place them next to the diagram where they fit.
- Tell students to do the same, using an individual strip for each sentence.
- Discuss and model how information can be added to give more detail (e.g., The water flows underground into the lake). Replace the original sentence strip with the new one.

**Secondary Grades**

*Complex to simple sentences activity:*

List one or more complex sentences of a paragraph in the table below. Each student gets a copy of the table and the paragraph.

*Example of Breaking Down and Unpacking Text Using the Gettysburg Address*

Original Text:

It is for us the living, rather, to be dedicated here to the unfinished work which they who fought here have thus far so nobly advanced.

| Original Text Chunked: | Rephrased for Unpacking Discussion: |
|---|---|
| It is for us | We |
| the living, | who are alive |
| rather, | [instead] |
| to be dedicated here | should commit |
| to the unfinished work | to finish the work |
| which | that |
| they who fought here | the people who fought here |
| have thus far | until now |
| so nobly advanced. | have moved forward with honor. |

You then show how you broke down the parts of the sentence into chunks and then discuss the meaning of each part, line by line.

Identify the NP, VP, and PP constituents and discuss what makes these sentences complex.*

With the students' input, compose simple sentences and write them in the appropriate row in the right column. Students copy them into their organizer.

Hand out the full passage and instruct the students to complete the organizer by identifying, analyzing, and deconstructing the complex sentences as in the co-constructed model sentences.

*NP, noun phrase; VP, verb phrase; PP, prepositional phrase.

| Elementary Grades | Secondary Grades |
|---|---|
| • Tell students to do the same with three or four sentences. Check for accurate level of detail during group work.<br>• Identify NP, VP, PP on your sample sentence and cut the strip between the constituents.*<br>• Tell students to do the same with their sentences.<br>• Write one sentence from each group, underlining the different constituents with different colors, until the entire diagram is described.[4]<br>• Hand out a short new passage about another known topic and have students identify the NP, VP, and PPs. | *Variations of the activity:*<br>• List all complex sentences from a paragraph on the table or a graphic organizer.<br>• Distribute sentence strips of simple sentences to each student.<br>• Model, with a think-aloud, selecting the simple phrases that together convey the meaning of the first complex sentence.<br>• Instruct students to do the same with the rest of the sentence strips.<br>• Stop the work when you see several strips not yet placed.<br>• Instruct the students to compare their completed table with a shoulder partner and negotiate where the missing strips would best be placed.<br>• Follow up with a discussion on the connections between the ideas of the complex sentence and the unpacked sentence. |

**Proficiency Level Differentiation**

The English learners should be paired or grouped with learners at varying proficiency levels, including native English speakers. English learners at the beginning level can be provided with sentence strips with a few words on each of them in order to participate in the activity. A native English speaker or an EL at level 3 or above within the group may be assigned the responsibility of drawing pictures associated with the unpacked sentences to help the English learner understand the discussion. Additionally, the English learner may be given a glossary with pictures of key words to serve as verbal and nonverbal support.

*NP, noun phrase; VP, verb phrase; PP, prepositional phrase.

## SUGGESTIONS FOR SUCCESS IN THE EL-INTEGRATED CLASSROOM

Teachers who unpack sentence grammar successfully have shared the following pointers.

### Universal, Supplemental, and Alternative Applications

This tool can be used appropriately with the entire class, including ELs at level 2 and above, as native English speakers benefit from learning or reviewing how to unpack complex sentences for reading comprehension.[5] In addition to acquiring this comprehension skill, ELs benefit from hearing the responses of classmates and learning different ways that sentences similar in meaning can be constructed. While native English speakers and English learners share their simple sentences, you can offer nonverbal support in the form of visuals to provide context for the sentences. You can also have students act out their sentences in addition to writing them.

### Pre-Teaching, Teaching/Co-teaching, and Post-teaching Variations

While the students unpack and repack the assigned sentences, you have the opportunity to check on your ELs and ask them to explain how they determined the constituents or why they think the simpler phrasing matches the more complex wording. As in all verbal interactions with English learners, we encourage you to employ leveled questioning (chapter 6) so that you enable them to comprehend your question and respond in a manner appropriate for their proficiency level; then you can elicit additional information if the response was uncertain or unclear. If there is not enough time to check with each EL or if some ELs show misconceptions during this practice session, make room for this discussion or for reteaching the concept shortly following the lesson.

## Collaborative Practices

Pre-teaching of important vocabulary in small groups prior to whole-class instruction can typically be assumed by the classroom teacher. The ELD teacher could be consulted as to whether the ELs in the class have the requisite knowledge to participate in meaningful ways in whole-class instruction. He could perform brief informal assessments during the time he typically works with the ELs and cover missing or superficial understanding, if found. Possible areas to investigate would be the most common parts of speech, as they likely will be brought up in the discussion of groups of words that are included in the noun phrases, verb phrases, or prepositional phrases (e.g., the big white house). Another area of investigation would be for ELs to show that they are able to respond to questions (especially *who, what, when, where, how,* and *how many*) when given simple sentences (e.g., Seven frogs hopped to the pond), since this understanding is indicative of word order and connections between words.

## Informal Assessment

To determine your ELs' understanding of simple and complex sentences, show them a long noun phrase and have them copy it onto their individual whiteboards. Instruct the students to break the complex noun phrase into shorter parts. For example, "The sole person for whom the cake was baked ate it all by himself" could be broken down by higher level ELs to "Someone baked a cake for one person. That person ate the whole cake." This activity offers a view into English learners' knowledge of English syntax and helps you see which EL needs additional assistance unpacking sentences. It also provides a discussion starter with the ELD professional about whether ELs are ready to move on to more complex sentences and how you can move them forward in constructing increasingly varied, complex, and longer sentences.

## ADDITIONAL INFORMATION AND RESOURCES

1. Robertson, K. "Increasing ELL Student Reading Comprehension with Non-fiction Text." Reading Rockets. 2008. www.readingrockets.org.

   This article describes effective ways of increasing EL students' comprehension of nonfiction expository text using evidence-based models of instruction such as the gradual release of instruction model.

2. My English Pages. "Noun Phrases." www.myenglishpages.com.

   Browse through this resource to read up on noun phrases and many other grammar points. The site also includes ideas and educational materials to support the teaching of grammar and related skills.

3. Nordquist, Richard. "Postmodifier (Grammar)." ThoughtCo. 2017. www .thoughtco.com.

   Access glossaries of grammatical and rhetorical terms with a focus on understanding and using modifiers: words or groups of words that describe noun phrases or restrict meanings in some way.

4. Nordquist, Richard. "How to Recognize and Use Clauses in English Grammar." ThoughtCo. 2017. www.thoughtco.com.

   Access glossaries of grammatical terms with a focus on understanding and using dependent and independent clauses.

5. Grammar Revolution. "What Are Helping Verbs and Verb Phrases." www.english -grammar-revolution.com.

   Access glossaries of grammatical terms and deepen your understanding of using helping verbs and verb phrases.

6. Brook, Erin. "Sentence Clarity: Nominalizations and Subject Position." Purdue OWL. 2015. owl.english.purdue.edu.

   The Purdue Online Writing Lab website is widely used in colleges and secondary schools as a resource to improve writing. This article provides ideas, tips, and strategies aimed at helping students to understand nominalizations and learn how and when to use them in sentences.

## Chapter 17

# Understanding Text Structures with Graphic Organizers

## DESCRIPTION

Text structure is used by readers to identify the most important information the author wants to convey to recall information and comprehend text. Unlike narrative text, informational or expository text may contain a variety of text structures within a passage or paragraph. Five major structures have been discussed by researchers: description, sequence, compare/contrast, cause and effect, and problem/solution.[1] English learners can benefit from direct teaching of these text structures with graphic organizers to help them organize information based on text patterns or structures provided in a text. Too often, English learners get lost in the sheer volume of words in a passage. Without a systematic way of assisting English learners on how to mentally organize information, reading comprehension will continue to be a major challenge for these learners.

## PURPOSE

Knowledge of text structures serves as clues to prepare readers to focus on information deemed important by the author. Focusing on specific information enables readers to recall and comprehend text. For example, if an author uses a descriptive structure, then the reader searches for the many describing words to understand the text. If a sequencing structure is used, then the reader expects to read a list of occurrences in a predictable or hierarchical order and will, therefore, focus on what happens first, second, third, and so on. Proficient readers identify signal words to inform them of the type of text structure the author is using. Words such as *first*, *next*, and *additionally* are often used in sequence structures. They inform the reader to pay attention to a series of events.

## CONTEXT OF USE

To help English learners visualize the structures, graphic organizers are a strongly recommended tool. Graphic organizers can be used with all academic subjects, as each subject area contains a variety of text structures.[2] To avoid confusion when introducing text structures to English learners, present one structure at a time.

| Text Structure | Definition | Signal Words | Graphic Organizer |
|---|---|---|---|
| *Description* | Many descriptions of a topic are provided. | *additionally, another, also* | |
| *Sequence* | Information is arranged in a specific order. | *first, second* | |
| *Compare and contrast* | Similarities and differences about people, events, animals, objects, etc. are discussed. | *different/ difference, same* | |
| *Cause and effect* | Results and reasons for a problem are provided. | *since, because* | |
| *Problem– solution* | A difficult situation or question is presented, followed by explanations of how the problem was solved. | *happens, occurs* | |

## MATERIALS AND PREPARATION

Select a text structure, a reading passage that contains the signal words of the text structure, and graphic organizers. Use a yellow highlighter to identify the signal words in the passage and write them on a graphic organizer. This tool should be modeled with an example prior to teaching it to English learners. WIDA level 1 and 2 students can read previously filled out graphic organizers and tables that use language at their proficiency levels to enable them to grasp the key points of a text. WIDA level 3 students can write key words and phrases on empty graphic organizer forms after reading a text. WIDA level 4 and above students can create a graphic organizer or table from scratch and complete it after reading a text. Keep these considerations in mind when selecting materials.

## THE FOUR PS OF TARGETED LANGUAGE AND LITERACY INSTRUCTION

### Pitch

The pitch of the selected text, and the discussion of the text, is very level sensitive. It is important to select a text that is challenging but not frustrating for an individual student, based on the student's overall English proficiency level as well as his reading level as measured by a test designed for ELs (e.g., WIDA ACCESS). Identifying signal words and reading or completing graphic organizers can be done at all levels, but the language used to explain the content or to give directions should be attuned to students' English proficiency levels.

### Pace

The pacing of using this tool will be affected by the need to define, paraphrase, and give examples of terms and phrases in the text that ELs are not familiar with. In addition, comprehension checks should be frequent to determine whether the EL understands the structure of the text even if she does not understand all of the details.

### Portion

The amount of text used would differ depending on the student's English proficiency level as well as the complexity and density of the text. In general, shorter texts with shorter paragraphs and sentences work better with level 1 and 2 ELs, and graphic organizers that are short and simple match well with these text types. Longer, more complex texts are appropriate for levels 3 and above, and the intricacy and detail of the graphic organizer would rise as well.

One structure and one graphic organizer type at a time should be presented with many opportunities for the learners to practice using the tool.

## Perspective

Text structure can be different in languages other than English, so it is helpful to discuss structural or rhetorical contrasts in terms of differences rather than correct or proper text structure. For example, some languages organize compare-and-contrast texts with a back-and-forth, sometimes meandering process. When showing how that structure works in English, a teacher can ask if it is different in anyone's home language and how. To support students in connecting signal words with text structure, teachers can show typical sentence patterns (grammar focus) that begin with certain signal words, such as "*Despite* the law that prohibited alcohol, consumption of spirits continued in the US," showing what *despite* is frequently followed by (a noun phrase).

## APPLICATION IN PRE-TEACHING, TEACHING/CO-TEACHING, AND POST-TEACHING

### TEXT STRUCTURE

### Elementary Grades

In this activity English learners identify the signal or clue words in a paragraph that will help them recall and comprehend the most important information in the text.

#### Text structure: compare and contrast

Tell the ELs that they will become language detectives because they will learn to see clues in paragraphs when they read. Those clues will eventually show them what they need to know and, as detectives, they will see and understand the entire message. But first, they will need to understand what the clues mean.

Define *different* and *same* by presenting pictures that are different and pictures that are the same while saying the words. Repeat the activity until they can differentiate between *different* and *same*.

Tell the learners that anytime they see these words, the author wants them to compare two things, so they should pay particular attention to the things that are being compared.

Show a compare/contrast reading passage on a document camera and highlight the clue words *same* and *different*.

### Secondary Grades

Readers in secondary grades benefit from using text structure activities to understand the macro or top-down elements of challenging text.

For example, after reading an article about improving writing instruction, readers can complete a table such as the following:

| Heading and Paragraph # | Topic | Function |
|---|---|---|
| *Introduction* | | |
| Paragraph 1. | Introduction to the article | Describes the article's content |
| *Academic Writing* | | |
| Paragraph 2. | Writing in general | Describes good writing |
| Paragraph 3. | Importance of writing | Persuades why writing must be taught |
| Paragraph 4. | Writing for academic purposes | Compares academic to nonacademic writing |
| Paragraph 5. | Features of academic writing | Transitions to writing pedagogy |

By completing the table, the reader makes an elaborated outline of the text's contents and can see how the argument progresses, paragraph by paragraph.

Another way to examine the structure of a text is to complete a character map.

Distribute a Venn diagram and the compare/contrast reading passage and model writing a few examples in each segment of the diagram, using the doc cam so all can see. Direct students to continue filling out their Venn diagrams as they read the text.

For a character-driven story, such as *The Picture of Dorian Gray*, a character map like the following can be completed:

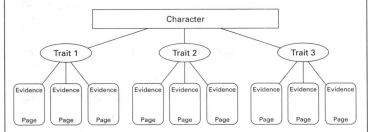

Seeing where details about the character's traits are provided throughout the story can highlight features of narrative structures.

**Proficiency level Differentiation**

Analyzing text structure with graphic organizers works with all levels of English proficiency. To target instruction to ELs' needs, leveled books would be most appropriate. When using this tool with reading materials that are above ELs' proficiency levels, different details can be stressed. At the beginning level more emphasis will be placed on vocabulary words in general and the signal or clue words more specifically. At the intermediate level, key vocabulary words should be reviewed and signal words emphasized. At the advanced level, vocabulary words, signal words, and text structural patterns should be discussed.

## SUGGESTIONS FOR SUCCESS IN THE EL-INTEGRATED CLASSROOM

Teachers who use graphic organizers to help students understand text structures have shared the following pointers.

### Collaborative Practices

Collaboration with a reading coach strongly benefits English learners through activities that reinforce text structural patterns and signal word vocabulary.

### Informal Assessment

This tool very easily lends itself to informal assessments. Since all expository textbooks contain varying text structural patterns, any book can be used to assess ELs' knowledge of text structures. Teach learners how to scan the pages of any book in search of signal words. Periodically, ask the learners to tell you whether or not they see any signal words on a page. At levels 1 and 2, ELs can copy and write the signal words they find in order to study them. At level 3, ELs can be asked to state the signal words and the name of the text structure the words represent. At levels 4 and above, ELs can be asked to identify the signal words, text structural patterns, and the author's intended message. These assessments should be used to determine whether comprehension skills are improving. In addition to focusing on signal words, graphic organizers can be used to assess students' comprehension of a reading passage, with variations of which graphic organizer and how to use it (e.g., student creates one from scratch versus filling in a preselected one) depending on proficiency level of the student and linguistic complexity of the text.

## ADDITIONAL INFORMATION AND RESOURCES

1. Akhondi, Masoumeh, Faramarz Aziz Malayeri, and Arshad Abd Samad. "How to Teach Expository Text Structure to Facilitate Reading Comprehension." *Reading Teacher* 64, no. 5 (February 2011): 368–72.

    This practitioner-oriented article describes how to teach upper-elementary-grade students to develop an awareness of how information is organized in expository texts, and how to use knowledge of text structure to facilitate reading comprehension.

2. Dymock, Susan. "Teaching Expository Text Structure Awareness." *Reading Teacher* 59, no. 2 (October 2005): 177–81.

    In this article learn about four common expository text structures and how you can teach them to your students to help them develop an understanding of text structure.

3. Peregoy, Suzanne F., and Owen F. Boyle. "English Learners Reading English: What We Know, What We Need to Know." *Theory into Practice 39* no. 4 (Fall 2000): 237–47.

    This article explains important English reading processes among native and non-native English speakers, along with recommendations for teaching English learners to read and understand texts in English.

4. Read, Sylvia, D. Ray Reutzel, and Parker C. Fawson. "Do You Want to Know What I Learned? Using Informational Trade Books as Models to Teach Text Structure." *Early Childhood Education* 36, no. 3 (December 2008): 213–19.

    Read this article to find out how to use "well-structured" expository trade book titles to teach text structure to your students. A lesson plan template and an extended example of an explicit lesson on ordering/sequencing are provided.

5. Williams, Joanna P. "Instruction in Reading Comprehension for Primary-Grade Students: A Focus on Text Structure." *Journal of Special Education* 39, no. 1 (2005): 6–18.

    This article explains how teaching the text structure compare/contrast through clue words, discussions, vocabulary development, graphic organizers, and summary writing facilitated reading comprehension of at-risk second- and third-grade students.

**6.** Williams, Joanna P., et al. "Close Analysis of Texts with Structure (CATS): An Intervention to Teach Reading Comprehension to At-Risk Second Graders." *Journal of Educational Psychology* 108, no. 8 (March 2016): 1061–77.

Read this article to learn about how to teach the five basic text structures (sequence, comparison, cause-effect, description, and problem-solution), along with linguistic signals (clue words such as *but*, *finally*, *because*), graphic organizers, and generic questions that help students to focus on essential textual information.

## Chapter 18

# Grammar, Spelling, and Vocabulary Mini-Lessons

## DESCRIPTION

A language development mini-lesson teaches language or about language. It focuses on a skill or concept that students need to know and be able to use to be successful in a larger lesson or assignment. For example, a teacher might lead the whole class or a small group of ELs in a mini-lesson on the passive voice prior to reading a scientific text. In addition, mini-lessons can be provided as a follow-up to individual areas of difficulty, as with teacher feedback about grammatical errors in written compositions (chapter 19) and their students' responses to the feedback. Mini-lessons should not exceed fifteen minutes because they serve as a just-in-time type of tutorial to support language development and accuracy. With the use of technology, these lessons can bring fun, excitement, and discovery to the lesson. Some of the technology-based mini-lesson options can be used as individual tutorials as well as small-group or whole-class activities, using an interactive whiteboard.

## PURPOSE

Knowledge of grammar, spelling, and vocabulary are core skills needed to acquire any language. These skills may be very challenging for English learners and often require direct instruction. Mini-lessons allow learners to focus specifically on the skills needed. With the added use of technology, ELs can work at their own pace while using the many visuals provided to support their language development.

## CONTEXT FOR USE

Certain technology-assisted apps may be used for mini-lessons in all subject areas. For example, a screencast is simply a video recording of one's computer screen and the teacher's voice-over narration. Screencasts can be used effectively in presenting any mini-lesson. A teacher can record a screencast for the mini-lesson he or she intends to teach, showing media content such as PowerPoint slides on the computer screen while talking over the instructional points. Screencast-assisted mini-lessons save teachers' instructional time in class and provide students with unlimited access to the content being taught. In other words, the learners can review the mini-lessons at any time to recall or reinforce content or language, and once teachers create them, they can be used again and again.

## MATERIALS AND PREPARATION

Teachers and students can use commercial, open access computer-based tutorials, games, and quizzes, or teachers can create them so they are tailored to their students' needs. To make these tools, teachers need a computer with a microphone as well as presentation and screencast software. Prior to creating or selecting a mini-lesson, teachers should make note of any spoken or written errors often made by the English learners. The errors then become the focus of the mini-lessons.

## THE FOUR PS OF TARGETED LANGUAGE AND LITERACY INSTRUCTION

### Pitch

Technology-based mini-lessons allow ELs to focus on grammar points that are appropriate for their level of proficiency. Using technology with mini-lessons also works with learners at all proficiency levels, because many apps contain visuals that support language found in the lessons. Additionally, using technology provides learners with control over how much support is needed as they engage in the lessons. They may proceed with a lesson by referring to the visuals if they are at the beginning level but at the intermediate and advanced levels, the learners may choose to answer questions without those visuals. However, teachers should continue to provide additional language and instructional support as needed.

### Pace

Using technology can adjust the amount of explanation and practice given to the learner since the learner will control the amount of language support needed. Therefore, students engaging in mini-lessons with technology assistance should be encouraged not to rush. Allow the learners to explore and interact with the various technologies to familiarize themselves with the apps. This familiarity will provide learners with the confidence needed to answer questions and solve problems independently. When teaching or recording mini-lessons, teachers should pace their speech according to proficiency level, with slower speech for beginners.

### Portion

Mini-lessons provide small portions of language study, and the lower the level, the smaller the portion. The teacher simply needs to select the mini-lesson on the strategy, skill, or content the learner needs to know. The specific focus of skills is the benefit of using this tool. The lessons are brief and to the point.

## Perspective

English learners have some needs in common with non-ELs, but many grammar points that need to be taught to ELs have been acquired without instruction by non-ELs (for example, using gerunds vs. infinitives in sentences, such as, "I want *to read* [infinitive] *The Wizard of Oz*" instead of "I want reading [gerund] *The Wizard of Oz*). The English learner's proficiency level affects the grammar points of focus. For example, beginning ELs can work on the verb *be* (I am, they are), and advanced ELs can study the passive voice.

| APPLICATION IN PRE-TEACHING, TEACHING/CO-TEACHING, AND POST-TEACHING | |
| --- | --- |
| **Elementary Grades** | **Secondary Grades** |
| *Vocabulary and Spelling* | *Grammar* |
| Mini-lesson using a flashcard app such as Cram, Quizlet, AnkiApp, Vocabulary.com, or StudyBlue | A low-tech approach to teaching the passive voice is a syntax clothesline activity. This could be used with English learners exclusively, or it could also include non-ELs. |
|     The teacher begins by guiding one or a pair of students through a flashcard app focusing on vocabulary and/or spelling. As the app presents new words and photos, students write the words in flipbooks and draw a picture for each, orally describing and defining them in English or their first language to a partner or the teacher, depending on proficiency level. |     Before the activity, the teacher needs to find or write pairs of sentences in the active and passive voices; for example, "John baked the cake. The cake was baked by John." Then the teacher prints the individual words of the sentences, using a bold marker, on index cards so each word is big enough for students to see across the room. Using different colored index cards can help code key words (e.g., *by*, *was*) for passive voice.[1] |
| *Using Sentence Frames to Teach Grammar* |     The teacher runs a four- to five-foot string across an empty space and attaches it to a wall or stable fixture, just above students' eye level. Students will hang their word cards on this "clothesline." After fastening the string, the teacher attaches ten clothespins to it. |
| Kate Kinsella offers a multitude of activities and resources for using sentence frames to teach grammar. When leaving spaces for students to write missing words or phrases in the frame, Kinsella identifies the parts of speech. For example: |     The teacher then puts the index cards for "John baked the cake" in sequence, leaving a little room between each card. Then a student volunteer comes to the clothesline and changes the sentence from active to passive voice by changing the word order and adding keyword index cards. After the first sentence, the teacher can ask another student to use the list of active sentences to pin a sentence to the clothesline so a classmate can then transform it into the passive voice. As each sentence pair is placed on the clothesline, the class copies them into their notebooks. |

We celebrate _____ by _____.
           Noun         Verb + ing
                       (gerund)

We celebrate New Year's Eve by dancing.

As students see examples and label their elements with the appropriate part of speech, they learn to analyze grammar in English.

| Elementary Grades | Secondary Grades |
|---|---|
| | The clothesline activity could also be used for changing affirmative sentences to negative ones or to questions. Sentences can include grammatical word forms, such as adding index cards that have been cut in half vertically and have printed *-ed/-d* or *-ing* word endings on them that can be inserted after the main verb.<br><br>After the whole-class activity, individual students can continue studying and practicing changing sentences from active to passive voice on the tutorials and exercises available at Englishpage.com. |

**Proficiency Level Differentiation**

Most students, EL or otherwise, enjoy interacting and using technology. Therefore, native English speakers can also benefit from these types of mini-lessons. In the grammar and vocabulary areas where English learners and non-ELs both need instruction, such as the difference among their/there/they're, using technology-based mini-lessons is a perfect opportunity to have English learners at different levels of proficiency, as well as non-ELs, work collaboratively on selected lessons. English learners can use the visuals in the apps for support and minimally depend on the native speakers for assistance.

The teacher may group students based on their knowledge of the content and use of the technologies as opposed to language groups. An English learner could be at the beginning level with limited English but know how to navigate certain apps much better than the native English speaker. The collaboration would enable both to learn from each other.

## MORE EXAMPLES OF TECHNOLOGY-BASED GRAMMAR MINI-LESSONS

| Grammar Mini-Lesson Screencast | Promethean (Smart) Board Grammar Mini-Lesson |
|---|---|
| The following is an example of a mini-lesson on grammar that can be created and used with a screencast. Although the actual video of the screencast mini-lesson has not been included, the lesson can be used with a voice-over narration using a computer cursor to highlight the narrator's main points. This could be made with a PowerPoint and Screencast-O-Matic, or an integrated program such as Explain Everything or Doceri.<br><br>Many teachers share their vocabulary, spelling, and grammar tutorials in Explain Everything and Doceri. You can search vocabulary, spelling, or grammar to find other teachers' ready-made tutorials.<br><br>*Count and Noncount Nouns*<br>English nouns can be categorized as count or noncount.<br><br>Count nouns can be singular or plural. In other words, count nouns can have a number in front of them, as in 3 cups or 1 spoon.<br><br>*Count Noun Examples:*<br>I ate *an* apple. (*An* indicates one.)<br><br>She has *two* bicycles. (Two indicates the number of bicycles.)<br><br>Noncount nouns cannot have a number or the article a/an in front of them. They can stand alone in a phrase, or they can be the object of a prepositional phrase, like *a cup of* sugar.<br><br>*Noncount Noun Examples:*<br>Americans love freedom. (*Freedom* stands alone.)<br><br>I bought *a pound of* beef. (*Beef* is the object of the prepositional phrase.) | Using **interactive whiteboards (also referred to as smartboards)** in the classroom is effective when teaching grammar and vocabulary. While many of its capabilities can be recreated using a dry erase board or chalkboard or even just a projection of the computer screen, interactive whiteboards allow the teacher to stand at the front of the class rather than sit at the computer or have their backs to the students when using the board.<br><br>When using a smartboard to study grammar, learners can be encouraged to use the specialized pen feature to write sentences in various colors. Colors can easily be changed by tapping on the screen or a color bank before writing. The different colors can be used to identify parts of speech (red for nouns, green for verbs, blue for adjectives, etc.). A color key can be provided to allow teachers to easily assess learners' work by simply glancing at the smartboard from any area of the classroom. |

| Grammar Mini-Lesson Screencast | Promethean (Smart) Board Grammar Mini-Lesson |
|---|---|
| Some types of noncount nouns can be categorized. This will help you remember them. There are five key groups that most noncount nouns fall under (i.e., not all words that pertain to these groups are uncountable, but most noncount nouns are found in these five categories):<br><br>1. foods (e.g., meat)<br>2. liquids (oil)<br>3. ideas (peace)<br>4. nature (thunder)<br>5. group nouns (luggage)<br><br>Many other nouns are count or noncount for no reason; for example, fruit is noncount, but vegetable is count. These must be memorized.[2] | |

## SUGGESTIONS FOR SUCCESS IN THE EL-INTEGRATED CLASSROOM

Teachers who use grammar, spelling, and vocabulary mini-lessons successfully have shared the following pointers.

### Collaborative Practices

Using various technological tools allows opportunities for collaboration between ELD and classroom teachers in many subject areas. Together, teachers from different content areas may decide on mini-lessons to teach. As learners work in groups or individually, both teachers can circulate around the room to assist learners. The classroom teacher can confer with an ELD specialist to preview certain grammar points prior to a lesson or to review them as a follow up.

### Informal Assessment

The Socrative.com app can be used as an exit ticket. Socrative allows teachers to create assessments and to see student results live. It also creates reports and even spreadsheets to track student progress overall as well as on a question-by-question level to find areas of difficulty for English learners. Kahoot is a fun app for creating and giving quizzes that students take on their devices.

## ADDITIONAL INFORMATION AND RESOURCES

### Websites, Apps, and Podcasts for Teaching Vocabulary, Spelling, and Grammar to English Learners

1. Busuu. www.busuu.com.

    The free version of this gamified mobile app helps users to learn three thousand words on a variety of topics.

2. Duolingo. www.duolingo.com.

   This gamified freemium app is organized by topics that are further divided into isolated grammar and vocabulary lessons.

3. Education.com. "Sentence Builder: Proper Nouns." www.education.com.

   This website offers an interactive game designed to promote students' use of grammar knowledge to build correct sentences. Other grammar elements such as pronouns, adjectives, and adverbs are also available.

4. ESL HELP! Desk. "English Grammar HELP and Podcasts for the Inquisitive ESL Student: We're Interactive!" 2006. www.eslhelpdesk.com.

   Through its Library link, the website offers written grammar explanations as well as podcasts about grammar points for English learners. The free podcasts can also be downloaded directly from Apple iTunes.

5. English Page. "Free Online English Lessons and ESL/EFL Resources." www.englishpage.com.

   This website offers comprehensive tutorials on various grammar points.

6. One Stop English. www.onestopenglish.com.

   This website presents grammar tutorials, such as nouns and noun phrases, as well as lesson plans for various grade levels.

7. Phrasalstein. "Phrasalstein: Phrasal Verbs Horror." Cambridge University Press. phrasalstein.cambridge.es/english.

   This app, available for Apple and Android devices, gives students the opportunity to learn the meanings of phrasal verbs and test their understanding. Translations are available in five languages.

8. English Banana. www.englishbanana.com.

   This website provides free podcasts that teach idioms in ten minutes and others that focus on grammar points.

9. University of Victoria English Language Center. "Study Zone." University of Victoria. www.uvic.ca.

   This website provides leveled grammar, reading, and vocabulary lessons and exercises as well as puzzles that use or focus on language appropriate for five different proficiency levels.

10. Woodward English. "Tag Archives: Grammar." www.woodwardenglish.com.

     Many of the grammar points on this website have an explanation, an on-line game, and worksheets and answers. Use this site for assessing your students' knowledge or to preview for yourself the grammar point you are going to teach next.

## Websites, Apps, and Podcasts for Teaching Vocabulary, Spelling, and Grammar (not specifically for ELs)

1. No Red Ink. www.noredink.com.

   This website offers adaptive grammar and writing exercises on the most common errors. Each tutorial includes a diagnostic assessment, a practice activity, and a quiz. A free account is required. The site also offers a paid membership version.

2. Hunter College Rockowitz Writing Center. "Grammar and Mechanics." City University of New York. www.hunter.cuny.edu.

   This website provides explanations and examples of correct and incorrect sentence structure, verbs, adjectives and adverbs, articles and determiners, nouns and pronouns, prepositions, punctuation and capitalization, spelling, and vocabulary.

3. Simmons, Robin L. "Grammar Bytes! Grammar Instruction with Attitude." www.chompchomp.com.

   This website defines grammar terms, offers exercises, and provides a Massive Open Online Course (MOOC) about grammar.

4. Khan Academy. www.khanacademy.org.

   On this website you will find screencast tutorials on a wide variety of grammar and writing topics. Some resources come with a unit test at the beginning that pinpoints the lesson a learner should watch based on the test results.

5. Brain Pop. "Grammar." www.brainpop.com.

   This section of the popular Brain Pop website offers tutorials and quizzes on common issues, such as the distinction between *their*, *they're*, and *there*.

## Websites, Apps, and Podcasts for Creating Mini-Lessons

1. Explain Everything. https://explaineverything.com.

   This app allows teachers to create screencasts and share them with others. The paid membership for educators starts at five users and costs $24.95 per year. The app is available for Apple, Android, and Microsoft devices.

2. Doceri. doceri.com.

   This app allows teachers to create, control, and present tutorials on their tablets or desktop computers. The desktop license is $30; the iPad and Windows apps are free.

3. Screencast-O-Matic. https://screencast-o-matic.com.

   This website allows teachers to create and save video recordings of their computer screen, from the webcam, or both at the same time. The free version is limited to fifteen minutes. Additional features, including editing and longer recordings, are available for single users in the pro version for $18/year.

## Chapter 19

# Responding to Sentence-Level Writing Errors

## DESCRIPTION

Writing can be challenging for English learners. Proficiency in writing depends on multiple factors, including organization of topics and ideas, evidence and support for arguments, and style and voice. These elements of good writing apply to English learners and non-English learners alike. However, English learners have an additional challenge when writing that non-ELs don't have. English learners' stage of English language development affects their use of English vocabulary and grammatical forms (e.g., adding -ed to verbs to make them past tense) and structures (e.g., sequencing auxiliary verbs correctly before the main verb). Successful writing demands adherence to rules of English grammar that an EL writer may not have acquired in speaking or in writing. In other words, there are developmental constraints to ELs' use of English grammar as they progress from beginning to advanced levels of English proficiency. This has a profound effect on their writing skills in English.

Responding appropriately to writing errors is a critical skill for teachers of English learners. Addressing ELs' sentence-level writing strategically has been shown to be beneficial for developing their writing skills in English.[1] By the term *sentence-level*, we mean everything required to make a sentence correct, including word choice, spelling, word endings, punctuation, word order, and completeness.

## PURPOSE

Responding strategically to sentence-level errors that ELs at different English proficiency levels make is a key instructional technique that supports writing development. Even though response to an EL's writing may seem like a grading issue, its purpose is primarily instructional, similar to a grammar lesson. Carefully selecting an appropriate response to an EL's writing error targets the instruction (feedback) to the specific areas of language development with which the student needs direction. It is one of the most powerful ways that teachers can provide instructed second language acquisition to their English learners. Through engaging in meaningful writing, revision, and reflection, English learners internalize new forms and structures of English grammar.

## CONTEXT FOR USE

Correcting the writing errors of English learners is the responsibility of all teachers who give assignments that involve writing. Therefore, all teachers must be aware of the errors often committed by English learners. With the assistance of the ELD specialist, meaningful activities can be created to provide learners with the information needed to acquire correct forms of English grammar. Internalizing correct forms of writing in English takes time, but once acquired, learners develop the skills to self-correct.

## MATERIALS AND PREPARATION

Depending on whether the response to student writing occurs on paper or electronically, a variety of materials can be used. Feedback codes can be provided to all students so they recognize recurring error types and attempt to self-correct. Some useful error coding schemes can be found by web-searching Writing Correction Code BBC, and there any many sources of editing and proofreading codes (search for "proofreading and editing symbols"). In addition, teachers can make their own feedback codes tailored to their students' needs.

For responding to writing errors on paper, using different color pens and highlighters can help identify specific issues by color coding. For online response, simple tools like the comments function of Word are helpful, but there are more powerful screencast tools such as Jing or Screencast-O-Matic that allow for recorded spoken feedback while using the pointer or highlighter to direct attention to the area needing correction.

## THE FOUR PS OF TARGETED LANGUAGE AND LITERACY INSTRUCTION

### Pitch

Because writing is language focused and proficiency-level dependent, error correction needs to be strategic by proficiency level. It is crucial to first know the learner's WIDA proficiency level and then employ error-correction strategies appropriate for the specific level when using this technique. For example, when addressing pronoun errors, feedback should differ by level. At beginning levels (WIDA 1 and 2), the focus of feedback might be on using the correct personal pronouns (*he* versus *she*, *I* versus *me*, etc.) or, more specifically, what they are and what role they play in a simple English sentence. At intermediate levels (WIDA 3 and 4), learners' attention can be directed to antecedents and the pronouns they represent in longer, more complex sentences. Follow-up to the feedback about pronouns and antecedents can include matching pronouns with their correct antecedents. At advanced levels (WIDA 5 and 6), learners can conduct a peer review of a paragraph, looking specifically for errors between personal pronouns and the antecedents they represent, and making the appropriate corrections within the paragraph.

## Pace

The pace of responding to EL errors is not unlike pace for non-ELs. Pace may be slower when discussing written feedback on a composition with an EL because the explanations of form and structure may take more time than simply pointing out that, say, a period is missing at the end of a sentence. It is important to remember that error correction for ELs does not lead to immediate, consistent use of the correct form. The desired outcome takes longer because of the second language acquisition process. As ELs are exposed to more forms and structures through listening and reading, and as they attempt to use these new forms and structures in writing, they will make errors.

## Portion

We recommend that teachers not point out every writing error made by learners, as this will be overwhelming and may discourage students from writing or from taking risks using more complex language. Errors should be noted and analyzed to determine which ones are being self-corrected and which ones are repeated. Those in the latter group should be corrected and the correct forms should be taught. In other words, select and teach only the errors that are at risk of becoming fossilized or permanent.

## Perspective

The perspective on EL writing errors is different from that on non-EL errors. As shown in the following section, ELs make many of the same errors as non-ELs, but there are numerous errors that only ELs make. Anticipating these errors, and employing the right strategies to respond to them, is essential for teachers of ELs. The native language can be taken into consideration if the teacher wants to conduct a contrastive analysis to determine the differences in grammatical structures. Identifying the differences may help learners understand which grammatical structures exist in their native language (for example, certain verb tenses).

---

### APPLICATION IN PRE-TEACHING, TEACHING/CO-TEACHING, AND POST-TEACHING

#### ERROR TREATMENT APPROACHES

Elementary ELs in intermediate grades and ELs in secondary grades benefit from teacher responses to sentence-level errors. The response approach and the type of errors may differ by age, but many of the same grammatical errors occur for both age groups.

According to Dana Ferris, the main types of errors that English learners make can be categorized as:[2]

1. **Noun:** For example, use of definite article when not needed ("I love the running") or not using it when needed ("I went to restaurant by your house") and wrong plural form ("She has two childs")

2. **Verb:** For example, wrong tense ("I live here since 2015") and wrong form ("She teached me English")

3. Word choice: For example, wrong preposition ("I went for see the movie") and faulty word combinations ("Californian, young, five actors" instead of "five young, Californian actors")

4. Sentence structure: For example, word order ("Why you didn't come yesterday?") or missing words ("I not feeling good lately")

Ferris points out that ELs also make mistakes that first language writers commit, such as errors in punctuation, sentence boundaries (fragments, run-ons), spelling, and so on.

According to Ferris, which feedback strategies are useful depends on various circumstances. The following table gives definitions of feedback types and Ferris's recommendations for their application.

| | When should which feedback type occur in the writing process? | What types of errors should be responded to in which way? | For which level should different feedback types be used? |
|---|---|---|---|
| **Who corrects the error?** | | | |
| **Direct** Teacher | *Varies* | *Example:* word choice (e.g., prepositions, which can be arbitrary) | Beginning English learners |
| **Indirect** Teacher points out error but student corrects | *Varies* | *Example:* word form (e.g., adding an *-s* to *like* in "She like pizza") | Advanced English learners |
| **How many errors are responded to in the student's text?** | | | |
| **Comprehensive** Correct all errors | Final drafts | *Varies* | *Varies* |
| **Selective** Mark certain errors only | Early in writing process | *Varies* | *Varies* |
| **How specific is the feedback about the error or its correct form?** | | | |
| **Explicit** Note error type or rule | *Varies* | *Varies* | *Varies* |
| **Implicit** Underline error | *Varies* | *Varies* | *Varies* |

In his book *Keys to Teaching Grammar to English Language Learners*, Keith Folse offers more details regarding key grammar points that English learners struggle with:[3] (1) forms of the verb *be* (e.g., *am, is, are, was*, etc.); (2) verb tenses that express present, past, and future; (3) count (e.g., one dollar, two dollars) and noncount nouns (e.g., *some money* but not *one money*); (4) prepositions; (5) articles; (6) adjective clauses and reductions; (7) infinitives (e.g., I want *to be* a teacher) and gerunds (e.g., I like *being* a teacher); (8) phrasal verbs (e.g., *put up with*, meaning tolerate); (9) modals (*can, could, would, should*); (10) word forms (e.g., adding s to present tense verbs for *he/she/it*); (11) passive voice; (12) conditionals (*if* clauses); and (13) negating.

He also identifies twenty areas where English learners need explicit explanations of the rule (when responding to student writing, this could mean explicit correction and follow-up instruction): "(1) adjective word order; (2) inverted word order with double negatives; (3) spelling words with double consonants; (4) *used to*; (5) present unreal conditional sentences; (6) *had had*; (7) adverbs of frequency word order; (8) *will* in *if* clauses; (9) contractions; (10) verb forms in past tense questions; (11) *since* versus *for*; (12) noun clauses as embedded questions; (13) *another, other*, and *others*; (14) adverb clauses; (15) *gonna* (informal and formal language); (16) present perfect tense; (17) possessive forms; (18) comparison of adjectives; (19) *do* versus *make*; and (20) adverbs of degree word order."[4]

**Using Errors to Develop Sentence-Level Writing Skills in English**

After noting specific error patterns that English learners make, teachers can use a number of tactics to help each student acquire the correct form and structure. Ferris recommends different ways for students to apply or extend what they learned from teacher or peer responses to their writing.

One way is to assign students to reflect on the errors and feedback in their papers, making a plan for improvement. If they are given an assignment to thoughtfully consider the feedback, they are more likely to read and apply it.

Another option is for students to complete an error analysis, looking for error patterns in the composition. They can count or code the errors or error types and consult grammar references to compare the correct form with their erroneous version.

To examine repeated errors across multiple compositions, students can complete an error chart. For example, a general chart could include Folse's thirteen points across the top and the writing assignment names or numbers down the side.[5] For each composition, students can check off the errors that were pointed out in the feedback. This gives them a good idea of which grammar rules to study and practice so they are eventually acquired. A more specific type of chart could also be made, identifying the particular error type that the EL makes. For example, "Verb tenses that express past" could be broken down into past perfect continuous ("I had been writing early that morning when . . .") if the EL has made recurrent errors using that tense.

Teachers can develop and/or select tutorial grammar mini-lessons (see chapter 18 for more information) based on the common errors their students make. Then, when an individual student has a repeated grammatical error across multiple compositions, the teacher can assign the specific mini-lesson so the student completes explicit instruction on the rules for application.

**Proficiency Level Differentiation**

Correct forms of sentences can be taught at all levels of proficiency. Learners at different levels will commit different errors that must be addressed on an individual basis.

It is important that all learners be engaged in meaningful reading and writing activities. At the beginning level, the teacher needs to first teach vocabulary words, then have the learners write very simple subject–verb sentences. For students at the intermediate and advanced levels, the teacher might provide sentences written incorrectly and ask the ELs to rewrite them correctly. Both activities can also serve as informal assessments to check for understanding of these concepts.

## SUGGESTIONS FOR SUCCESS IN THE EL-INTEGRATED CLASSROOM

Teachers who respond to ELs' sentence-level writing errors successfully have shared the following pointers.

### Pre-Teaching, Teaching/Co-teaching, and Post-teaching Variations

Prior to teaching grammar lessons, teachers should collect various writing samples from their English learners to identify errors and to determine whether patterns exist. Those errors that occur most often should form the focus of grammar lessons, as they signify the learners' need for additional instruction. While teaching the lesson, the key will be to break down the grammatical concepts into simple and concrete language the learner can understand. Simple sentences and visuals should be used as often as possible throughout the lesson. After the lesson, teachers should continue to collect student writing samples to determine if grammatical concepts taught are being used by these learners to self-correct.

## Collaborative Practices

It is strongly recommended that teachers collaborate with the ELD specialist at their schools for assistance with best practices. ELD specialists typically have extensive backgrounds in English grammar and in addressing grammar issues with English learners.

## Informal Assessment

An informal assessment that uses sentence-level grammar correction is the Language Experience Approach (LEA). LEA is often used when groups of learners have a shared experience and provide teachers with spoken sentences to explain that experience. As the learners state sentences to the teacher, the teacher writes them on the board. Some have argued whether teachers should correct errors prior to writing the sentences on the board, or allow the students to correct the errors after they have been written. When using this activity with ELs, it is recommended that the teacher write the sentences verbatim, errors and all. The number of sentences to be written will depend on the students' proficiency level. If the student is at the WIDA levels 1 and 2, two or three sentences will suffice; three to five sentences for learners at WIDA level 3; and five or more for learners at WIDA level 4 and above. Once the sentences are written on the board, the teacher may use one of them to model how to correct grammatical errors. The teacher should use a think-aloud strategy to allow the learners to observe why and how corrections are made. Then the teacher should let students discuss and correct the remaining errors in small groups. While they are discussing the errors and their corrections, the teacher should make note of key points from the discussions and assess the learners' corrections.

## ADDITIONAL INFORMATION AND RESOURCES

1.  Robertson, Kristina. "Improving Writing Skills: ELLs and the Joy of Writing." Colorín Colorado. www.colorincolorado.org.

    In this article the author explains how to differentiate writing activities for English learners at different proficiency levels through the Language Experience Approach, quick writes, or writing cinquain poems.

2.  Santa Barbara City College Writing Center. "Common Error Types for English Language Learners." www.sbcc.edu/clrc/writing_center.

    This handout, provided to writing tutors, lists the twenty most common errors found in papers written by English learners.

3.  Zainer, Leanne. "Prioritizing Common Sentence-Level Errors." University of Minnesota Writing Center. writing.umn.edu.

    Read this article to find out about common writing errors made by EL and non-EL students and which errors are more problematic.

4. Shoebottom, Paul. "Understanding Written Mistakes." Frankfurt International School. esl.fis.edu.

   This article points out the types of errors English learners make most often and provides practice exercises to correct them. Review the identification of errors and the general description of writing levels of writing samples under the "Mistakes Analysis" link for a better understanding of proficiency level abilities.

## Chapter 20

# Planning Writing with Graphic Organizers

## DESCRIPTION

Graphic organizers, sometimes referred to as concept maps, cognitive maps, or content webs, are communication tools that can be used to visualize and organize information. Graphic organizers facilitate learning and instruction in a powerful way because they allow teachers and students to visually organize, connect, and present concepts, ideas, and information. Through visual learning, graphic organizers not only help language learners comprehend and/or summarize language input effectively, but also encourage students' creativity and productivity in their language output. This chapter illustrates how graphic organizers can be used to support students' writing in language arts classrooms.[1]

## PURPOSE

K–12 students, whether native English speakers or English learners, often have difficulty organizing information. The main purpose of a graphic organizer is to help students clearly envision how ideas are organized within a text or evolved from an abstract concept. By creating a clear picture, graphic organizers enable learners to literally see connections and relationships between facts, theories, and terms, thereby facilitating students' development in higher-level literacy and writing skills.

There is a wide variety of graphic organizers. According to the way information is arranged, organizers can be hierarchical, conceptual, sequential, or cyclical. They can take the forms of drawings, webs, or maps. Graphic organizers are frequently used as prompts for students to fill in the blanks. In this way, they guide students in brainstorming, organizing, and outlining essential concepts and ideas.

## CONTEXT FOR USE

Commonly used in grades K–12, graphic organizers as learning and instructional tools have been found to be successful at all grade levels and in every content area. There is great flexibility associated with graphic organizer usage.

By integrating text and visual imagery, graphic organizers actively engage ELs. In a writing class, they can be used to support ELs' writing every step of the way, from brainstorming to organizing information to writing a draft, by breaking down a writing project into a set of segmented yet interconnected tasks.

## MATERIALS AND PREPARATION

When planning a writing class, teachers can use graphic organizers that are ready-made, teacher-made, or student-generated.

Free, readily printable graphic organizers are available in textbooks and online at websites such as Teach-nology (search "Teach-nology worksheet graphic"). Meanwhile, teachers can always duplicate, customize, or create forms, web diagrams, and maps when they feel inspired or when the predesigned forms are not entirely appropriate for the teaching task at hand. Customizable graphic organizers can be found at Daily Teaching Tools (search "language arts graphic organizers daily teaching tools") while user-friendly computer software such as Inspiration and Kidspiration provide excellent tools for creating graphic organizers, as do the drawing and painting programs in common word processing programs. William & Mary School of Education provides some basic design principles of graphic organizers (available by searching "William & Mary graphic organizers").

After a specific graphic organizer has been selected or designed for a writing project, students can interact with the graphic organizer individually or cooperatively, in class or after class, in a traditional paper-based manner or by using mobile devices such as tablets. Normally, students will complete or reproduce the provided visual with their own ideas, knowledge, or information that can eventually support their writing output. It may be helpful or even necessary to choose or design different versions of the same graphic organizer to suit students with specific needs in the same class. Depending on the proficiency level of their students, teachers may also consider translating the graphic organizers into the students' home language before asking for them to be completed.

## THE FOUR PS OF TARGETED LANGUAGE AND LITERACY INSTRUCTION

### Pitch

Leading English learners through the process of brainstorming, planning, and organizing information for a written composition can be done for any level of English proficiency. This is possible because the identification and visual representation of the sequence or relationship of key topics or points reduces the amount of language needed for an EL to begin organizing information. Rather than trying to free-write a draft, a beginning EL can complete a teacher-selected premade graphic organizer by supplying one or two words or even a drawing for each box, and a more advanced EL can select a graphic organizer that is appropriate for the type of composition they're working on and write key points in sentence form, even drafting preliminary topic sentences for each box representing a paragraph. The only parts of using graphic organizers to support writing that are sensitive to ELs' English proficiency level are the language the teacher and student use to discuss the task as well as the eventual writing the student produces after the organizational stage.

Even though English learners need individualized support and consultation during the writing process, each student in an EL-integrated class will be learning the same rhetorical structure of different writing assignments, and therefore both ELs and non-ELs can complete graphic organizers—just somewhat differently, depending on English proficiency level.

## Pace

Pacing during completion of the graphic organizer is not greatly affected by English proficiency level because this stage is more about organizing thoughts, be they in picture or simple verbal form, than discussing, unpacking, or composing complex language. The subsequent stage of fleshing out the organizational structure with sentences formed into coherent paragraphs requires a slower pace due to the additional support English learners need (providing and explaining templates, frames, and other sentence-level scaffolds) to express their complete thoughts in written language.

## Portion

While beginning English learners are typically expected to write shorter compositions than native speakers, there is no reason why they can't plan (and write, with proper support and concomitant extended time) longer passages. Therefore, portion does not vary greatly by English proficiency level for planning a written composition with graphic organizers.

## Perspective

For secondary students, contrasts in rhetorical style and organization between their native language and English can be an issue. Graphic organizers of texts in both languages can give a concise overview of these contrasts so the EL understands that both are valid as well as what the student should do differently from what is customary in their native language when composing in English. For example, some languages' expository text is less direct than the approach that American rhetoric takes. To an English speaker, essays in these languages might seem like they are meandering and obscuring the main points, but that is the accepted style of writing (in some cases a more direct writing style is considered disrespecting the reader's sophistication). The American English style of rhetoric that moves directly from point A to point B to point C is not a universal element of good writing, so that style needs to be taught to ELs and planned for with graphic organizers prior to their writing.

# APPLICATION IN PRE-TEACHING, TEACHING/CO-TEACHING, AND POST-TEACHING

## DESCRIPTIVE WRITING AND BRAINSTORMING

### Elementary Grades

Creating graphic organizers with a fun theme can help to improve the motivation of your younger students. For example, you can provide a blank graphic of an ice cream cone with four scoops, such as the "Ice Cream Graphic Organizers Worksheet" available at English-linx.com. With the final product of a basic descriptive paragraph in mind, have each student choose a topic and write specific details on each scoop of the ice cream cone. You may choose to require a different type of detail for each level, such as size, color, shape, texture, etc.

A more traditional way to have students organize thoughts and descriptions about a given topic is with a cluster/word web,* though uses for both of these organizers are countless in all subject areas.

### Secondary Grades

While the basic cluster web can still be used for secondary students, the increased complexity of the writing required at these levels necessitates additional details in paragraphs and five-paragraph essays. Webs, such as the one below,* can be used for students to elaborate thoughts in any rhetorical pattern—descriptive, cause/effect, persuasive, compare/contrast, and informative.

Instruct students to add more bubbles as necessary to their organizers. You can also have them create their own versions on the computer or draw them by hand. Circulate and check all work to ensure that everyone is on track; they should not move on to their final writing task before successfully completing a web that displays clear thinking and logic.

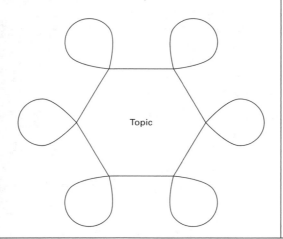

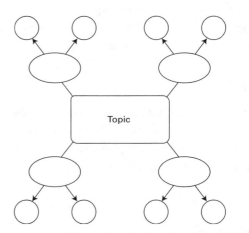

### Proficiency Level Differentiation

Encourage students at lower WIDA proficiency levels to draw pictures in the bubbles around the word web. The ice cream cone can be colored and changed to reflect the descriptive qualities of the topic—does something have stripes? The student could draw stripes across that scoop. Is it blue? That particular scoop could be colored blue. As always, provide word banks and space for lower-level students to copy terms to describe their pictures. Elementary students at a high overall proficiency level can be given the more advanced word web from the second column and vice versa.

## STRUCTURED PARAGRAPHS AND FIVE-PARAGRAPH ESSAYS

### Elementary Grades

Using a hamburger graphic organizer, such as the one available at teacherspayteachers.com, preface the introduction of the graphic organizer with a discussion about a burger. What is needed on the outside, and how many pieces? What do these two pieces of bread do? (Keep

### Secondary Grades

As students begin to routinely write five-paragraph essays, elaboration and increased support for their major points should be explicitly elicited by the graphic organizer, as it is more effective to do so early than when the writing process has already begun. Make it clear everything together.) Ask students if they can predict what keeps a *paragraph* together (the introduction and the conclusion). Next, what does a good burger have? Just one piece of lettuce or many ingredients? Compare this idea to body paragraphs adding "meat" to their writing and to their argument. After they choose a topic, have them complete the hamburger organizer by filling in the topic on the top bun, the first detail or event on the lettuce, the second on the tomato, the third on the meat patty, and so on, and ultimately the conclusion on the bottom bun. This graphic organizer is suited for any rhetorical pattern.

At higher elementary-grade levels, a more traditional approach to paragraph writing, and eventually five-paragraph essay writing, may be taken to suit the age of the class.* At this stage, ensure that students have a clear thesis statement and adequately supported details.

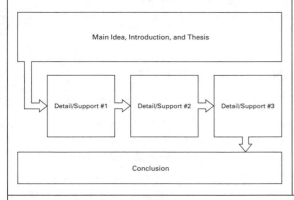

to the students that each of their details requires specific examples and explanation.

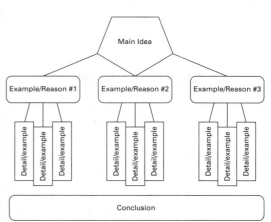

Depending on the rhetorical pattern being focused upon in your class (compare/contrast, informative, cause/effect, persuasive, etc.), it may also be necessary to complete a preliminary organizer, such as a T-chart or Venn diagram, which allows students to gather their initial thoughts and ideas.

**Proficiency Level Differentiation**

At lower WIDA proficiency levels in elementary grades, EL students may write a few words or phrases (chapter 10) rather than more complete sentences. Within each category, you may need to provide a basic sentence frame or blanks for them to fill in. Give as much individual attention as possible to each EL student to guide them through the process. A simpler organizer can also be given to select secondary students who are having trouble with the one suggested here.

*Adapted from teachervision.com.

## SUGGESTIONS FOR SUCCESS IN THE EL-INTEGRATED CLASSROOM

Teachers who use graphic organizers to support writing have shared the following pointers.

### Pre-teaching, Teaching/Co-teaching, and Post-teaching Variations

Preface any use of a language arts graphic organizer with a class discussion of the rhetorical writing pattern of focus and the key elements you intend for them to produce in their work. For all students in your class, provide a model of a successfully completed graphic organizer and discuss exactly why it was successful, asking the opinion of the students. For ELs, particularly those at WIDA levels 1–3 in the elementary grades, consider providing a printed handout of the completed model and/or word banks and sentence frames.

### Informal Assessment

Graphic organizers can and should be used as informal—and even graded—assessments. Do not allow students to begin writing before you have looked over their work. This allows you to gauge each student's level of understanding and discern what might still need to be reviewed with the class as well as to prevent students from beginning to write before they are ready, which can prove a frustrating and disheartening experience. Grading graphic organizers for clarity and completion, particularly at higher grade levels, also increases the chances that students will put forth their best effort.

## ADDITIONAL INFORMATION AND RESOURCES

1. TeAchnology. "General Graphic Organizers Worksheets." www.teach-nology.com.

   This site offers a well-categorized collection of ready-to-use graphic organizers designed for K–12 teachers for reading, science, writing, and math classes, as well as for general classroom use. Blank printable templates like graph paper, dot arrays, and other useful diagrams can be downloaded.

2. Inspiration Software, Inc. "Visual Learning Overview." www.inspiration.com.

   Teachers and students can use this commercial software for visual learning to create graphic organizers along with other visual supports as they brainstorm ideas, gather information, arrange materials, and find connections. The tool requires a license, which many schools have.

3. Houghton Mifflin Harcourt. "Graphic Organizers." www.eduplace.com /graphicorganizer.

   This website provides free graphic organizers for teachers to print and copy for the classroom. These can be used not only for writing projects but also for activities such as vocabulary building and brainstorming. All the graphic organizers listed are available in English and Spanish.

4. Haynes, Judie. "Graphic Organizers for Content Instruction." EverythingESL. www.everythingesl.net.

   This site contains downloadable graphic organizers to support EL student reading and writing of various types of texts.

**5.** McKnight, Katherine S. *The Teacher's Big Book of Graphic Organizers: 100 Reproducible Organizers That Help Kids with Reading, Writing, and the Content Areas.* San Francisco: Jossey-Bass, 2010.

> This book includes graphic organizers for use before, during, and after learning activities across the content areas.

**6.** Jacobson, Jennifer, and Dottie Raymer. *The Big Book of Reproducible Graphic Organizers: 50 Great Templates to Help Kids Get More Out of Reading, Writing, Social Studies and More.* Jefferson City, MO: Scholastic, 1999.

> This strategies book includes fifty reproducible templates along with simple how-tos and student samples.

# Tools and Techniques in Practice

Now that you've reached the end of the book, you have learned very specific applications of the twenty tools and techniques to meet the unique needs of English learners at different proficiency levels. You know how to avoid the common "ESOL strategies" trap that so many teachers and administrators fall into. At this point, it's important to revisit how these tools and techniques work in the context of a lesson, so here we offer a recap of their place in our two protocols and offer suggestions for expanding your use of the tools.

## *SHOW* AND *TELL* TOOLS AND TECHNIQUES
## FOR ACADEMIC SUBJECT INSTRUCTION

English learners studying academic subjects benefit from the same instructional practices as other students, but as we have shown with the *Show* and *Tell* tools and techniques, they need something more to be able to learn the content. Communication support, differentiated by level of English proficiency, helps ELs take in new information, interact with others to process the information, and express their understanding of the new information. This is what we call supporting communication *for*, *between*, and *of* English learners. Providing this support through our *Show* and *Tell* tools and techniques not only helps the new information break through the noise of incomprehensible language (i.e., language well above the EL's current English proficiency level), but it also helps ELs acquire greater English proficiency.

## *BUILD* TOOLS AND TECHNIQUES FOR LANGUAGE
## ARTS AND LITERACY INSTRUCTION

When ELs study language arts, or when they are learning to develop listening, speaking, reading, or writing skills in a variety of subjects, their ELD teachers use many of the same tools and techniques that are effective for non-ELs. However, ELs who are developing listening, speaking, reading, and writing skills in English need instruction targeted specifically to their proficiency levels. This ELD instruction can take place in different settings and configurations, but one aspect is consistent across all types.

Language arts instruction must be targeted to the current proficiency level while reaching toward indicators of the next proficiency level.

What we call *targeted language arts instruction* can be challenging to provide for ELs during whole-class instruction in the EL-integrated classroom. It occurs naturally in early grade levels where all students are learning simple, concrete new concepts and their vocabulary; for example, shapes, colors, and numbers. Other topics and competencies that are also less level-sensitive, such as learning sound-symbol correspondences or simple punctuation, don't depend on the student's ability to form or understand new sentences of varying complexity in English (a key element of English proficiency). In addition to the type of topics and competencies of a lesson, ELs' proficiency level also affects whether the whole-class language arts instruction is within their targeted area. Generally, English learners at the most advanced levels of proficiency, and those who have exited the classification of English learner but continue to be monitored, benefit from the same type of language arts instruction as non-ELs, but with some adaptations and support for specific language and cultural differences.

The *Build* tools and techniques in this book are used to provide targeted language instruction. Some of them are very level-sensitive (for example, Listening Skill Development: Building Comprehension at Word, Sentence, and Discourse Levels), while others are less so (such as Writing Skill Development: Planning Writing with Graphic Organizers). In either case, language arts teachers in EL-integrated classrooms have a number of options for providing targeted instruction for their EL students. When the lesson for non-ELs is within the targeted area for the ELs in the class, whole-class instruction can include ELs as well. In other instances, the lesson for all may be just outside of the ELs' targeted language area, but if the teacher is able to provide support before, during, or after the lesson, the EL can participate meaningfully to develop the skill of focus. The premise of the *Build* tools and techniques is that except for language arts instruction in early-childhood classrooms or for ELs at the highest levels of English proficiency, these tools will be used the way they are presented here with ELs exclusively, either in small-group instruction or activities, or in one-on-one consultations with the teacher. They may also be used in ELD classes that are solely for ELs at certain proficiency levels, when the number of ELs at a particular school is large enough to afford that possibility.

Whether a lesson's primary focus is on learning academic subjects or on developing listening, speaking, reading, and writing skills, our two protocols for differentiation, the Academic Subjects Protocol and the Language Arts Protocol, can help teachers provide the most accessible and appropriate instruction for their ELs, given the resources at hand. Where possible, collaboration among classroom teachers, ELD teachers, bilingual aides, reading and writing coaches, and other school personnel enables all educators to provide the most communication support and targeted language instruction for ELs, and both protocols lay out a decision-making pathway for this sort of collaboration. However, many classroom teachers don't have those resources, so the protocols also offer guidance in how teachers can provide communication support and targeted language instruction on their own.

## HOW TO GET STARTED USING THE TOOLS AND TECHNIQUES IN YOUR LESSONS

Now that you know about the Academic Subjects and Language Arts Protocols and the *Show*, *Tell*, and *Build* tools and techniques that are part of them, it's time to start using them.

If you were teaching the water cycle, for example, you would start with the ASP (see figure I.2 in the introduction), moving from left to right and top to bottom to plan the necessary support.

### Start with the ASP

Begin with Phase I: Understanding the Task and the Student. Look at your lesson plan (either obtained from another source or created yourself) and complete step 1. Read the lesson plan descriptions of what the teacher and students are doing during each part of the lesson, and analyze how many of the verbs are SLIDE (nonverbal) and TREAD (verbal). Highlight the TREAD verbs because that is where you will likely need to add support for your ELs.

Then go on to step 2 of the ASP and look at the assessment profiles of your EL students. Depending on your district and state requirements, you will be given assessment information that indicates an overall English proficiency level and possibly composite and individual skill scores for each English learner in your class. Review the proficiency descriptors for your students' levels and keep these data and resources in a readily accessible place.

Now, look again at the TREAD verbs in the lesson and compare them to the proficiency levels of your ELs as you move to phase II to plan the support. The easiest way to start using the *Show* and *Tell* tools and techniques, what are referred to in the diagram as nonverbal (*Show*) and verbal (*Tell*) support, is to try out one of the *Show* ones. This can be done universally, with the entire class, or it can be a supplement or an alternative to an activity or assignment for one or more ELs. Universally, you could search for an infographic for a topic that you will be teaching and distribute it to all students along with the associated readings from the textbook. Your beginning and intermediate ELs will benefit from having the graphics and the reduced amount of text to convey the main points, and your advanced ELs and non-ELs will appreciate having a summary of what is in the grade-level text. This simple act can be a very strong start to using the new tools in your toolbox and techniques in your repertoire. You're on your way!

For the next lesson, you'll begin with a SLIDE/TREAD analysis, highlighting the TREAD-heavy parts where your ELs will need support, but this time you will already know the proficiency levels of your EL students (you put the information in a readily accessible place, remember?).

Then, depending on your ELs' English proficiency levels, you can select a *Tell* tool or technique, such as using a leveled text for your beginning and intermediate ELs. As you read in chapter 8, there are many free resources for leveled text on a plethora of topics, so you can select a beginning and an intermediate-level text on the lesson topic (say, climate change) and give those texts to your ELs at those levels so they can work in small groups with you or a collaborator when the non-ELs are working with the grade-level text. Now you're getting the hang of using the ASP for planning and the *Show* and *Tell* tools and techniques for differentiating for your EL students!

You can continue trying out new *Show* and *Tell* tools and techniques—a good goal might be to use one new one per week in addition to layering the ones you've already tried. So you might continue to use infographics as a supplement to your lesson text for all students, and then also give your beginning and intermediate ELs leveled texts to use as alternatives to the grade-level text. Your advanced ELs will benefit from the infographic, and if any of these students struggle with the grade-level text, you could provide the intermediate level one as a supplement. Remember that the bigger the communication gap between the language demands of classroom instruction and your ELs' English proficiency levels, the more layering you will need to provide (and the more individualized support your ELs will need—ask for bilingual aides, parent volunteers, and others who can give extra one-on-one support).

## Learn About Second Language Development Before Using the LAP

We highly recommend reading our earlier book—*Educating English Learners: What Every Classroom Teacher Needs to Know*—which explains what's different about teaching English learners. It details the background knowledge you need to understand *why* and *for whom* you should use the tools and techniques; we present the *how to* in *Show, Tell, Build*. This is especially critical for using the Language Arts Protocol and the *Build* tools and techniques because language arts instruction for ELs at different English proficiency levels requires a deeper understanding of second language development. By knowing what to expect from ELs in terms of their comprehension of (listening and reading) and expression in (speaking and writing) English, you will be able to adjust the pitch, pace, portion, and perspective of the lesson to meet their needs. You will make those adjustments when using any of the *Build* tools and techniques to teach language skills.

## Using the LAP in Collaboration

Once you are more knowledgeable about second language acquisition, you can start using the LAP (see figure II.2 in part II). Phase I, Understanding the Language Skills and the Student, begins with analyzing a language arts lesson plan, looking at the listening, speaking, reading, writing, and language conventions instruction (whichever are the focus of the lesson), in comparison to each EL's proficiency in that domain. As noted in the ASP description above, you should be able to locate assessment data that separates proficiency indicators into the four skill areas; this will be even more useful in planning language arts instruction for ELs. Carefully consider the descriptors for each English learner, noting whether the student's listening, speaking, reading, and writing skills are developed enough to participate in all parts of the lesson.

Next comes phase II, Targeted Language Instruction. When you use a tool or technique in a lesson intended to develop one or more of your ELs' language skills, you will need to adjust its pitch, pace, portion, and perspective (step 1) to the students' English proficiency level. Each *Build* tool and technique includes suggestions for making those types of adjustments. At this point you should consider whether these adjustments are compatible with the lesson for the whole class (universal), or if they need to occur as a supplement or alternative to it (step 2). If the latter, then you should move to step 3: consider when they can be provided (before, during, or after the lesson for all) and by whom (you—the classroom teacher, a bilingual aide, an ELD teacher, and so forth).

As noted previously, the best *Build* tools or techniques to start with on your own are those that are less level sensitive (i.e., they need less adjustment in pitch), such as Exploring the Meaning, Form, and Relationships of Words. If your lesson focuses on teaching derivational morphemes (segments of words that change their part of speech, such as *-al* in *national*, and segments of words that change the word's meaning, such as *un-* in *unbelievable*), even your beginning ELs can learn how to combine root words and affixes to create new words. If your main activity is to complete a derivational morpheme table together, in looking at pitch, you will not need to modify the language content of the lesson, but you might need to adjust how you explain the concept and how you expect your ELs to apply what they learn. The pace of the lesson used for all should be fairly similar to what is appropriate for your ELs because the focus is on combining parts of words, a simple grammatical exercise. The portion of the lesson might be reduced somewhat for your beginning ELs, as they may need to translate words into their native language to understand their meaning and need a limited number of words to do that successfully in the time allotted. The perspective could be different if the word roots and affixes have cognates in the students' native languages, such as *-tion* in English and *-cion* in Spanish. Those features are important to point out to emerging bilingual students so they can draw on the assets of their first language in learning their second.

When you do have a collaborator, such as an ELD teacher, the possibilities increase for adjusting the four Ps to target the *Build* tool or technique to your English learners' proficiency levels. If you are not able to collaborate with a colleague, then you can be creative in carving out time to work exclusively with one or more ELs before or after the lesson, and you can also structure class time to include group activities during which you can devote more time to targeting language and literacy instruction to their English proficiency level.

## EXPANDING YOUR USE OF THE TOOLS AND TECHNIQUES

If you are an elementary or language arts and literacy teacher, start with the *Show* and *Tell* tools and techniques, and later move to the *Build* tools and techniques. Remember that most, if not all, *Show* and *Tell* tools and techniques can be used together with the *Build* ones, such as using gestures (e.g., showing with your hands how the be verb is next to the main verb) and leveled questioning (e.g., Does the main verb go first?) when providing feedback for your ELs' spoken errors.

If you are a secondary mathematics, science, social studies, or other academic subject teacher, the *Show* and *Tell* tools and techniques will address most of your ELs' needs for communication support. Stick with these tools and techniques and make using them a habit.

If you are an ELD teacher, you are likely to be well versed in applying most tools and techniques to meet your EL students' needs, so use these chapters as a starting point for collaborating with your colleagues. Begin by selecting a tool or technique together, plan to co-teach the first time it's used, and give your colleague constructive feedback and encouragement afterward.

To view demonstration videos of teachers using many of the tools and techniques with English learners, visit our website at englishlearnerachievement.com. Seeing them in use with real students in EL-integrated classrooms will help you feel confident to try them with your own EL students. Keep trying out as many of these tools and techniques as you can, and bring everything you've learned together in your daily instructional routines. Before you know it, you will have become an amazing teacher for your English learners!

# The Language Demands Posed by Academic Standards

The first two things academic subject area teachers need to be aware of when thinking about how to reach English learners in their classrooms are that, first, learning a second language takes considerable time, and support must be provided that is appropriate for the learner's current level of proficiency. Second, it is important to keep in mind that language used in everyday conversation is substantially different from language that is used in an academic setting.

## SOCIAL AND ACADEMIC LANGUAGE

Sometimes, to their teachers' surprise, ELs who converse fluently in social settings perform very poorly academically. Jim Cummins revealed two constructs that help subject-area teachers understand the fundamental difference between social and academic language demands: basic interpersonal communication skills, or BICS, and cognitive-academic language proficiency, or CALP.[1]

 ## KEY TERMS

❖ **BICS** is the language required for face-to-face social communication. ELs usually acquire it in one to three years of full immersion or full-time study, and they typically learn BICS from their classmates, day-to-day interactions, and Internet or traditional media (e.g., TV, YouTube). These types of social interactions rely on ample context clues, such as gestures, real objects, facial expressions, and so on.

❖ **CALP** is the language used in the academic classroom. It is usually acquired in five to seven years (some researchers extend the range up to ten years).

CALP is more cognitively demanding as context becomes increasingly reduced and is both a result and a condition of school-based learning.[2]

✦ Full proficiency in BICS does not indicate full proficiency in CALP. When teachers understand the difference between these two types of language proficiency, they are more likely to understand their ELs' needs to concurrently acquire content knowledge and help them develop academic language in English.

## THE ELEMENTS OF ACADEMIC LANGUAGE: A FOCUS ON SUBJECT-AREA VOCABULARY

A critical component of language proficiency, the academic language used in subject-area materials and instruction can potentially be very hard for ELs to understand. By definition, academic language represents the language that students need to learn and use to participate and engage in meaningful ways in the subject area.[3] There are three language dimensions that teachers need to consider as they plan how to support student learning of academic content and language.[4]

 ## Key Terms

✦ **Discourse** (organization and thinking skills): Two important concepts related to discourse are coherence and cohesion. For example, in writing, **coherence** refers to organization, including developing and supporting an argument or a thesis, as well as stating and clarifying ideas. Yule defines coherence as all elements fitting together well, while **cohesion** refers to the grammatical and vocabulary connection of ideas at both the sentence and paragraph levels using cohesive ties.[5] For example, for listing or sequencing language functions, we use words like *first*, *second*, *third* or *next*, *then*. When we want to transition to a new point, we use *now*, *as far as . . . is concerned*, *with regard/reference to*, or *turning to*.

✦ **Syntax** (sentences and grammar): One construct frequently associated with syntax is **grammatical accuracy**, or the degree to which speaking and writing are grammatically correct.

✦ **Lexical** (vocabulary): In addition to the **vocabulary of a subject area**, teachers need to consider the presence of **idioms** in both social (BICS) and academic (CALP) language. Idioms are phrases or groups of words that have a meaning different from the individual words. For example, "the ball is in your court" means that you need to make the next decision or take the next step, not that a ball is literally on your side of the basketball court. One special category of idioms is represented by phrasal verbs (i.e., verb + preposition such as *up/down/in*), where the meaning changes after the preposition is added to the verb. For example, compare "I *ran* two miles today" with "I *ran out* of milk yesterday."

Knowledge of subject-area vocabulary, part of the lexical dimension of academic language, is essential for ELs who want to communicate in academic settings successfully. There are several published categorizations of academic vocabulary, but let's focus on the inventory containing three types of vocabulary—general, specific, and technical.[6]

**General** vocabulary is represented by words that are used across disciplines, such as *analyze*, *assume*, and *compare*. **Specific** vocabulary contains words and phrases with subject-specific meanings that differ from meanings used in everyday life; for example, *table* as in math table, solution as in a chemical solution, or *bank* as in a river bank. The third class of academic vocabulary, **technical**, comprises words and phrases that are subject-specific, such as *atoll*, *butte*, or *geography* in social studies.[7]

ELs who function very well in social settings might have difficulties comprehending academic language. An example of vocabulary misunderstanding was provided by a subject-area teacher who reported that an EL in her class drew a picture in the response box of a homework assignment. Rereading the directions of that assignment, the teacher noted it required students to *draw a conclusion*. The EL had taken the social meaning of the word into account and had started drawing the answer! However, in subject-area instructional materials, the verb *draw* mostly occurs in combination with (in other words, it collocates with) the noun *conclusion* and therefore has nothing to do with the physical act of drawing.[8]

## EL-SPECIFIC LANGUAGE DEMANDS AND ACADEMIC SUBJECTS

Language demands are affected by the discipline and the grade level. During early grades, content is presented using large amounts of pictures, visual communications, and hands-on objects and experiences. The more ELs progress in grade level, the more information is presented through text that is not always accompanied by visual support.

## Essential Points

- **Language demands** include listening, speaking, reading, and writing. Language becomes more complex as content becomes more complex and abstract while less supported by context-embedded instruction.

- In earlier grades, subject-area content is taught using less language (i.e., lower volume and complexity) and more hands-on experiences. In this case, the instruction is what Jim Cummins terms *context-embedded* because it relies on context that is closely related and integrated with academic content.[9] This is what we call **SLIDE** (show, look, investigate, demonstrate, experience) verbs, those that describe the use of senses and modalities beyond simply using language to teach and learn.

- As students progress to upper grades, language becomes the principal means of teaching academic content. Verbal classroom communication with very limited nonverbal support makes the presentation of academic content *context-reduced* due to the absence of contextual support.[10] We identify this through **TREAD** (tell, read, explain, ask/answer, and discuss) verbs because they denote listening, speaking, reading, and writing in the language of instruction. In this case, high academic-language proficiency (CALP) is vital for ELs in order to acquire subject-area competency.

Figure A.1 illustrates the gradual but inevitable transition from more nonverbal, more context-embedded teaching to verbal, more context-reduced instruction throughout the preK–12 cycle.

## EXAMPLES FROM SOCIAL STUDIES, SCIENCE, AND MATH

The differences in social and academic language demands have an influence on oral and written language use in the subject-area classroom as well.

FIGURE A.1
**Proportion of Verbal and Nonverbal Communication Across Grades**

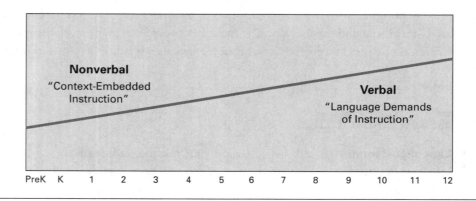

Nonverbal
"Context-Embedded Instruction"

Verbal
"Language Demands of Instruction"

PreK   K   1   2   3   4   5   6   7   8   9   10   11   12

## ESSENTIAL POINTS

- Social studies texts often contain a lot of complex sentence structures and vocabulary. This brief sentence from *TimeLinks: Third Grade* illustrates how complex social studies language can be: "She [Jill Staton Bullard] serves seven counties in North Carolina and feeds more than 5,000 people a day with donations."[11] In addition to the fact that the sentence is complex because it consists of two separate clauses linked by the coordinating conjunction *and*, it also uses the word *donations* in combination with the verb *feeds*. ELs may take word meaning literally and wonder how people can be fed with donations and not with food.

- The language of science can pose problems for English learners because it often uses everyday vocabulary but with different meanings. For example, ELs may know that they can put food on a plate, but the term *plate tectonics* is completely unrelated. Other everyday words that have different meanings in science are *cell* (as in cell phone), *tissue* (something to use when you sneeze), and *organ* (an instrument).[12]

- Some language patterns specific to mathematics may be unfamiliar to ELs. For example, the sentence "The number $a$ is five more than the number $b$" is often translated by ELs as $a + 5 = b$, when it should be $a = b + 5$. The reason for this error is that ELs may try to read and write mathematical sentences in the same way they read and write narrative text.[13]

## GRADE LEVEL NATIONAL AND STATE STANDARDS

The Every Student Succeeds Act (ESSA) is the most recent education initiative that puts instructional standards and accountability for all students front and center. Replacing the No Child Left Behind Act (NCLB) of 2001, ESSA requires that all public school students be taught to achieve high academic standards that will prepare them to succeed in college and careers. The Common Core State Standards (CCSS) many states adopted describe the knowledge and skills that public school education should provide to students so that they graduate college- and career-ready. One of the states that has adopted the CCSS is Florida, which now uses Mathematics Florida Standards (MAFS) for teaching and assessment. However, not all states have adopted the CCSS. Virginia is one of the states that have decided to create their own Standards of Learning (SOL) to be used in instruction and assessment. [14] When we compare Florida's CCSS-inspired standards to Virginia's SOL in table A.1, the similarities (marked in bold) between the two sets of standards are unsurprisingly more evident than the differences.

TABLE A.1

**A Two-State Comparison of Kindergarten Mathematics Standards for Count and Cardinality**

| Mathematics Florida Standards (MAFS) | Virginia Mathematics Standards of Learning (SOL) |
|---|---|
| **Count to 100 by ones and by tens.**<br><br>Cognitive Complexity: Level 1—Recall | **The student will**<br><br>a. **count forward to 100 and backward from 10;**<br>b. identify one more than a number and one less than a number; and<br>c. **count by fives and tens to 100.** |
| **Count forward beginning from a given number within the known sequence (instead of having to begin at 1).**<br><br>Cognitive Complexity: Level 1—Recall | **The student will**<br><br>a. **count forward to 100 and backward from 10;**<br>b. **identify one more than a number and one less than a number;** and<br>c. count by fives and tens to 100. |
| **Write numbers from 0 to 20. Represent a number of objects with a written numeral 0–20 (with 0 representing a count of no objects).**<br><br>Cognitive Complexity: Level 1—Recall | **The student, given a set containing 15 or fewer concrete objects, will**<br><br>a. **tell how many are in the set by counting the number of objects orally;**<br>b. **write the numeral to tell how many are in the set; and**<br>c. **select the corresponding numeral from a given set of numerals.**<br><br>The student will<br><br>a. count from 0 to 100 and write the corresponding numerals; and<br>b. **group a collection of up to 100 objects into tens and ones and write the corresponding numeral to develop an understanding of place value.** |

## LARGE-SCALE ASSESSMENTS

Academic standards are reflected in the way academic content is presented and assessed. Assessment takes many forms, but educational outcomes are generally measured through large-scale tests administered toward the end of the academic year. English learners are required to participate in standardized assessments, including state-administered tests designed for determining their language proficiency levels and their progress in acquiring English. Therefore, ELs take additional assessments that non-ELs do not take. For progress in academic areas and literacy, ELs take the same state exams as native English speakers but have access to test accommodations. We have defined accommodations as the support provided to ELs who have not reached full proficiency in English to help them access the English content of the assessment so they can demonstrate their true knowledge of academic content unhindered by language obstacles.

According to Mihai and Pappamihiel, test accommodations for ELs can be divided into several categories of support:[15]

1. nonlinguistic
   a. time and scheduling (schedule changes, breaks, and additional time)
   b. location (preferential seating and a private setting)

2. linguistic
   a. directions (read aloud in student's native language or in English)
   b. presentation (translated test items or translated test that can be read to the student, audio test versions, video test versions, and text-to speech software)
   c. support (access to bilingual dictionaries, English dictionary, translated glossary for construct-irrelevant items, English glossary, and thesaurus), and
   d. response (use of the EL's native language and allowing the EL to point to the responses in English)

Of these accommodations, the three most common types are allowing ELs to use a bilingual dictionary during the test, giving them more time to take the exam, and letting them take the exam in a separate setting.[16]

While ELs need accommodations to make the standardized tests accessible, several problems with their use have come to light. The first is blanket implementation. Often states make the same accommodations available to *all* ELs regardless of their proficiency level. However, research has shown that an accommodation can be effective for one level but not very effective for another.[17] A second issue is the familiarity of accommodations. If state-approved accommodations are not used frequently during instruction by academic-area teachers, they will not be very effective during testing, which defeats the purpose of reducing the language barrier that may prevent ELs from showing their true knowledge of academic content. Teachers should therefore emphasize in their teaching and assessment those accommodations that the ELs will be given during standardized assessments in addition to implementing a variety of tools and techniques to make content comprehensible and reduce the language barrier for their ELs.

## USING ASSESSMENT ACCOMMODATIONS AND LANGUAGE PROFICIENCY DATA IN INSTRUCTION

To help content-area teachers make the complex language demands of their academic subjects accessible to English learners, we recommend a multistep process that accounts for English proficiency levels in instruction and assessment. Sequentially, these are the steps.

### Step 1

To use accommodations effectively, academic-area teachers need to identify what accommodations are approved at the state level. There is no set of federally approved accommodations that all states are required to use in their academic-area assessments. Each state has its own set of accommodations, and these may vastly differ from state to state. An example of the accommodations allowed for English learners enrolled in Florida is listed in table A.2.

Arkansas has, for the most part, approved the same accommodations as Florida, but the state allows ELs one additional accommodation: test responses may be dictated in English using scribe or speech-to-text software for math assessments. This additional accommodation may be very beneficial to ELs at lower levels of proficiency, who may be able to demonstrate their math knowledge orally but have trouble expressing themselves in writing.

## Step 2

Once subject-area teachers identify the approved accommodations in their respective school districts, they should start incorporating them in the instruction and assessment of their ELs. An accommodation is effective only if ELs are familiar with it and have used it consistently in class before taking large-scale tests. Additionally, academic-area teachers should try to focus more on those accommodations that have the potential of drastically reducing the language barrier for ELs. For example, using approved dictionaries during class instruction and allowing ELs to have access to them when taking classroom-based tests makes the ELs familiar with their use, which potentially improves their test performance.[18]

In order to implement the state-approved accommodations in effective ways, teachers need to know the language proficiency level of their ELs and, more importantly, understand what the data means in terms of what they can expect their ELs to comprehend and produce at each proficiency level. All states are required to administer

TABLE A.2

**Approved Accommodations for Florida's Large-Scale Assessments**

| Accommodation | Description |
|---|---|
| *Flexible setting* | ELs may be tested in a separate room with the English Language Development (ELD) or heritage language teacher acting as test administrator. |
| *Flexible scheduling* | ELs may take the test during several brief periods within one school day or be provided with additional time. |
| *Assistance in the heritage language* | ELs may be provided limited assistance by ELD or heritage language personnel using the student's heritage language for all directions and for specified portions of tests. |
| *Approved dictionary* | ELs may have access to approved dictionaries during the test. These dictionaries provide word-to-word translation only and must not provide definitions in the heritage language or in English. |

a language proficiency test to monitor the progress of their ELs enrolled in K–12 public schools. There is no single language proficiency test that is administered nationwide for this purpose. Instead, each state is allowed to choose a language proficiency assessment as long as it is valid, standardized, and administered consistently. The majority of states belong to one of two consortia that have established English language proficiency standards and assessments, although a few states, such as California and Texas, have devised their own tests.[19] Teachers receive scores from these tests that show where on the English language proficiency continuum their students fall in listening, speaking, reading, and writing.[20] When comparing them against the standards, they see what each EL is currently able to process and produce. Because English language development specialists have advanced knowledge of the standards and of second language acquisition, we recommend that teachers meet with the specialists at the beginning of each school year to study the scores and plan individualized testing accommodations practice opportunities.

## Step 3

With the knowledge of state-approved testing accommodations and their individual English learners' formal and classroom-based language proficiency information, teachers are better equipped to increase ELs' active engagement with the content and acquisition of the academic language specific to each content area by using the instructional tools and techniques that are detailed in this book, which will foster students' achievement.

# Assessment of English Proficiency

**M**any different standardized tests are used to measure English proficiency. These tests provide useful information for a variety of purposes. The primary purposes are identification and placement (entering the program of services for ELs), measurement of progress, and reclassification (exiting the EL category).

Thirty-nine state education agencies belong to the WIDA Consortium, which means that they use English language proficiency standards and assessment materials created by the WIDA organization. WIDA offers a number of standardized English proficiency tests for different purposes. Some states, districts, or schools use other tests for placement, measurement of progress, and reclassification of ELs. Older tests include the IPT, MacII, LAS, and CELLA. There are also state-specific tests, such as the CELDT in California, the ELDA, LAS Links, NY-SES-LAT in New York, the SELP, and the TELPAS in Texas.

It cannot be overemphasized that one test alone should not determine placement, measurement of progress, or reclassification of ELs. The test results should be considered in light of other factors, such as teacher observations of, and interactions with, the EL, as well as informal classroom assessments. These other factors are discussed in a different part of this appendix; the following text addresses the types of data teachers can use to learn about their ELs from standardized assessments.

## WIDA SCREENER/W-APT AND ACCESS 2.0

Because the WIDA tests are used by the majority of states, this section presents WIDA examples to describe listening, speaking, reading, and writing (the four skill domains) scores as well as composite scores for oral proficiency, literacy, and overall proficiency.

WIDA offers placement tests (W-APT and WIDA Screener) as well as progress and reclassification tests (ACCESS 2.0). WIDA tests are aligned with the WIDA standards, focusing on social and instructional language and on the language of language arts, mathematics, science, and social studies. Both screening tests measure each language domain separately and provide an overall score.

The W-APT is an individually administered, paper-based identification and placement test that offers versions for grades K, 1–2, 3–5, 6–8, and 9–12. The WIDA Screener is a paper- or computer-based, individual or group-administered identification and placement test for grades 1–12. Screening tests are administered on demand, when a new student enters the school system. Along with other measures, they assess whether a student qualifies as an English learner and places them on the continuum of WIDA levels 1–6.

The WIDA ACCESS for ELLs 2.0 is designed to indicate an EL's current level of English proficiency and locate it on the continuum of English language development (ELD). It is intended for use in determining whether program support is required for ELs to engage in academic content instruction and in informing ELD instruction. The Individual Student Report displays the student's proficiency levels separately in the four language domains of listening, speaking, reading, and writing as well as four composite proficiency levels in oral language, literacy, comprehension, and overall. Proficiency levels are reported on a continuum of 1.0 to 6.0.

Proficiency scores in listening and speaking are combined into the oral language composite score, 50 percent of which is contributed from each of the two domains. The literacy composite score is weighted the same way, with 50 percent of the score from reading and 50 percent from writing. Composite comprehension scores indicate how well a student understands spoken and written language, and the weighting is 70 percent reading and 30 percent listening. The overall score combines listening, speaking, reading, and writing, with the majority of weight on reading (35%) and writing (35%), and the remainder divided equally between listening (15%) and speaking (15%). The weighting of the composite and overall scores is based on the assumption that literacy is stressed more at school and therefore contributes more to educational success than oral language.

Depending on an individual student's exposure to English instruction or time spent in an English-speaking environment, as well the amount of formal education in any language and the student's literacy level in the native language, English learners can have different proficiency levels in the four language domains. From our research at elementary schools, we have found that many English learners develop proficiency in listening and speaking that becomes more advanced than their reading and writing skills. For example, we have seen numerous instances of English learners who begin with comparable oral language and literacy scores in the range of 1 to 2, but over time the rate of oral language development exceeds that of literacy, with splits such as oral language 3 and literacy 1, or oral language 5 and literacy 3. Conversely, we have seen students assessed initially with fairly strong literacy skills in English due to formal study, but their oral language skills lagged behind. This, however, has been a rarer occurrence. Access to test results that are broken down by language domain provides crucial information that offers insights into their progress and tells teachers of ELs where extra instructional emphasis may be needed.

All four language domains are important elements of English proficiency, and while the overall score is helpful in suggesting the type of general support ELs need for academic subject instruction, the individual domain and the three composite scores give more meaningful information regarding the student's language development. By knowing exactly where the student is on the continuum of second language development, the teacher or a collaborator can provide language instruction targeted to the student's proficiency in each domain.

Teacher reports include the student's scores in the language domains and composites as well as raw scores reported as the number of correct items for comprehension (listening and reading), speaking, and writing. The comprehension scores are reported for social and instructional, language arts, mathematics, science, and social studies language. The speaking task is administered individually and presents scores in three groups—social and instructional, language arts/social studies, and mathematics/science. The writing task presents scores in the same groups and is individually scored, with points broken down by linguistic complexity, vocabulary usage, and language control (grammar, word choice, and mechanics).

The Writing Rubric of the WIDA Consortium (table B.1) provides useful details regarding expectations for linguistic complexity, vocabulary usage, and language control at each level. The progression from the beginning, or Entering level, to approaching reclassification, or the Reaching level, shows the growing complexity, variety, and mastery of language use. English learners move through levels starting with single words and set phrases copied or adapted from a model all the way to writing original, cohesive paragraphs with precise vocabulary and grammatical accuracy and complexity.

TABLE B.1
**The Writing Rubric of the WIDA Consortium**

| WIDA WRITING INTERPRETATIVE RUBRIC Grades 1–12 | | | |
|---|---|---|---|
| | **Discourse Level** *Linguistic Complexity* | **Sentence Level** *Language Forms and Conventions* | **Word/Phrase Level** *Vocabulary Usage* |
| Level 6 Reaching | Text is fully comprehensible and appropriate to purpose, situation, and audience; comparable to the writing of English-proficient students meeting college- and career-readiness standards; and includes: | | |
| | • extended connected text (single or multiple paragraphs) that is organized and shows tight cohesion in the precise expression of ideas <br> • clear evidence of consistency in conveying an appropriate perspective, register, and genre | • a full range of sentence patterns and grammatical structures matched to content-area topics <br> • consistent use of appropriate conventions to convey meaning, including for effect | • consistent usage of just the right word or expression in just the right context related to content-area topics <br> • facility with precise vocabulary usage in general, specific, or technical language |
| Level 5 Bridging | Text is comprehensible and related to purpose; generally comparable to the writing of English-proficient peers; and includes: | | |
| | • extended connected text (single or multiple paragraphs) that is organized and shows a cohesive and coherent expression of ideas <br> • clear evidence of conveying an appropriate perspective, register, and genre | • a broad range of sentence patterns and grammatical structures matched to the content-area topic <br> • nearly consistent use of appropriate conventions to convey meaning, including for effect | • usage of technical and abstract content-area words and expressions as appropriate <br> • usage of words and expressions with precise meaning related to content-area topic as appropriate <br> • vocabulary usage that fulfills the writing purpose |

*continues*

TABLE B.1
**The Writing Rubric of the WIDA Consortium** (*continued*)

| WIDA WRITING INTERPRETATIVE RUBRIC Grades 1–12 | | | |
|---|---|---|---|
| | **Discourse Level** | **Sentence Level** | **Word/Phrase Level** |
| | *Linguistic Complexity* | *Language Forms and Conventions* | *Vocabulary Usage* |
| Level 4 Expanding | Text is generally comprehensible at all times; approaches comparability to the writing of English-proficient peers; and includes: | | |
| | • connected text (sentences or paragraphs) that shows an organized expression of ideas with emerging cohesion<br>• some evidence of conveying an appropriate perspective, register, and genre | • a range of sentence patterns and grammatical structures characteristic of the content area<br>• generally consistent use of appropriate conventions to convey meaning | • usage of specific and some technical content-area words and expressions as appropriate<br>• usage of words and expressions with multiple meanings or common collocations and idioms across content areas as appropriate<br>• vocabulary usage that generally fulfills the writing purpose |
| Level 3 Developing | Original text is generally comprehensible (though comprehensibility may from time to time be compromised in more complex original text) and includes: | | |
| | • text that shows developing organization in the expression of an expanded idea or multiple related ideas<br>• evidence of a developing sense of perspective, register, and genre | • a developing range of sentence patterns and grammatical structures common to content areas<br>• developing use of conventions to convey meaning | • usage of some specific content words and expressions as appropriate<br>• usage of common cognates, words, or expressions related to content areas as appropriate<br>• vocabulary usage that attempts to fulfill the writing purpose |
| Level 2 Emerging | Some original text and text adapted from model or source text is generally comprehensible (though comprehensibility may often be compromised in attempts at more complex original text) and includes: | | |
| | • text that shows emerging organization of an idea or ideas and may demonstrate some attempt at organization<br>• some amount of text that may be copied or adapted | • repetitive sentence and phrasal patterns and formulaic grammatical structures used in social and instructional situations or across content areas<br>• variable use of conventions | • usage of general content words and expressions<br>• usage of social and instructional words and expressions across content areas<br>• possible usage of general vocabulary where more specific language is needed |
| Level 1 Entering | Text that is copied or adapted from model or source text is generally comprehensible (though comprehensibility may be significantly compromised in original text) and includes: | | |
| | • language that represents an idea or ideas<br>• varying amounts of text that may be copied<br>• adapted text that may contain some original language | • words, chunks of language, or simple phrasal patterns associated with common social and instructional situations<br>• possible use of some conventions | • usage of highest frequency general content-related words<br>• usage of everyday social and instructional words and expressions |

## USING ORAL PROFICIENCY AND LITERACY COMPOSITE SCORES TO INFORM TARGETED INSTRUCTION

Standardized test scores, such as WIDA ACCESS 2.0, are useful in measuring where an English learner is on the continuum of English language development. Knowing that a student is, for example, at the Emerging level of speaking gives the teacher specific information about what the student can utter in English. At this level, an EL speaks using language chunks (on the table), repetitive phrase patterns (I like music, I like chocolate, I like money, etc.), formulaic grammatical structures (How are you?), and general vocabulary (chair).

Instructed second language acquisition depends on targeting language study and use to students' proficiency in listening, speaking, reading, and writing. These four skills are mutually supportive. Listening and speaking skills are referred to as oral proficiency, and reading and writing skills are referred to as literacy. From another angle, listening and reading are considered receptive skills, meaning that information is received through them, and speaking and writing are considered productive (also called expressive) skills, indicating that they are used to express information.

For second language learners, receptive skills typically precede productive skills, but there is a complex interaction between an oral skill and its literacy counterpart. To be able to understand a sentence we read, we would need to understand that sentence if it were spoken (with the exception of those who are hearing impaired). The converse, however, is not generally true. We don't typically need to comprehend the written sentence to be able to understand the same sentence in speech. The same type of relationship is true for productive skills. We should be able to spontaneously say the same sentence we can write spontaneously, but we don't need to be able to write that sentence to be able to say it.

In both these cases, ELs' literacy in English is inextricably linked to their oral proficiency in English (as well as their literacy in their first language, depending on age). As they move through the process of second language acquisition, they acquire new vocabulary and phrases as well as implicit knowledge of how words are formed and how they combine to make sentences. This process begins with their ability to comprehend common words and simple phrases and to concurrently or subsequently combine them into one-word and short phrasal spoken and written utterances, depending on age and first language literacy experiences.

It's probably clear by now that sentences are the main unit of verbal comprehension and expression for English learners as they acquire their second language. While there are many other factors beyond the scope of this discussion (discourse and text coherence, pragmatic and cultural elements of communication, etc.), sentence-level development in all four skills becomes increasingly complex.

Sentence-level errors in comprehension and expression are a predictable part of that development. The sentences ELs create spontaneously, without support, are sometimes referred to as learner language or interlanguage, and they are markers of progress through the stages of second language acquisition.

Teachers can use both the individual language domain scores and the composite oral language and literacy scores to plan and provide targeted English language development activities for their English learners. Phase I of the Language Arts Protocol takes teachers through the process of ascertaining whether the components of grade-level language arts lessons are targeted to the English learners' proficiency levels, or if supplemental or alternative activities are needed to hit the target area. In general, the lower the grade level (e.g., preK and K), the more likely that the activities that are appropriate for non-ELs will also be targeted to English learners' needs, especially those who have moved beyond Entering or Emerging levels of English proficiency. Also, ELs at the highest levels of proficiency, Bridging and Reaching, benefit from most of the language arts instruction planned and provided for non-ELs, with occasional supplemental activities needed.

Where language arts instruction in the EL-integrated classroom gets tricky is when English learners at the earlier stages of language development are enrolled in upper grades. In these circumstances, it is not likely that the activities planned for non-ELs can benefit ELs because their language demands are beyond the ELs' level of proficiency and therefore are not targeted English language development. Sometimes this means that supplemental or alternative activities for ELs can take place at the same time as the activities for non-ELs, under the supervision of the classroom teacher alone, as when students are working in groups or pairs. Other times this means that supplemental or alternative activities for ELs can take place at the same time as activities for non-ELs, but in this case there needs to be a collaborator, such as a bilingual aide or ELD teacher, to work with a group of ELs while the classroom teacher leads the rest of the class in an activity. Different circumstances might dictate that the classroom teacher must provide these additional activities before or after those for non-ELs, because the gap between the lesson activities and the ELs' proficiency level is too large, and because the classroom teacher is the only instructional provider available.

## USING AND DEVELOPING CLASSROOM ASSESSMENTS OF LISTENING, SPEAKING, READING, AND WRITING

At the beginning of this appendix we presented standardized and commercially available English proficiency tests. These tests assess ELs' listening, speaking, reading, and writing skills in English. Classroom teachers use the data from these tests to determine the areas where support is needed and to measure student progress, but they are just one of many sources teachers rely on. Students may perform differently under formal testing circumstances, and testing usually takes place at certain times of the year, so it is important to have multiple measures of students' proficiency and their growth in all language domains.

Much of what students do in the classroom can be a form of language skill assessment, whether it be how well they comprehend a presentation, participate in a discussion, make inferences about a reading passage, or write a persuasive argument. Within any of these examples, there are opportunities to look at students' command of both broad and narrow language elements, such as identifying the main idea or specific details in a listening or reading activity, or planning and composing the content of a presentation or an essay. In addition, all of these types of listening, speaking, reading, and writing activities provide opportunities to assess ELs' developing English proficiency within each domain, directing attention to their growth in vocabulary, grammatical complexity and accuracy, and discourse competence. Collecting these classroom assessments in a portfolio or other organizing system can provide helpful insights into growth areas as well as persistent errors and challenges. Assessing a sample speaking or writing item periodically by referring to the WIDA rubrics for each domain can help track progress.

## Listening

Teachers can use existing assessments or develop their own assessments of listening skills in a variety of ways.

- To assess whether students comprehend and identify main points during a presentation, ELs can take open notes or use a note-taking format such as Cornell notes, and teachers can collect and review them for completeness. Notes can be taken in English or in the student's dominant language (if the teacher or a collaborator knows the language).
- To assess beginning students' listening for details, students can be given a fill-in-the-blank song lyrics form that omits key words in each line; then they can listen for the missing words and write them when the song is played.
- A nonverbal way to assess listening skills is Total Physical Response, or TPR, which is discussed in chapter 4. It is especially useful for level 1 ELs, although it can be adapted to different levels.
- Quizzes using drawings or diagrams are other nonverbal ways to assess listening skills without assessing speaking, reading, or writing skills. For example, the student can listen to a Podcast about a restaurant and then has to choose a drawing of a library or a restaurant to indicate the setting of the listening passage.

With receptive skills, the objective of the activity differs based on the EL's listening proficiency and the complexity of the spoken or written language. For example, a teacher might develop a listening activity for the EL's level, such as a simplified description of the water cycle, and the student would be expected to listen for main ideas as well as important details. In other cases, the content of the listening activity might exceed the EL's listening proficiency level, such as a historic speech, so the teacher would only expect that the EL would grasp the gist of the recording rather than a full understanding of every detail. Both types of listening tasks are important for ELs to develop the ability to focus on the big picture and supporting details as well as a tolerance for not understanding everything but still being able to extract the overall meaning and certain details.

## Speaking

There are many opportunities to assess ELs' proficiency in speaking.

- Teachers can observe an EL's spoken language during a small-group discussion about academic content and then complete a checklist or rubric of their speaking proficiency, noting various qualities of the phrasing, such as grammatical accuracy and complexity, proper register (argumentation phrasing versus description phrasing), and ability to take turns and engage in extended discourse.
- The technique of leveled questioning, presented in chapter 6 of the *Tell* section, can be the basis of a number of informal assessments of EL students' proficiency in speaking. Teachers can write a set of questions that elicit responses requiring increasingly advanced language proficiency to understand and respond to. The questions can be on an interview form, and the teacher can mark which questions the student understood and could respond to successfully. For example, after a lesson about Ponce de Leon:

### Beginning Level of English Proficiency Questions

Who is this (teacher points to an illustration of Ponce de Leon standing on a ship, dated 1531)?

Is he in a house or on a boat?

What is the boat's name?

What year is it (in the picture)?

What country is Ponce de Leon from?

### Intermediate Level of English Proficiency Questions

Where did Ponce de Leon travel? Describe his journey.

What was Ponce de Leon looking for? Describe his search.

How did Ponce de Leon pay for his journey?

Do you think Ponce de Leon is a hero? Why or why not?

What qualities does an explorer like Ponce de Leon need to be successful?

### Advanced Level of English Proficiency Questions

Was Ponce de Leon's journey a success? Justify your answer.

If you were Ponce de Leon, what might you have done differently?

Looking at Ponce de Leon's journey from today's perspective, what modern discoveries could have helped his voyage to the New World?

Are there any explorers today who are searching for something like Ponce de Leon? Describe them and their goals.

What might have happened if Ponce de Leon hadn't reached Florida? How might that have changed history?

The teacher can create a form that lists each question and then provides a line to note the student's answer verbatim. Depending on the student's formal assessment of proficiency data, the teacher can begin the questioning at the student's current level and move upward from there.

## Reading

Classroom reading assessments in the primary grades that focus on early basic reading skills, such as phonological processing, word reading, and spelling, provide valuable information about beginning reading skills for both ELs and non-ELs.[1] Assessments that include reading comprehension, however, are less universally applicable, especially for ELs at beginning to intermediate levels of oral language or overall language proficiency.

There are a number of individually administered classroom assessments of reading.

- One common classroom assessment that many teachers use with their native-speaking students is an informal reading inventory. These assessments include spoken directions in English as well as comprehension questions, so it is important to remember that the student's level of comprehension in oral language (listening) and expression in oral language (speaking) have a profound effect on their comprehension of written language (reading). It is also possible that the student's non-native accent could cause the administrator to count a word response as incorrect, such as pronouncing the word *live* as *leave*.
- Another approach to assessing ELs' reading in the classroom is to use think-aloud protocols to prompt ELs to read a passage (silently or aloud) and recount their understanding and thinking process at designated points in the text. It can be very telling to hear their confusion over embedded phrases (e.g., "She told me the person who brought her the money was her brother") or phrasal verbs (a verb plus one or more prepositions, whose meaning is different from the sum of its parts—e.g., *brush up on* does not mean to use a brush in an upward motion on something).
- It's also important to remember that ELs have different levels of reading ability in their native language, and assessing their native language reading provides information about the potential transfer of reading skills from one language to another. Formal reading assessments in the major languages of ELs exist, but in some cases ELs speak a less common home language, and reading assessments in that language may not be available. Some teachers of older students with interrupted formal education have found reading passages in multilingual websites such as Wikipedia and have asked the student to read the passage aloud in their home language and explain it to the teacher in English.

## Writing

Classroom writing assessments in the primary grades that focus on early writing skills such as forming lowercase and uppercase letters and using basic punctuation and word-level spelling offer insights into the development of ELs' and non-ELs' writing skills.

Similar to reading assessment, many types of writing assessment require comprehension of and expression in oral language.

Beyond the primary grades, writing assessments range from writing one-word answers to writing a research paper. Writing assessment can take place with scaffolding such as sentence frames, or simply with a blank piece of paper, a pencil, and a prompt to respond to.

Examples of potential classroom writing assessments for ELs include:

- Using templates to write a short paragraph that includes phrasing for a specific discourse type, such as disagreeing with someone's point, then attempting to write the same type of argumentation at a later time without referring to the templates. The two versions can be compared, with discussion of why the template's phrasing of a point that the student wrote incorrectly without support is grammatically accurate.
- Completing sentence starters with original utterances.
- Paraphrasing a printed text without plagiarizing.
- Responding, without templates or other support, to a simple prompt that elicits language targeted to the EL's level of proficiency. The writing can be assessed with a rubric that emphasizes variety and complexity of language use (such as the rubric in table B.1), and any persistent errors can be addressed with explicit feedback.
- Responding, with templates, word banks, and model texts, to a more complex prompt that elicits language beyond the EL's level of proficiency. The writing's organization and supporting details can be evaluated with a rubric.
- Teachers can use ELs' independent writing practice activities as well as classroom assessments of writing in portfolios collected over time.
- It is also helpful to assess EL students' writing in their native language, so a prompt can be translated and the written response can be reviewed by a native speaker to get a sense of the student's first language literacy.

## USING LANGUAGE DOMAIN SCORES TO SET GOALS

Second language acquisition takes place over time and is affected by multiple factors, some that teachers can impact and some that they can't. If instructed second language acquisition is provided through targeted language arts instruction, English learners' language acquisition process may be accelerated and their ultimate level of attainment (i.e., achieving at or above grade level standards in language arts) may be elevated.[2]

Various studies of K–12 ELs in the past thirty years have shown that, on average, English learners reach grade-level proficiency in English over a period of five to seven years.[3] In a more recent review of research, the National Academy of Sciences reports five research-based conclusions regarding how long it takes an EL to become a former EL:[4] (1) becoming proficient in English is a complex process that occurs over multiple years; (2) the younger the EL upon entry into an English-speaking environment, the faster the progress toward full proficiency in English; (3) there is considerable variation among individual ELs in the ultimate level of proficiency attained; (4) even after many years in US English-medium schools, a relatively high percentage of ELs do not achieve grade-level proficiency; and (5) long-term English learners, meaning those who do not achieve proficiency within seven years of enrollment in US schools, are negatively affected by schools' lack of appropriate support.

Of these research-based findings, perhaps the greatest takeaway for educators is the importance of providing appropriate support for achieving proficiency in a timely manner. Although second language acquisition in the EL-integrated classroom happens over the course of years, English learners don't have unlimited time to acquire the language necessary for academic success in classrooms where instruction takes place in their second language. Because second language acquisition is not tied to a certain age or grade level like literacy development in the first language is, and because ELs enter US classrooms at different grade levels and different levels of first language literacy, there are no national standards that link progression from one proficiency level in oral language or literacy and a specific time frame, such as from the beginning of one school grade until the next. This doesn't mean, however, that teachers and students have to look at second language acquisition as a process that takes its own sweet time, for which no goals or time lines should be created. In fact, as all students gain more ownership of their progress toward meeting rigorous standards, shouldn't ELs be able to see an end toward which they should aspire?

Schools have adopted different approaches to supporting English learners' goal setting. One school district developed a one-page "English Learner's Road to Proficiency" form at the elementary, middle, and high school levels to structure conversations between teachers and their EL students and parents.[5]

At the beginning of each year, the ELD specialist meets with each student and shares the form with current test score information, including specifics about their scores and subscores on tests of English proficiency. The form asks the student to set English proficiency goals, to identify what steps they can take to accomplish them, and to suggest how their teacher and parents can support them in reaching their goals.

At midyear, the teacher and student meet again to discuss the student's reflection on their progress in meeting their goals and what may be helping or hindering them. The same process happens at the end of the year, with plans made for taking advantage of summer enhancement and remediation opportunities provided by the district specifically for English learners. The form is translated into multiple languages and is shared with parents during scheduled conferences so they are able to track and encourage their child's progress. It is also submitted to the school administration and the district, where the student's progress and potential need for additional support is monitored and reported.

In breaking down the practical meaning of the English proficiency score data used to set goals, teachers can refer to performance definitions (WIDA) or other descriptors that describe the EL's current proficiency levels as well as those of the subsequent level.[6] This gives a concrete depiction of what the student and teacher need to work on as the EL progresses in English proficiency. For example, EL students at a WIDA level 2 in speaking and writing can express ideas in phrases or short sentences, using formulaic grammatical structures and repetitive sentence patterns. They use general content words as well as social and instructional words. An example of the type of support that they would need is being allowed to draw and label to describe what they have learned, using models and vocabulary cards with illustrations. The teacher can show the student how their writing reflects these specifics, identifying the short sentences (I like dogs. Dogs are nice.), formulaic structures (I don't like cats), and repetitive patterns (I like____, I don't like____, etc.).

To set reasonable goals for progress, the level 2 ELs and their teacher can look at the performance definitions for WIDA level 3. Here a student can express ideas in expanded sentences with emerging complexity and can do so with grammatical structures that are more varied. They can also use content language and expressions with multiple meanings. At this level they need less support; for example, they can describe their pets using sentence frames. Teachers can share sample writing that reflects growth from level 2 to level 3, such as, "Pets enhance our lives by *verb* + *-ing* us *adverb*" (e.g., Pets enhance our lives by loving us unconditionally").

Teachers can use the same type of description to set goals for listening and reading, the receptive language skills. They can also use these types of examples of current and subsequent performance definitions to target literacy skills, especially when the student has reached higher levels of oral proficiency but lags behind in literacy by one or more levels. If a student has a concrete sense of where he is and where he is going, he can see a clearer purpose to the specific activities that the teacher recommends to move ahead more quickly.

In planning the actions that will further attainment of the student's goals, the teacher can provide both general and specific suggestions. For example, in improving speaking and writing, a general suggestion might be to read and listen to/watch teacher-selected materials on a daily basis, which can help expand the student's repertoire of sentence patterns and formulaic expressions. A specific suggestion might be to write and submit a weekly paragraph focused on a prompt and supported by sentence frames. The teacher can then give specialized feedback on persistent grammatical errors or can suggest expanded vocabulary and phrasing that the student can use in a revision, thus providing instruction targeted to their precise level. This can be accompanied by a grammar mini-lesson (chapter 18) on the error of focus so that the student can attempt to use that grammatical structure in subsequent paragraphs correctly.

## STUDENT-DIRECTED GOAL SETTING FOR ENGLISH LANGUAGE DEVELOPMENT

Figure B.1 shows a sample "road to proficiency" form that high school students complete with their teacher and review with their parent or guardian (hence the title Road to Graduation). A discussion of a more detailed goal-setting process that uses WIDA-based performance definitions follows the form.

FIGURE B.1
**Sample "Road to Proficiency"**

### English Learner's Road to Graduation — HS

**About me:**

Name: ____________________ Grade: _____ Language: ______________ Country of Birth: ____________________

What makes me unique: ________________________________________

My goal is to achieve proficiency:

_______ ACCESS for ELLs 2.0—overall English language proficiency level 4 and above
_______ ACCESS for ELLs 2.0—reading proficiency level 4 and above
_______ FSA ELA level 3 and above, or a concordant score in ACT or SAT
_______ ALG I EOC, or earn a concordant score on the PERT

**My current proficiency levels are . . .**

| **ACCESS for ELLs 2.0 Data English Proficiency Levels** | **FSA** | **ACT** Concordant Score (19) | **SAT** Concordant Score Reading (24) | **SAT** Concordant EBRW (430) | **PERT ALG** (97) |
|---|---|---|---|---|---|
| 4, 3, 2, 1, 0<br>Listening, Speaking, Reading, Writing<br>☐ 2016–2017 | 3, 2.5, 2, 1.5, 1, 0.5, 0<br>Reading Level | 20, 15, 10, 5, 0<br>ACT | 20, 10, 0 | 400, 300, 200, 100, 0 | 100, 80, 60, 40, 20, 0 |

**Am I On Track to Graduate?**

| Math Credits (out of 4): | ELA Credits (out of 4): | Science Credits (out of 3): | Social Studies Credits (out of 3): | GPA (min. 2.0): |
|---|---|---|---|---|
| | | | | |

**Based on my data, my areas of focus this year will be . . .**

| **Semester** | **What are two areas I want to improve in? (Language Goals)** | **What steps can I take to accomplish these goals?** | **How can my teacher support me in attaining my goals** | **How can my parent(s) support me with my goals at home?** |
|---|---|---|---|---|
| **1:** | 1 ______<br>______<br>2 ______<br>______ | ______<br>______<br>______<br>______ | ______<br>______<br>______<br>______ | ______<br>______<br>______<br>______ |
| **Reflection** | Am I making progress toward my goals? (Why?/Why not?) | | | |
| **2:** | 1 ______<br>______<br>2 ______<br>______ | ______<br>______<br>______<br>______ | ______<br>______<br>______<br>______ | ______<br>______<br>______<br>______ |
| **Reflection** | Did I reach my goals? (Why?/Why not?) How can I use Summer Bridge to help me achieve my goal? | | | |

To help students set appropriate language goals, the student's WIDA ACCESS 2.0 level and descriptions can be used. For example, a student at the Developing level (3) in writing currently uses simple and expanded sentences with emerging complexity, general and some specific content-area language, and may make errors that may impede comprehensibility when writing more complex text. At the subsequent Expanding level (4) in writing, the student should be able to write sentences of varying lengths and complexity in a cohesive paragraph, use specific and technical language in a content area, and may make errors that don't affect comprehensibility.

For the student to set goals related to reaching level 4, each dimension can be broken down further. In the area of linguistic complexity, the student can focus on examining models of sentences of different lengths and complexity, using a resource such as *They Say, I Say* to identify sentences to emulate.[7] When writing, the student can review first drafts of his own work by analyzing the length and complexity of each sentence and then consult with the teacher to brainstorm more advanced ways to, for example, write stronger and more academic sentences. In other writing assignments, the student can focus on finding and using more precise and varied vocabulary. In addition, the student could ask the teacher to point out a specific grammatical error so he could reflect on the proper form and rule and practice writing sentences that use it correctly. These are all steps the student can take to accomplish the goal of achieving level 4 writing skills during the academic year.

# Notes

## Introduction

1. Joyce W. Nutta, Carine Strebel, Kouider Mokhtari, Florin M. Mihai, and Edwidge Crevecoeur Bryant, *Educating English Learners: What Every Classroom Teacher Needs to Know* (Cambridge, MA: Harvard Education Press, 2014).
2. Collaborators are English language development specialists, bilingual teachers, paraprofessionals, or classroom volunteers.
3. We discussed M.A.K. Halliday's descriptions of language use in schooling—learning through language, learning the language, and learning about language—in our previous book, *Educating English Learners: What Every Classroom Teacher Needs to Know* (pages 22–23).
4. Of course, early childhood and elementary teachers have been prepared to teach both academic subjects and language arts, so they should use each protocol according to the focus of their lesson and move between the two protocols within an integrated unit.
5. The four Ps of targeted language instruction are explained in *Educating English Learners: What Every Classroom Teacher Needs to Know*, on pages 129–132. They are also explained in the introduction to part II of this book.
6. We chose the WIDA English Language Development Standards as our guidepost because roughly two-thirds of US states have adopted these standards. However, since the Academic Subjects Protocol and the Language Arts Protocol are designed as overlays to lesson planning and design, the *Show*, *Tell*, and *Build* tools and techniques can be used in conjunction with other standards, such as ELPA21, used in Arkansas, Iowa, Nebraska, Ohio, Oregon, Washington, and West Virginia; or individual states' standards, such as CA ELD in California.

## Part I

1. Joyce W. Nutta, Carine Strebel, Kouider Mokhtari, Florin M. Mihai, and Edwidge Crevecoeur Bryant, *Educating English Learners: What Every Classroom Teacher Needs to Know* (Cambridge, MA: Harvard Education Press, 2014).
2. The Language Arts Protocol will be presented in part II.
3. If you open your classroom to students enrolled in teacher education programs to gain clinical experience, consider asking them to assist with pre- or post-teaching the English learners with the support you developed.
4. The ASP can be used when adapting a unit, lesson, or activity plan for English learners, even plans that indicate that they are differentiated for English learners, but which often do not provide adequate support. The ASP can also be referred to when developing a unit, lesson, or activity plan as a reminder of important considerations for every segment of the instructional sequence. We frequently refer to its use for adapting a lesson, but for purposes of brevity, we use the term *lesson* to encompass a collection of lessons (a unit) or a part of a lesson (an activity). Figure I.2 offers a visual overview of the Academic Subjects Protocol.
5. Your state may have selected another English language development framework. Please check with an ELD specialist in your district or school about how you can best cluster the levels so that they correspond with ours.
6. One of the authors (Carine Strebel) had preservice teachers who dubbed the addition of universal nonverbal support "SLIDE-ification," a term that has stuck. Her students' first task after identifying the language demands, even before considering the gap, is to SLIDE-ify those aspects of the lesson where pictures or gestures are easily woven in. This addition of nonverbal support is considered universal, because it is good for non-ELs as well as for English learners.
7. These students are identified as SLIFE, or students with limited or interrupted formal education.

## Chapter 2

1. Video demonstrations are similar to animation in showing the steps of a process in motion.
2. Although the term *cement* is often used interchangeably with *concrete*, cement technically refers to the mixture of water and paste that is the binding element of concrete.

## Chapter 3

1. These are also known as artifacts, props, and ephemera.
2. Jim Cummins, "The Role of Primary Language Development in Promoting Educational Success for Language Minority Students," in *Schooling and Language Minority Students: A Theoretical Framework,* ed. Charles F. Leyba (Los Angeles: California State University, Evaluation, Dissemination and Assessment Center, 1981), 3–49.
3. Chapter 10 in the *Tell* section describes how sentence frames or starters and word banks can be used to support writing.

## Chapter 4

1. James Asher, *Learning Another Language Through Actions*, 7th ed. (Los Gatos, CA: Sky Oaks Productions, 2009).
2. Michael Byram and Adelheid Hu, *Routledge Encyclopedia of Language Teaching and Learning*, 2nd ed. (New York: Routledge, 2013).
3. According to Asher, students can "assimilate 12 to 36 new lexical items depending upon the size of the group and the stage of training." Asher, *Learning Another Language Through Actions*, 42. The acronym BICS stands for Basic Interpersonal Communication Skills, and CALP is short for Cognitive Academic Language Proficiency. These terms are further explained in appendix A.
4. Blaine Ray and Contee Seely, *Fluency Through TPR Storytelling: Achieving Real Language Acquisition in School*, 7th ed. (Berkeley, CA: Command Performance Language Institute, 2015).

## Chapter 5

1. In second language instruction, the term *teacher talk* is sometimes used synonymously with *foreigner talk*, which means simplified speech that is slower and clearer, uses less slang and contractions, and states the same information in multiple ways, including gestures and pointing. When we use the term *teacher talk*, we are referring to this specific type of speech used by second language teachers.

## Chapter 6

1. For ELs at beginning levels of English proficiency, first language use can complement English instruction, allowing students to express complex thoughts in their dominant language.
2. WIDA Consortium, *2012 Amplification of the English Language Development Standards: Kindergarten–Grade 12* (Madison, WI: Board of Regents of the University of Wisconsin System, 2012).
3. It is important to note that when questioning the whole class, normal questioning procedures should be used for non-ELs and leveled questioning for ELs should be interspersed throughout the questioning period. For example, the teacher may choose to ask open-ended questions to the entire class, direct them to think quietly for a moment, and then ask for volunteers to answer. An advanced EL could likely volunteer an answer just as a non-EL would, but a beginning or intermediate EL would be less likely to volunteer. To engage ELs with leveled questioning in this context, the teacher would call on an individual beginning or intermediate EL and then ask the leveled question. Calling on the student prior to asking the question signals to other students to allow the EL to respond. After that EL-directed question, the teacher can resume asking open-ended questions to the entire class before calling on individuals.
4. Teachers can provide support between ELs and between ELs and non-ELs by preparing group discussion questions according to level.
5. Teachers can use the leveled questioning technique to help ELs form questions through sharing templates and sentence frames of question types.

## Chapter 7

1. Office of Research, US Department of Education, *Consumer Guide*, June 1992, www2.ed.gov/pubs /OR/ConsumerGuides/cooplear.html.
2. Oakland Unified School District, *Family Engagement Toolkit*, www.ousdfamilytoolkit.org/wp-content /uploads/2014/09/ Definition-of-Quality-Academic-Discussions.pdf.
3. Suzanne H. Chapin, Catherine O'Connor, and Nancy C. Anderson, *Classroom Discussions in Math: A Teacher's Guide and DVD*, 3rd ed. (Sausalito, CA: Math Solutions, 2013).
4. Jeff Zwiers and Marie Crawford, *Academic Conversations: Classroom Talk That Fosters Critical Thinking and Content Understandings* (Portland, ME: Stenhouse Publishers, 2011).
5. Nicole Knight, "Why Are Academic Discussions So Important for Our ELLs?" *Teaching* Channel, 2014, www.teachingchannel.org/blog/2014/10/24/academic-discussions-and-english-language -learners-ousd/.
6. Zwiers and Crawford, *Academic Conversations*.

## Chapter 8

1. A general discussion of word/phrase, sentence, and discourse complexity can be found in in appendix A. The *Build* tool on grammatically unpacking sentences provides a description of how phrases and clauses make text dense and linguistically complex.
2. They will likely help you examine the WIDA Performance Definitions, English Language Proficiency Standards by the Council of Chief State School Officers, or English Language Development standards developed by your state.
3. English learners typically do not encounter exactly the same reading difficulties as their non-EL peers. Therefore, we do not recommend the use of a readability index, such as the Flesh-Kincaid Grade Level Test, because those do not include measures for English language proficiency.
4. At times, texts with very dense phrasing or those that treat highly abstract concepts cannot be sufficiently simplified to make them accessible to the English learners who recently arrived with very little knowledge of English or those with limited prior schooling. Too many and too substantive alterations of such texts may even render them more obscure. These students are better served by being exposed to the content through an entirely different text, including in the native language, or even an alternative format, such as a video with subtitles in the native language, or a video in the native language only.
5. Available at http://teachingamericanhistory.org/library/document/by-aiding-britain-we-aid -ourselves-our-own-democracy-is-threatened/.

## Chapter 9

1. While most of today's informational texts include images, with or without labels, they are typically insufficient for English learners because the link between image and text may not be obvious. (We recall a textbook chapter on states' rights in the western United States that began with an image of the Grand Canyon as the introductory picture, but the relationship of the Grand Canyon to water rights was made three pages later.) Additionally, one image without some form of text simplification (see chapter 8) or without modification is not sufficient for ELs, who, by definition, cannot yet comprehend grade-level text independently.
2. Chapter 16 provides a brief overview of terms encountered in grammar books.
3. Schweizerische Eidgenossenschaft, "Hydropower," Swiss Federal Office of Energy, www.bfe .admin.ch/themen/00490/00491/index.html?lang=en.
4. In this reading assignment, the beginning English learner can benefit from images, which can easily be found through searches on Yahoo! Images (http//images.search.yahoo.com/) or on Google Images (https://images.google.com/).
5. Although a beginning-level English learner likely mistakes the term *plant* for a flower or tree, since it is more commonly used in this context, the synonym *station* would not be a good choice because the term *plant* is used in the original text that the collaborative group members read. Therefore, if the word in the context of power production has not already been taught to the entire group in preparation for the lesson, the teacher would need to pre-teach it explicitly, possibly by translating it.

6. The fact that only hydropower plants that produce more than 300 kilowatts/hour are included in the number 643 is not an important detail to convey in the modified text. The peers can include the information in their poster or PowerPoint presentation.

## Chapter 10

1. In appendix A, we describe and provide examples of the three types of academic vocabulary: general, specific, and technical.

## Part II

1. Early childhood and elementary teachers typically teach academic subjects and language arts, but at the secondary level English language arts teachers have primary responsibility for language arts instruction. We recommend addressing language development in all academic subjects, but the degree of focus on either element tends to differ by grade level (i.e., early childhood and elementary teachers balance the focus more consistently than secondary teachers because of subject specialization).
2. If you open your classroom to students enrolled in teacher education programs to gain clinical experience, consider asking them to assist with pre- or post-teaching the English learners with the support you developed.
3. We do not include level 6 (Reaching) in the adjustment decisions since ELs at that level require fewer, less extensive adjustments to reach the same language sophistication as their non-EL peers.
4. William Saunders, Claude Goldenberg, and David Marcelletti, "English Language Development: Guidelines for Instruction," *American Educator,* Summer 2013, 13–25, 38–39.

## Chapter 12

1. Claude Goldenberg, "Instructional Conversations: Promoting Comprehension Through Discussion," *Reading Teacher* 46, no. 4 (1992): 317.

## Chapter 13

1. In the public domain.

## Chapter 14

1. Some English learners, especially in secondary grades, may prefer that you bring their errors to their attention rather than correcting them implicitly. It never hurts for a teacher to ask their students' preference, while also explaining that there are times when explicitly correcting an error and providing an explanation interferes with the flow of the lesson because it is not pertinent to the task. Error correction varies by culture. It is, therefore, important first to inquire about the practices in the home country of a student who recently arrived in your class, and later explain how and why you choose to address errors explicitly or implicitly.
2. Rod Ellis, *The Study of Second Language Acquisition*, 2nd ed. (Oxford, UK: Oxford University Press, 2008).

## Chapter 15

1. From "Living Language. The Accent Is on You" website. www.livinglanguage.com/blog/2015/11/16/closer-than-you-think-cognates-in-arabic-english-and-spanish/.

## Chapter 16

1. Newcomer ELs whose first language follows the same word order as English may be able to participate as early as WIDA level 1.5, if an ELD specialist deems this appropriate based on their command of English vocabulary and overall literacy skills.
2. Isabel L. Beck, Margaret G. McKeown, and Linda Kucan, *Bringing Words to Life: Robust Vocabulary Instruction*, 2nd ed. (New York: Guildford Press, 2013). See also their article "Choosing Words to Teach" on the Reading Rockets website at www.readingrockets.org/article/choosing-words-teach.
3. It is important to inform students that unpacked sentences may be written in different ways, as long as the author's intended meaning does not change.

4. For additional practice, you could ask the students to draw the diagram in a notebook and copy the final sentences (with the constituents identified) from the board.

5. As we explained earlier, English learners at level 1 proficiency do not benefit from learning this tool.

### Chapter 17

1. Joanna P. Williams, "Instruction in Reading Comprehension for Primary-Grade Students: A Focus on Text Structure," *Journal of Special Education* 39, no. 1 (2005): 6–18.

2. See chapter 1 for graphic organizers in academic content instruction and chapter 20 for graphic organizers to support writing.

### Chapter 18

1. A great visually enhanced resource for grammar examples and explanations is the book *English for Everyone: English Grammar Guide* (New York: DK Publishing, 2016).

2. The explanations and examples were adapted from Keith Folse, *Clear Grammar* (Ann Arbor, MI: University of Michigan Press, 2010).

### Chapter 19

1. Dana R. Ferris, *Treatment of Error in Second Language Student Writing*, 2nd ed. (Ann Arbor, MI: University of Michigan Press, 2011).

2. Dana Ferris and Keith S. Folse, "Preparing Teachers to Treat Errors in the K-12 Classroom" (interview), *Tapestry*, 2013, http://tapestry.usf.edu/responding_to_errors/.

3. Keith S. Folse, *Keys to Teaching Grammar to English Language Learners: A Practical Handbook* (Ann Arbor, MI: University of Michigan Press, 2016).

4. Ibid.

5. Folse divides grammar errors of ELs into sixteen categories. For our purposes, we combined verb tenses of past, present, and future, condensing them to thirteen categories.

### Chapter 20

1. For information on using graphic organizers in academic content instruction, see chapter 1, and for their use in understanding text, see chapter 17.

### Appendix A

1. Jim Cummins, "BICS and CALP: Empirical and Theoretical Status of the Distinction," *Encyclopedia of Language and Education, Vol. 2. Literacy,* ed. Brian Street and Nancy Hornberger (New York: Springer, 2008), 71–83.

2. Jim Cummins, "Knowledge, Power and Identity in Teaching ESL," in *Educating Second Language Children: The Whole Child, the Whole Curriculum, the Whole Community,* ed. Fred Genesee (Cambridge, UK: Cambridge University Press, 1994).

3. WIDA Consortium, *2012 Amplification of the English Language Development Standards: Kindergarten–Grade 12* (Madison, WI: Board of Regents of the University of Wisconsin System, 2012).

4. Susan O'Hara, Robert Pritchard, and Jeff Zwiers, "Identifying Academic Language Demands in Support of the Common Core Standards," *ASCD Express* 7, no. 17 (2012), www.ascd.org/ascd-express/vol7/717-ohara.aspx.

5. George Yule, *The Study of Language*, 6th ed. (Cambridge, UK: Cambridge University Press, 2017).

6. James F. Baumann, and Michael F. Graves, "What Is Academic Vocabulary?" *Journal of Adolescent & Adult Literacy* 54, no. 1 (2010): 4–12, Douglas Fisher and Nancy Frey, *Word Wise and Content Rich: Five Essential Steps to Teaching Academic Vocabulary* (Portsmouth, NH: Heinemann, 2008); Janis M. Harmon, Karen Wood, and Wanda B. Hendrick, "Vocabulary Instruction in Middle and Secondary Content Classrooms," in *What Research Has to Say about Vocabulary Instruction,* ed. Alan E. Farstrup and S. Jay Samuels (Newark, DE: International Reading Association, 2008), 150–81; Elfrieda H. Hiebert, and Shira Lubliner, "The Nature, Learning, and Instruction of General Academic Vocabulary," in *What Research Has to Say about Vocabulary Instruction,* ed. Alan E. Farstrup and S. Jay Samuels (Newark, DE: International Reading Association, 2008), 106–29.

7. Robin Scarcella, *Academic English: A Conceptual Framework. Technical Report 2003-1.* (Santa Barbara: University of California Linguistic Minority Research Institute, 2003); Susan Ranney, "Defining and Teaching Academic Language: Developments in K–12 ESL," *Language and Linguistics Compass* 58, no. 9 (2012): 560–674.

8. Florin M. Mihai, *Assessing English Learners in the Content Areas: A Research-Into-Practice Guide for Educators* (Ann Arbor, MI: University of Michigan Press, 2017).

9. Jim Cummins, *Bilingualism and Special Education: Issues in Assessment and Pedagogy* (Clevedon, UK: Multilingual Matters, 1984).

10. Ibid.

11. Macmillan McGraw-Hill, *Time Links. Third Grade: Communities* (Columbus: Macmillan McGraw-Hill, 2007).

12. Wayne Wright, *Foundations for Teaching English Language Learners: Research, Theory, Policy, and Practice* (Philadelphia, PA: Carlson Publishing, 2010).

13. Gladis Kersaint, Denisse R. Thompson, and Mariana Petkova, *Teaching Mathematics to English Language Learners*, 2nd ed. (New York, NY: Routledge, 2013).

14. Virginia Department of Education, *Comparison of Virginia's 2009 Mathematics Standards of Learning with the Common Core State Standards for Mathematics*, 2011.

15. Florin M. Mihai and N. Eleni Pappamihiel, "Accommodations and English Learners: Inconsistencies in Policies and Practice," *The Tapestry Journal: An International Multidisciplinary Journal on English Language Learner Education* 6, no. 2 (2014): 1–9.

16. Mihai, *Assessing English Learners in the Content Areas*.

17. Jamal Abedi et al., "Language Accommodations for English Language Learners in Large-Scale Assessments: Bilingual Dictionaries and Linguistic Modification," *CSE Tech. Report No. 666.* (Los Angeles: University of California's National Center for Research on Evaluation, Standards, and Student Testing, 2005).

18. Michael J. Kieffer, Mabel O. Rivera, and David J. Francis, *Practical Guidelines for the Education of English Language Learners: Research-Based Recommendations for the Use of Accommodations in Large-Scale Assessments,* 2012 Update (Portsmouth, NH: RMC Research Corporation, Center on Instruction, 2012).

19. WIDA, a consortium of thirty-nine states, uses the ACCESS for ELLs 2.0 as a yearly progress measurement, while seven states use the ELPA21.

20. WIDA also includes composite scores for oral language (listening and speaking) and literacy (reading and writing), and an overall proficiency score.

**Appendix B**

1. Nonie K. Lesaux, Orly Lipka, and Linda S. Siegel, "Investigating Cognitive and Linguistic Abilities That Influence the Reading Comprehension Skills of Children from Diverse Linguistic Backgrounds," *Reading and Writing: An Interdisciplinary Journal* 19, no. 1 (2006): 99–131.

2. Rod Ellis, *The Study of Second Language Acquisition* (Oxford, UK: Oxford University Press, 2008).

3. Jim Cummins, "The Role of Primary Language Development in Promoting Educational Success for Language Minority Students," in *Schooling and Language Minority Students: A Theoretical Framework*, ed. Charles F. Leyba (Los Angeles: California State University, Evaluation, Dissemination and Assessment Center, 1981), 3–49; Kenji Hakuta, Yuko Goto Butler, and Daria Witt, "How Long Does It Take English Learners to Achieve Proficiency?," *The University of California Linguistic Minority Research Institute Policy Report*, 2000 (1).

4. Suzanne Le Menestrel, *Promoting the Educational Success of Children and Youth Learning English: Promising Futures* (Washington, DC: National Academy of Sciences, 2017).

5. Natasa Karac, Pinellas County School District.

6. WIDA, www.wida.us/.

7. Gerald Graff and Cathy Birkenstein, *They Say/I Say: The Moves That Matter in Academic Writing*, 3rd ed. (New York: W. W. Norton, 2016).

# Acknowledgments

We are grateful to many people who helped shape this book. First and foremost, our deepest appreciation goes to editor extraordinaire, Caroline Chauncey. She shepherded us through this process by challenging us to write more succinctly, to provide more context, to find that uniform voice as we transformed our individual class notes and professional development presentations, handouts, and favorite application activities into the *Show*, *Tell*, and *Build* tool and technique chapters. Caroline's insights and probing questions during the development phase, guidance following draft versions, and phenomenal advice in response to specific inquiries were without parallel!

To the many committed and brilliant professionals at Harvard Education Press, thank you for your expert suggestions in copyediting, attention to detail in artistic design, and creative marketing skills and plans. You are a key part of this book's success.

We deeply appreciate the enthusiasm with which doctoral students Lauren Raubaugh and Charlene (Ying) Xiong accepted our request for assistance with the *Build* chapter application tasks. They diligently researched best practices and proposed many great ideas from which we had the luxury of building the activities.

We want to extend a big thank-you to Troy Scrimgeour and Marco Nutta for their attention to detail in checking our references and resources, and "Chicago-izing" them all. Without your help, the publication of this book might well have been delayed.

We greatly benefitted from the artistic talents of Wendy Williams, who, for the third time now, worked meticulously to turn our vision of graphics into what you see in this book. Thanks also go to TeacherVision for allowing us to adapt some of their popular graphic organizers for this book, and to Junia Braga for her technology suggestions.

Special thanks go to Natasa Karac, head of the English for Speakers of Other Languages programs in Pinellas County Schools (Florida) for sharing the "English Learners' Road to Graduation." Joyce and Carine are also appreciative of her invitations to provide professional development for teachers in the district. They thoroughly enjoy working with these dedicated educators, always learning a little more about what points deserve additional emphasis and connections to practice and where to tread more lightly to maximize the valuable exchanges.

Similarly, we are fortunate to count Minnie Cardona, district coordinator of ESOL and World Languages in Seminole County Public Schools (Florida), among our friends. She fully embraced our previous publication, *Educating English Learners: What Every Classroom Teacher Needs to Know*, and pushes her general classroom teachers to support their English learners at every step.

# About the Authors

**Joyce W. Nutta** began her fascination with second languages before elementary school, listening to French- and Spanish-speaking tourists at her parents' ten-unit motel in west central Florida. In the ninth grade, she and her parents moved to a small town in the Dolomites of Italy, where she was enrolled in an Italian-speaking high school even though she knew nothing of the language or culture. She spent two years in the ninth grade and although her social language developed by the end of her second year, she was unable to pass the rigorous essay exams of academic subjects and language arts in Italian and returned to Florida to continue high school. After volunteering to help immigrant students learn English in her academic classes, she began her profession as an English as a second language teacher and eventually a teacher educator. She earned teaching certification followed by a master's degree in applied linguistics and a PhD in second language acquisition/instructional technology. She is currently professor of English for Speakers of Other Languages (ESOL) Education and the ESOL endorsement and TESOL PhD track coordinator at the University of Central Florida. Her research interests include the integration of English learner issues into teacher preparation and professional learning and the use of technology to teach second languages. Nutta has received over $7,000,000 in research and training grants. Her research has been published in the *Journal of Teacher Education*, *Hispania*, *Foreign Language Annals*, *TESOL Journal*, and *CALICO Journal*, among other publications.

**Carine Strebel** is assistant professor of education and coordinator of English for Speakers of Other Languages (ESOL) at Stetson University. A native of Switzerland who spent the first three years of school in Paris, she pays tribute to her parents for sparking her love for different cultures and language learning. While fulfilling field experience hours in an elementary classroom, she noticed a tiny girl sitting by herself in the back of the room, largely ignored by the teacher and classmates, and instinctively selected her to be the focus of her case study (although the teacher warned she would not "get enough out of it" to earn a good grade on the assignment). Although communication proved to be difficult, the experience was powerful and rewarding. The two grew close as they worked on below-grade-level vocabulary and math problems, and at the end of the semester their goodbyes were difficult. While teaching French and German in the United States, Strebel's thoughts repeatedly returned to this girl, and she decided to help immigrant children become successful in American schools by becoming a teacher educator. Strebel holds a master's degree in French and a PhD in instructional technology with a focus in ESOL, and has experience mentoring practicing teachers around the world online on the implementation of language learning technologies. She has coauthored previous books with Harvard Education Press, is a cofounder and coeditor of *The Tapestry Journal: An International Multidisciplinary Journal on English Language Learner Education*, and serves on the advisory board for a US Department of Education grant. Her current research focuses on preservice teachers' development of self-efficacy of teaching English learners, assessment of and feedback to preservice teachers' field experience teaching performance, and faculty and teacher professional development.

**Florin M. Mihai** grew up in Iasi, Romania. In second grade, he started learning English and became fascinated by it. After he earned a BA in English and Romanian from Alexandru Ioan Cuza University in Iasi, he taught English as a foreign language at a private language school in his hometown for several years. Because he wanted to further his education and pursue a postgraduate degree, he enrolled in the Multilingual and Multicultural Education program at Florida State University, where he earned a master's and a PhD. His research interests include language and content-area assessment for English learners, grammar instruction, pre- and in-service teacher education, and curriculum development in global contexts. He is the author of *Assessing English Language Learners in the Content Areas: A Research-into-Practice Guide for Educators* (2nd ed., University of Michigan Press, 2017) and a coauthor of *Course Design for TESOL: A Guide for Integrating Curriculum and Teaching* (University of Michigan Press, 2016), *Educating English Learners: What Every Classroom Teacher Needs to Know* (Harvard Education Press, 2014), and *Language and Literacy Development: An Interdisciplinary Focus on English Learners with Communication Disorders* (Plural Publishing, 2012). Mihai is a coeditor of *The Tapestry Journal: An International Multidisciplinary Journal on English Language Learner Education*. Currently, he is professor and director of the TEFL undergraduate certificate in the Teaching English to Speakers of Other Languages (TESOL) program at the University of Central Florida.

When **Edwidge Crevecoeur Bryant** immigrated to the United States from Haiti with her family, she had no idea what awaited her. Upon arriving in New York, in the winter, she expected neither to see "white things" fall from the sky that caused her toes to feel numb nor to ride to school on a noisy bus with children laughing and talking instead of walking! Even more startling, she did not expect to paint all day, every day, while the other students did work that she had previously done in Haiti. She could not understand the language but knew she could do the work if the teacher just gave her a chance. At the age of seven, during one of those "painting in the back of the classroom" moments, she decided that she would become a teacher to help students who could not speak English. Taught English by her father, she became that teacher! Crevecoeur Bryant was the first student in the United States to earn a BS in bilingual education with an emphasis in Haitian Kreyòl and English; she then earned a master's degree in educational administration and an EdD in applied linguistics with an emphasis in bilingual/bicultural education. She has coauthored five bilingual English-Haitian Kreyòl dictionaries, serves as codirector of five literacy centers in Petit Goâve, Haiti, and is the educational director of the Technology and English Learning in Leogane Project in Haiti. Crevecoeur-Bryant has devoted her career to improving the lives of English learners through directly teaching ESOL as well as undergraduate and graduate students. She is an associate professor, ESOL coordinator, and director of the Collaborative Online Mentoring Partnership for English Learners program in the Education Department at Flagler College.

**Kouider Mokhtari** grew up in Morocco, a multilingual country, where he learned to read in two languages: Arabic and French. Outside of school, he spoke Moroccan Arabic, which is a colloquial version of Modern Standard Arabic that is rarely written or used in any formal communication. His fascination with the nature of language and its role in learning to read and write intensified in the first year of high school when he started learning English. After completing teacher certification, he taught English as a foreign language in high school in Rabat and Casablanca, Morocco. He earned a master's degree in applied linguistics and an interdisciplinary doctorate from Ohio University. His research focuses on the acquisition of language and literacy by first and second language learners, with particular emphasis on children, adolescents, and adults who can read but have difficulties with reading comprehension. Mokhtari is a coauthor of *Preparing Every Teacher to Reach English Learners: A Practical Guide for Teacher Educators* and *Educating English Learners: What Every Classroom Teacher Needs to Know* (both with Harvard Education Press). He is a coeditor of *The Tapestry Journal: An International Multidisciplinary Journal on English Language Learner Education* (Harvard Education Press), which is dedicated to the advancement of research and instruction for English learners. He currently serves as the Anderson-Vukelja-Wright Endowed Professor of Education within the School of Education at the University of Texas at Tyler, where he engages in research, teaching, and service initiatives aimed at enhancing teacher practice and increasing student literacy achievement outcomes.

# Index